The Emerging Power
of Japanese Money

The Emerging Power of Japanese Money

Aron Viner

DOW JONES-IRWIN
Homewood, Illinois 60430

To Doris and Bob

Dow Jones-Irwin is a trademark of Dow Jones & Company, Inc.

Acquisitions editor: Richard A. Luecke
Project editor: Susan Trentacosti
Production manager: Carma W. Fazio
Jacket design: Sam Concialdi
Compositor: Eastern Graphics
Typeface: 11/13 Times Roman
Printer: Arcata Graphics/Kingsport

Library of Congress Cataloging-in-Publication Data

Viner, Aron.
    The emerging power of Japanese money.

    Bibliography: p.
    Includes index.
    1. Finance—Japan. 2. Investments, Japanese.
3. Japan—Commerce. 4. Money—Japan. 5. Japan—
Economic conditions—1945–   6. International
finance. 1. Title.
HG187.J3V56 1988   332.1′0952   87–73190
ISBN 1-55623-071-0

Printed in the United States of America

2 3 4 5 6 7 8 9 0 K 5 4 3 2 1 0 9 8

PREFACE

Like the sudden appearance of a volcanic island bursting through the surface of the ocean, the emerging power of Japanese money promises to be a new system of still indefinite shape and temporality. Perhaps the island will rise for a short time only to enjoy a brief existence before sinking below the waves. Perhaps the island will provide the base for a new financial empire.

I chose to write this book because if this island does provide the base for a durable economic force, we in the West need to understand the implications of that development. Such understanding will not be easily acquired. The representatives of Japan, the United States, and the European Community are far, indeed, from mutual understanding. The gulf that separates Japanese and Western views shows many signs of deepening rather than disappearing.

Protectionism and antiforeign sentiments can only be destructive to all members of the world economy. While technology is swiftly uniting the separate national worlds of finance into a single global nexus, political differences and unilateral economic concerns conspire with cultural biases to undermine free trade.

* * *

This book is intended to raise issues and provoke thought. It begins by exploring opposing views of some of the major trade issues that have resulted in disputes between Japan and the West. Chapter 1 offers a Western perspective, while Chapter 2 provides an indication of Japanese views. Thus, many of the opinions presented in these chapters are not mine. My intention is to describe ongoing trends in Japan's economic relationships with the world. Chapter 3 provides a historical context and a contemporary framework that I believe will influence the unfolding of Japan's participation in the financial sector. I think that these discussions will help foreshadow and clarify the future financial trends and current financial activities presented in the book's remaining three chapters.

Chapter 4 focuses on a few recent changes in world finance and on the implications of those changes. Chapter 5 describes current Japanese approaches to finance and corporate structure within the context of international investment. Chapter 6, the conclusion, considers Japan's preeminent role in the new world of international finance that is now emerging.

ACKNOWLEDGMENT

Hilary McLellan worked on parts of this book with me. As far as I'm concerned, she was a coauthor. However, she declined to be recognized as such.

I have drawn upon interviews conducted in Tokyo, New York, and Washington during 1986 and 1987. I am indebted to all of those who took the time to speak to me.

Aron Viner

CONTENTS

INTRODUCTION

IS JAPAN POOR?

Is Japan poor? Perhaps this is an odd question to pose at the beginning of a book that claims to be about the emerging power of Japanese money. Nonetheless, it is a question made serious by the majority of Japanese economists, who are persuaded that in many ways—the ways that matter most—Japan is poor.

There is no shortage of evidence to support pessimism about Japan's immediate prospects. The economy has been in a "growth recession," albeit a mild one. Economic growth in 1986 declined to 2.6 percent. This was the second lowest growth rate since the first oil crisis in 1973 and a far cry from the double-digit growth of the heady 1960s. Although corporate profits recovered dramatically during the second half of 1987 and economic growth will rise significantly above the doldrums of 1986, continued appreciation of the yen could undermine all gains.

Seasonally adjusted unemployment reached 3.2 percent in May 1987, the highest rate since 1953, when such statistics were first compiled. In remote locations, such as the northern island of Hokkaido, unemployment exceeded 4.5 percent. According to the Japanese government definition of unemployment, a person who works as little as one hour per week is considered employed.[1] By U.S. or European Economic Community (EEC) methods of calculation, unemployment in Japan would have surpassed 5 percent. Many Japanese economists

---

[1] Part-time employees (who represent 5 percent of the employees of Japan's larger companies) who would like to work full-time are thus not considered unemployed. Unemployment statistics also do not include workers who have been laid off by their companies but continue to receive compensation. Graduating students who are given job offers in August for the financial year beginning the following April are also regarded as employed for statistical purposes.

believe that unemployment will double during the next several years and will triple in the manufacturing sector.

Mature industries such as shipbuilding, steel, coal, and textiles are closing plants and will fire tens of thousands of workers. "Rationalization" efforts by Japanese manufacturers are resulting in increased overseas production leading to fewer jobs at home. The strong yen seems destined to shatter forever Japan's export-based economy.

Because Japan's corporations gained their wealth primarily through the manufacture of superior and price-competitive products, it has been assumed that they will decline as the high yen (what Japanese term *endaka*) eliminates their competitive edge. Exports will shrink and corporate losses will consume excess liquidity. As a result, the Japanese manufacturing sector will contract and many sunset industries will dip below the horizon, never to rise again. In Japan, this process is known as "the hollowing out" (*kudoka*) of Japanese Industry. Thus, Japan is the apple and the high yen is the apple corer.

* * *

Perhaps if you have been too busy with immediate concerns to read about Japan, you may not know that Japan, the exporter of autos (Toyota) and electronics (Sony), has too many yen ("excess liquidity") and negligible consumer price inflation. Meanwhile, the yen appreciated against the dollar by 40 percent in 1985, the Year of the Ox, and continued strengthening throughout 1986 and 1987. That means that if Japanese assets are considered in terms of dollars, many Japanese corporations and financial institutions are exceedingly rich.

Here are five examples selected in order to impress you.

- **Stock Market.** Not only is the Tokyo stock market the biggest in the world (in terms of the capitalization of listed companies), but *just one* of the stocks listed on it (NTT) is worth more than all of the stocks listed on the West German Stock Market and the Hong Kong Stock Market combined. Moreover, the provincial Osaka stock market (13 percent the size of the Tokyo stock market) is the third largest stock market in the world.
- **Banks.** The five biggest commercial banks in the world (in terms of deposits) are Japanese. Japan's postal savings system, which isn't a bank at all, holds deposits equal to six times the deposits of Citibank, North America's largest commercial bank. More

than one third of *all* the global cross-border assets held by banks belonged to Japanese institutions in 1987. As a result, Japanese banks have become the world's biggest international bank creditors, with $1.1 trillion in cross-border assets, an increase of 100 percent over the 1985 level.

- **Leading Creditor.** Japan is the world's biggest creditor nation. Its net overseas credits increased in 1986 by 40 percent over the preceding year, reaching a record $180.35 billion. During fiscal 1986 (ended March 31), Japan's current account surplus reached $93.76 billion, up 70 percent over the year before.
- **Stockbrokers.** Japan is the home of four of the largest securities companies the world has ever seen. The biggest, Nomura Securities Company, is valued on the Tokyo Stock Exchange at $58 billion, which is far more than the market value of all U.S. securities firms combined. By itself, Nomura has been buying a major portion of the annual U.S. government budget deficit, which it sells effortlessly to its Japanese clients.
- **Corporate Cash.** Many leading Japanese corporations hold highly liquid assets. Toyota and Matsushita, for instance, each have liquid assets exceeding $12 billion.

You are impressed? Japanese economists are not. They believe that Japan, as the second largest economy in the free world with about 15 percent of the free world's gross national product (GNP), is bound to be the grazing ground of fat corporations and institutions. They perceive Japan's wealth as "paper riches," of no value to the Japanese people, whose standard of living they regard as not comparable to that of the West.

Furthermore, they are afraid that the recent appreciation of the yen against the dollar and other major currencies will result in sharply higher world prices for Japanese exports. Thus, the future will be determined by the foreign exchange markets: the higher the yen, the smaller Japan's global market share. Japanese exports will cease to be competitive, and the nation and its assets will soon decline.

Japanese economists fear that the newly appreciated yen will cause the Japanese export market to dry up. The economy will thus swiftly deteriorate, and Japan will return to the struggle for survival that characterized the grim years of postwar reconstruction. Although Japanese consumers have not yet begun to stockpile food for the imminent crisis, few Japanese believe that their nation's economic future is bright.

Many Japanese are convinced that Japan is about to follow the well-beaten path established by Britain and the United States: international trade declines, the government deficit increases, and the economy contracts. Welcome, Japan, to the exclusive club of industrial and financial leaders gone to seed.

* * *

American economists, on the other hand, view Japan as a superstar economy hindered by labyrinthine government regulations and antiquated distribution systems. They argue that if Japan would pause for a moment and modernize (deregulate and liberalize its regulatory systems), then the East Asian giant would become what MacArthur meant it to be: a rich and powerful U.S. ally capable of complementing and not competing with the U.S. economy. In a Japan with a truly open market, Japanese consumers could select products manufactured throughout the world on the basis of quality and price.

These economists point out that Japan must reform its restrictive tax system, relax its monetary policies, and open its financial markets. These issues aside, however, they argue that Japan is a supreme capitalist. Japanese manufacturers provide the United States with vital products and leading edge technology. Moreover, Japanese investors supply the U.S. economy with indispensable transfusions of cash. Indeed, U.S. interest rates would be substantially higher were it not for Japanese purchases of U.S. Treasury issues.

According to the jaded eyes of American economic observers, Japanese industry is *not* being crushed by an overvalued currency. Of course, Japanese companies are faced with an adjustment period resulting from the reality that the yen was undervalued during most of the period following the second "oil shock." This undervaluation can be demonstrated by a variety of measures of the exchange rate. Thus, overall, after a brief period of rationalization, the productivity of Japanese industries will be stimulated rather than retarded by the newly appreciated yen. Therefore, the Japanese term *endaka* or "high yen," is a misnomer. The yen is not high—to the contrary, it is at (or perhaps slightly above) sea level.

Some American economists have termed Japan neo-mercantilist. By this they mean that Japan favors exports over imports in a total system that concentrates wealth in selected institutions and provides individuals with little opportunity to spend money. Japan's policies have certainly displayed resemblances to the mercantilist doctrines of the 17th century. A strong national focus on exports and nontariff barriers that have discouraged imports has given Japan an economy based on "adversarial trade."

Japanese politicians and bureaucrats have been antagonized by the term *adversarial*. Nonetheless, for its critics, no epithet better captures Japan's trade relations with the West. Ordinarily, when nations conduct trade, all partners benefit. Yet, from the perspective of foreign economists, Japan's economic growth has opposed rather than complemented the economies of the major industrial nations. Japan exports maufactured products to the West (reducing the importer's demand for domestically produced goods) but imports little. Japan's surplus in telecommunications trade is an example of this. In 1985, the most recent year for which statistics of the Organization for Economic Cooperation and Development (OECD) are available, Japan exported $1.38 billion of telecommunications products but imported just $57.6 million of such products—thus, Japan exported 24 times as much as it imported. From this perspective, Japan has been a minor contributor to the total volume of world trade.

Although Japan has grown to be a multitrillion-dollar economy and is the biggest creditor nation, Japanese consumers pay exorbitantly high prices for nearly all commodities. The quality of life in Japan's cities is generally considered far inferior to the middle-class urban splendor of North America or Western Europe. A majority of the Japanese population considers itself poor. Just ask.

* * *

A common phrase in Japan, rapidly becoming a cliché in daily parlance, is "a rich country but a poor people." No one can deny that Japan, the nation, is rich. Its hefty surplus on the current account, the magnitude of its foreign investments, the sheer value of its corporations, and its expensive urban real estate all attest to the vast accumulation of physical and monetary assets. Yet, who owns Japan? Who owns Japan's corporations? Who owns the land of Japan? Who owns Japan's overseas investments?

Of course, the Japanese government owns land as well as a handful of national corporations (rapidly being privatized at great profit).

However, with a budget deficit equivalent to 4.1 percent of GNP in 1987 and a net debt approaching one third of GNP, the government is scarcely the proud owner of Japan's great liquid wealth. The Japanese government is chronically short of revenue. Thus, while Japan has an enormous trade surplus, it is all in the private sector.

The vast majority of Japan's major corporations are publicly held. The top 1,860 companies are listed on Japan's stock exchanges, while others are traded over the counter. Yet, only 23.9 percent (in 1986) of all the outstanding shares in these corporations are held by individuals. To make matters more perplexing, corporate profits are not redistributed as dividends. Dividends *are* paid to shareholders, but they are based on a tiny percentage of par value and there is little correlation between the dividends paid out and the magnitude of corporate profits.

Japanese workers are not highly paid in relation to the cost of living in Japan. The average Japanese family must spend roughly 30 percent of its disposable income on food alone. The costs of rent, clothing, education, and other necessities consume another 48 percent of disposable income. Japan's corporate profits are not redistributed to employees in the form of generously high salaries or profit sharing.

Much of Japan's choicest urban real estate is owned by major corporations. Indeed, a portion of the current high market value of Japanese stocks is the result of "hidden assets" in the form of real estate held by many blue-chip Japanese companies. Similarly, Japanese overseas investments are owned by Japanese companies. Japan's wealth is corporate wealth. The five examples of Japan's financial prowess listed above are manifestations of corporate wealth.

Thus, allegations of neo-mercantilism seem apt. Japan, the nation, is rich as a direct result of accumulated corporate surpluses derived from a pattern of trade with the world's nations that has favored exports far above imports. The Japanese people have little money to spend and therefore a limited choice about how to spend it. Nontariff barriers either exclude foreign-made products or raise their prices to match patterns within the domestic pricing system. For example, Japanese rice (discussed in Chapter 1) costs far more than Southeast Asian rice, but rice imports are banned.

* * *

So, is Japan rich or poor? The people are poor (at least by consensus and relative deprivation), the government is poor (just look at that debt), and the corporations hold the purse strings. What does this mean for Japan's future?

Today, corporate profits are invested in a range of financial market instruments and in plant and equipment. Recently, the expansion of corporate facilities has focused on the creation of *overseas* factories, offices, and networks. Offshore manufacturing in countries with lower labor costs is already well under way.

For example, in 1987 Matsushita Electric Industrial, Japan's biggest electronics firm, produced 14 percent of its products outside Japan and planned to increase overseas production to 25 percent by 1990. In 1986, the Aiwa Company, another major electronics concern, set up production facilities in Singapore (eliminating 1,000 jobs in Japan) in order to raise the portion of overseas production from 12 percent to 50 percent. Unlike the Aiwa Company, which has focused production in a single country, Canon, Inc. has spread its factories throughout the West. Canon plants in West Germany, the United States (Virginia), Italy (a joint venture with Olivetti), and France produce a total of 100,000 plain paper copiers per year.

Although only about 3 percent of total Japanese production occurred outside Japan in 1987, this percentage will increase from five to seven times during the next decade. Furthermore, a hefty portion of Japanese overseas production will be exported to Japan. In the future, many of Japan's biggest imports will be Japanese products produced outside the country.

Also in 1987, Japanese investors (primarily corporations and institutions) bought a net $90 billion in foreign securities and spent more than $6 billion on U.S. corporate acquisitions and investments. Indeed, Japanese corporations have become market movers throughout the world. The growing size of Japanese corporate investments as well as the expanding international role of Japanese banks and securities companies is giving these institutions considerable global power.

The contraction of the domestic manufacturing sector will serve to drive domestic corporations overseas into new areas promising high return. In 1986 and 1987, many Japanese corporations derived a major share of their profits from activities in overseas (and domestic) financial markets. Japan's major trading houses (*sogo shosha*) today own financial subsidiaries in Europe. At home, Sony Corporation, the famous producer of acoustic equipment, now operates a life insurance company and will soon be managing its own pension funds. By all indications, these trends will continue for quite some time.

Japan's service sector will expand. In the postindustrial era that is now under way, services will become increasingly more important than manufacturing. The purveyors of products ranging from hamburgers to movie reviews, from mortgages to life insurance, will satisfy domestic demand and represent a growing portion of the economy.

The leaders of the service sector, however, will be financial institutions. Barring a collapse of the Japanese economy, Japan's financial institutions and corporations, *because of the money that they control,* will become forces of increasing global influence. Indeed, long before the turn of the century they will have become the world's most powerful entities in finance, foreign exchange, and trade. As Japan's financial institutions and organizations rise to ascendancy, Tokyo as a world financial center will rise with them. Inhibiting regulations will be shed, uncovering Japan's new and toughly competitive financial skin.

* * *

China, Greece, Spain, England—each had its moment of glory, and today each is a second-rate power supported by a wobbly economy. That rich countries become poor and poor countries become rich, though a platitude, is true for all sovereign entities.

The United States, for example, enjoyed its heyday of riches and economic power during the 20th century. With the approach of a new millennium, it is on the threshold of a new era. Not much longer will it be the world's dominant financial power or the most technologically advanced nation. The United States is in the process of being superseded by the next global economic power—*Japan.*

CHAPTER 1

THE WORLD VIEWS JAPAN

FROM RICE TO STOCK

I had been living in Indonesia for nearly two years before I arrived at Tokyo's Narita airport in 1978. I had come to Japan to attend a conference about rice. I thought that rice was one of the most fascinating and important (and appetizing) things in the world. From my point of view, when it came to the growing of rice, the Japanese were inefficient but masterful artists.

I had brought a movie of Japanese farmers transplanting and harvesting rice to several dozen villages in North Sumatra. When I showed the movie, women sighed and men exclaimed with awe at the images of excellent yield and automated harvesting. My audiences marveled when I mentioned that Japanese farmers held more political clout than any other single group in Japan. When, however, I told them that the Japanese government bought virtually the entire national rice harvest at 10 times the Indonesian price, it was suggested (not always politely) that I was spinning a yarn. This was not the last time that my statements about Japan evoked such a response.

The day before I was scheduled to leave Tokyo, a fateful event occurred. An old school friend, who was then working for a large Japanese securities firm, offered to give me a tour of the Tokyo Stock Exchange. Because my friend was Japanese, I attempted to be Japanese in my phrasing of a refusal. I politely protested that he was very busy and his valuable time could be better spent. He insisted that the "TSE," as he called it, was the eighth wonder of the world and that under no circumstances could I be permitted to visit Japan without witnessing the stock exchange floor during trading hours. "You're an economist," he concluded, as though that fact clinched the matter.

Reluctantly, I agreed to meet my friend in Kabuto-cho, Tokyo's Wall Street, the following morning. In the 18th and 19th centuries, Kabuto-cho had been the home of Japan's rice warehouses. In those days, the government collected taxes in the form of rice. Rice trading predated the stock market and was the first commodities market in Japan as well as the first futures market in the world. I was intrigued by the historical connection between stock trading and rice trading.

I had been advised that traveling by subway from my hotel would be quicker than contending with "rush hour" traffic. When I emerged from the depths of the underground, I was certain I had gotten out at the wrong station. Surely, this motley collection of dingy concrete buildings, main thoroughfares, and narrow streets could not be the center of Japan's financial district. I wandered past little shops and paused to watch an old woman who sat on the sidewalk repairing shoes. Across the street, a young man wearing a white apron carried a tray of coffee cups into a building. The smell of raw sewage permeated the air, and for a second I thought I was back in Jakarta.

A passerby directed me to the stock exchange building, a seven-story circular structure. The building's Corinthian columns and Grecian facade reminded me of its counterpart in New York. My friend greeted me with a smile and led me inside.

From the visitors' gallery, I looked down upon a thronging melee of at least 2,000 people. Men in blue suits shouted and gesticulated, while men in brown suits shoved their way through the crowds as though intent upon some urgent personal mission. Suddenly, the mass of people seemed to coalesce into a single unit as everyone began to enthusiastically applaud.

"What's happening?" I asked my friend in bewilderment.

"The market just broke 6,000!" he replied excitedly. "This marks the market's full recovery from the oil shock."

"How much higher will the market go?" I naively inquired.

"There's no limit," he grinned. "The market will break 10,000 in a few years, it will surpass 20,000—even 30,000—within 10 years, 40,000 by the end of the century."

I knew that my friend's company made the lion's share of its profits from stock market commissions, so I disregarded his optimistic projections. He had once told me that by accepting a job with a Japanese securities company, he had become a minotaur—half bull and half human.

"Congratulations," I said sardonically. "You'll get rich."

"So can you," he replied. "Buy electronics: Sony, Matsushita, Hitachi, Toshiba; or automobiles: Toyota, Nissan."

I had invested my small savings in U.S. municipal bonds and had no intention of speculating in foreign stock markets. Later that day, I left Japan.

Japan, however, did not leave me. Every Monday, reports on the Japanese economy and the Japanese stock market arrived in the mail— courtesy of my friend. Soon, I found myself following the Japanese stock market with mounting interest. I subscribed to the *Japan Economic Journal* and the *Japanese Stock Journal*. Gradually, almost insidiously, Japanese finance became something of a preoccupation and my interest in rice began to wane.

I began to notice bizarre and enigmatic movements in the Japanese stock charts. A particular issue would move along a narrow box range for a long time. Then, suddenly, like a Nijinsky leap, the issue would rise dramatically, increasing in value by as much as 50 percent in a few weeks. Subsequently, succumbing to the force of gravity, the stock would drift to the ground. It crossed my mind that advance knowledge of these sudden jumps could make an investor very rich very fast. The idea intrigued me so much that I telephoned my friend in Tokyo to wish him a happy new year.

"By the way," I inquired, making my voice casual, "I've noticed that certain Japanese stocks double in value overnight and then return to previous levels before I can find an explanation for the rise."

"Nothing new about that," my friend replied.

"Well, U.S. stocks don't behave that way," I pointed out.

He laughed.

I tried again, "I really don't understand what is going on."

He laughed again. "Look at it this way," he said finally. "Climbing Mount Fuji is a good thing to do, but everyone can't do it at the same time."

The telephone call was costing me over a dollar a minute, and on my salary at that time this could easily add up to a formidable bill. Nonetheless, a minute elapsed before I could think of a response.

"Who decides who will climb and at what time?" I delicately inquired. Now, it was my friend who paused for a minute before answering.

"The best time to climb Mount Fuji is at night, so that you can see the sunrise from the summit," he clarified. "We will have to go together when you next visit Japan. By the way, I've just been promoted to section chief."

"Congratulations," I said without enthusiasm, "it's a great way to begin the new year." I hung up the telephone feeling perplexed.

As usual when dealing with the Japanese, I felt that there was more to this issue than met the eye. I decided to return to Japan for my next vacation.

* * *

Some years later, still intrigued by the Japanese, I found myself working for my friend's company in Tokyo. I discovered many interesting things. For example, the odor of raw sewage that I had detected in the vicinity of the stock exchange had a simple explanation. Many of the office buildings were not connected to sewers. Instead, a truck would arrive once each week to pump out the septic tanks located in the basements of the buildings. A comparable situation in Wall Street or in the City of London would be difficult to imagine.

In Japan, the contrast between advanced development and Third World characteristics never ceased to astound me. Nothing seemed to exemplify this odd contrast better than the Tokyo stock market. The Tokyo Stock Exchange utilizes state-of-the-art computer facilities tailored to the trading of shares in some of the most technologically advanced corporations in the world. Nonetheless, a kind of institutionalized corruption typical of the Third World is found in Japan's stock markets. For example, a host of marginal activities (trading on inside information, cornering the float of an issue, spreading false rumors, and systematically pushing certain stocks in order to fulfill marketing goals as well as government aims) are common practice.

These marginal activities are considered illegal and reprehensible in the United States and Europe. They are also illegal in Japan, where they are ignored by the regulatory authorities and condoned by the biggest securities companies. Everyone does it, everyone denies it, and no one discusses it.

THE WEST VIEWS JAPAN

Hazy as the horizon illuminated by the rising sun, everything east of the Urals has been considered for centuries a single vague homogeneous enclave known as the "Orient." To the average European or North

American, cultural characteristics distinguishing such broad ethnic groups as the Chinese, Japanese, and Koreans have frequently been too remote for recognition.

Since the Middle Ages, Asia has been a largely unknown but concrete entity—vast, populous, and exotic. Treachery and inscrutability are attributes that Europeans have long associated with "Orientals." Indeed, since Attila the Hun invaded the Roman Empire in the fifth century, Europeans have been wary of the power of the "yellow peril" erupting from the distant East.

Seven centuries after Attila was killed in France, swarms of Mongols riding fast horses overran what is today the Soviet Union, inspiring terror and threatening the West. Yet another seven centuries later, Tojo invaded Southeast Asia and bombed Pearl Harbor, demolishing the peace and stability of the Pacific.

Perhaps fallaciously, Asian military strategies have been commonly regarded as more devious, dangerous, and destructive than their European counterparts. "Life is cheap in Asia," and Asian wars are fought by rules different from those of the West. Thus, while European warfare stressed the openness of direct battles between opposing armies, with victory determined by superior strength and skill, in Asia more emphasis was placed on cunning in battle than on group strength. For example, Genghis Khan's cavalry sometimes feigned retreat and then turned back, rapidly surrounding and destroying the opposing forces. Marco Polo, a European witness, reported that "in this sort of warfare, the adversary imagines he has gained a victory, when in fact he has lost the battle."

As recently as the Vietnam War, popular American sentiment regarded guerrilla tactics as inappropriate. For years, American generals unsuccessfully used classic European strategies in combating the Vietcong's more effective techniques of concealment and surprise. Often, U.S. troops were deployed in a manner more appropriate to European terrain than to a jungle environment and did not conform to the recognized patterns of attack and withdrawal indigenous to the region.

* * *

Strategies of international trade are analogous to military strategies. European nations expect their trading partners to conform to agreements (often unwritten) regarding acceptable and unacceptable practices. On the other hand, Asian nations may utilize the most effective method, regardless of the expectations, needs, or desires of their trading partners.

In war, surprise and the confusion it inspires can be instrumental to victory. Some of the most dazzling military victories in history have been the result of surprise attacks, and, sometimes, the more shocking the surprise, the more rapid the victory. In trade, however, Western nations see surprise attacks as underhanded and illegal. Although such tactics may yield a crucial advantage, they are not ordinarily adopted in the West, where trade partners are regarded as allies, not as opponents.

Today, many Americans and Europeans are firmly convinced that "Orientals" play by different rules: They neglect agreements, reciprocate only when convenient, and invade markets with inexpensive products. From the textiles produced by cheap labor in Hong Kong, to the VCRs built in Taiwanese sweatshops, to the semiconductors mass-produced in efficient Japanese factories, Asian commodities are seen as flooding Western markets like cancerous cells that destroy the ability of indigenous industry to grow and prosper. Dumping, or predatory pricing, is sometimes viewed as an East Asian creation designed to kidnap market share from native producers. Thus, Japanese silicon chips have become a modern version of barbarian Huns theatening Rome or Mitsubishi Zeros invading U.S. airspace with impunity.

MADE IN JAPAN

Of course, the West is no longer as ignorant about the East as it was a century ago. Advances in cartography and printing have provided us with an abundance of accurate and colorful maps that enable Everyman to have a clear idea of the location of Taiwan, South Korea, and Inner Mongolia. Television, documentaries, and package tours have filled in the gaps in popular knowledge of the Far East.

However, nothing heightens awareness as well as the immediacy of danger. For example, as Japanese manufactured products began to rival those of the United States in the early 1970s, there emerged a desire to learn the rules that dictate business operations in Japan. Books about Japanese management techniques and Japanese industrial production have proliferated. The idea that Americans (or Europeans) should emulate Japanese methods has been proposed by a number of prominent

American writers as an obvious method of defending domestic interests against foreign threats.

The Japanese ability to manufacture products that are better and cheaper than those of their competitors in the West has been a major issue of the late 1970s and 1980s. The benefits of such Japanese institutions as "lifetime employment," consensus decision making, and quality control circles (an American invention) have been popularized in the United States at least since 1979. Innovative U.S. companies and managers have attempted to replicate certain features of Japanese corporate organization with varying degrees of success.

Clearly, the Japanese remain more adroit at using their own production and management techniques than we Westerners, despite a proliferation of English-language books and commentaries on the subject. By the 1980s, Japanese corporations dominated world production of products ranging from autos to semiconductors and from VCRs to ball bearings.

At the same time that Japanese manufacturers freely opened factories in the United States and Europe, foreign companies wishing to open plants in Japan encountered barriers. The Ministry of International Trade and Industry (MITI) often excluded foreign direct investment by insisting that it be confined to minority participation in joint ventures with Japanese corporations. Japan's protected industries thrived by freely combining the benefits of production *and sales* in Japan with unrestricted opportunities abroad. Thus, Japanese success was perceived as in part a result of unfair advantage.

Many Western producers disappeared as a consequence of overwhelming Japanese competition. In their wake, tens of thousands of unemployed American and European workers expressed mounting animosity toward Japan.

So great was the anti-Japanese sentiment that during a demonstration one group of American autoworkers used sledgehammers to ritualistically demolish a new Japanese car, which they then buried. Other hostile workers expressed their anger more directly by killing Chinese Americans whom they mistakenly identified as Japanese. The subsequent sentences were extremely lenient considering the magnitude of the crime. This is the setting that legislators in the United States consider when they draft protectionist bills aimed against Japan.

With an eye to their public, American legislators have been increasingly vehement in their expression of anti-Japanese sentiment and their hot tempers have given rise to protectionist trade policies. At such times, all it takes to ignite a conflagration is a Molotov cocktail thrown into the party. Toshiba Machine, a company little known in the United States, became such a cocktail in the spring of 1987.

OF MITI AND SUBMARINES

There is a marginal area where the separate activities of trade and war meet before they again diverge. In this gray, ill-defined area, the sale of military equipment can itself have great political impact or be an expression of political alignment. Victory in war is often determined by access to appropriate military hardware. Thus, the sale of weapon-related technology is never apolitical.

Manufacturing companies and governments sell weapons and the machinery to manufacture weapons to the highest bidder. Although the sale of weapons and related equipment is generally a legitimate sector of world trade, a portion of such selling occurs on the black market. Sometimes private corporations illegally sell classified equipment and information to an enemy. When this is done by individuals, it is termed *lèse majesté*. There is no term to describe such activity when a company engages in it.

Between December 1982 and June 1984, Toshiba Machine Company, one of the world's largest machine-tool makers (50.08 percent owned by Toshiba Corporation, Japan's second largest general electrical machinery producer) shipped some model MF–4522 milling machines to the Soviet Union. Under a contract with a Soviet trading concern (Techmashimport), numerical controllers, computers that guided the milling machines, were provided by a Norwegian arms maker (Kongsberg Vaapenfabrikk) and attached to the Toshiba machines prior to shipment.[1]

In June 1984, after the machines had been shipped by Toshiba Machine, a special computer program was given to the Soviets by

---

[1] As this book goes to press, recent revelations have indicated that Kongsberg Vaapenfabrikk shipped 140 numerical controllers (and necessary software) to the Soviet Union. Many of these shipments preceded Toshiba Machine's illicit sales of nine-axis milling machines to the USSR.

Toshiba Machine as the concluding portion of the package. The deal was arranged by C. Itoh & Co., one of Japan's major trading houses.

This series of apparently routine transactions would have gone unnoticed by the press were it not for an April 1987 report presented to the U.S. Congress by the Central Intelligence Agency (CIA). Perhaps not coincidentally, the report was released several days before President Reagan was scheduled to meet Prime Minister Nakasone in Washington.

The CIA would never have had occasion to prepare its report were it not for the disturbing discovery that for a period of time (unspecified) a number (undisclosed) of Soviet attack submarines had been evading U.S. detection with unprecedented success. Subsequent investigations determined that the computerized milling machines that Toshiba Machine had sold to the Soviet Union were not ordinary. Technologically superior to anything available in the USSR, the machines enabled the Soviet government to build ultraquiet submarine propeller blades. Those blades gave Soviet attack submarines the ability to evade detection so successfully that, according to Representative Duncan Hunter, they can now approach to within 10 minutes' missile flying time of the mainland United States.

Transfer of the milling machines to the Soviet Union was a violation of regulation IL 1091 of the Coordinating Committee on Multilateral Export Controls (Cocom), a Paris-based monitoring entity created by the United States and 16 allies, including Japan. Fully aware that the sale constituted an illegal diversion of high-technology goods to the USSR, Toshiba Machine executives misrepresented the machine tools' capabilities in their application for export permission from Japan's Ministry of International Trade and Industry (MITI).

Meanwhile, Toshiba Machine invited a team of Soviet technicians to examine and test the milling machines at the Toshiba Machine plant in Japan. Subsequently, Toshiba Machine employees went to the USSR and assembled at least one machine in the Baltic Ship Yard, outside Leningrad.

The U.S. response to the revelation was sharp and rapid. Five members of Congress introduced a bill banning all imports from Toshiba Corporation and its Norwegian accomplice. The U.S. Defense Department delayed the award of several electronic contracts (including a $100 million plan to supply the Air Force with 90,000 lap-top computers made by Toshiba Corporation) until the Japanese government conducted a satisfactory investigation of Toshiba's role in the debacle. Furthermore, the Pentagon objected to lax Japanese government supervision of exports to the USSR and other Soviet-bloc nations.

Following the congressional and Pentagon responses to the CIA report and on the same day that Reagan and Nakasone met in Washington, Japanese police searched all offices and factories belonging to Toshiba Machine Company. MITI lodged a complaint with the police against Toshiba Machine for violating a domestic ban against the exportation of strategic equipment to the USSR.

MITI also ordered a review of all outstanding export applications for computers, certain machine tools, and semiconductor manufacturing equipment valued at more than 100 million yen ($710,000). However, the effectiveness of such a move was moot. The export control inspection staff of MITI's Office of Security Export Controls consisted of 42 people (subsequently increased to 63 and at the end of 1987 to 100) who reviewed roughly 200,000 license applications per year. The small staff is perhaps an indication of the importance MITI attributed to export controls.

Several weeks later, Japanese police arrested two senior Toshiba Machine Company executives, the chief of the materials division and the vice director of a machine technology division, and charged them with violating Japan's foreign exchange and foreign trade control laws. Under Japanese law, a three-year statute of limitations prevented the government from charging these men with the illegal exportation of the machine tools and consequently they were only charged with the sale of the computer program. Although details regarding the computer program are classified, it is known that the program was indispensable for the production of the propeller blades. The maximum penalty for the executives, if convicted, would be three years in prison.[2]

The Pentagon praised the quick Japanese government action and congratulated MITI and the police. Stephen Bryen, deputy undersecretary of defense for trade security policy, commented that the Japanese government's vigorous role in the investigation represented "positive evidence that Japan views this problem with the same seriousness as we do." This public statement, designed to encourage Japan to strengthen

---

[2]Several months later, four additional employees of Toshiba Machine and three employees of Wako Koeki (a Tokyo-based trading firm) were arrested, bringing to nine the total number of individuals liable to be prosecuted.

its monitoring of strategic exports, masked hostile U.S. sentiment. Through its actions, Toshiba Machine Company had violated U.S. security and, according to the U.S. government, neutralized a critical part of U.S. antisubmarine technology, thus undermining a vital area of the North Atlantic Treaty Organization (NATO) defense system.

Two months later, in June 1987, Japanese investigators announced that more milling machines had reached the Soviet Union than the four that the CIA had mentioned in its congressional report. In addition to the four 200-ton milling machines already identified, four more milling machines (of even higher technical sophistication) were sent to the USSR in the spring of 1984. These machines should enable Soviet attack aircraft carriers to attain higher speeds and improved maneuverability. This new revelation left little doubt in Washington that Toshiba Corporation, parent of Toshiba Machine, knew about the orders. It was assumed that large and repeated sales to the USSR would have routinely come to the attention of the directors of Toshiba Corporation.

The revelations continued. Following Japanese press reports that Toshiba Machine Company had shipped a half-dozen propeller milling machines to the USSR before 1980, the firm admitted that it had begun selling such machines to the Soviet Union in 1974. According to a Pentagon report released on July 28, 1987, the Soviet Union started a program to reduce propeller noise in 1979 and by 1981 had acquired five-axis numerically controlled propeller milling machines that used numerical controls produced by Kongsberg.

Toshiba Machine Company knowingly gave the USSR critical technology that was immediately used against the defenses of the United States and other Japanese allies. Not stopping there, the company permitted Soviet experts to visit its factory and scrutinize the technology. Subsequently, Toshiba sent its own employees directly to a Soviet shipyard to assure that Soviet engineers would successfully adapt the technology to their attack submarines. C. Itoh, one of Japan's biggest trading houses, arranged at least some of the deals with full knowledge of their implications and illegality.

Given the gravity of the crime, what penalties were meted out to the corporations responsible?

- Toshiba Machine Company, which provided the technology, was barred from shipping goods to the Soviet bloc and China for a year. This could cost the company as much as ¥5 billion ($36 million) in sales—about 5 percent of its total annual revenue. However, the revenue that Toshiba Machine gained from the Soviet deal was not confiscated. Details of the profits deriving from the transaction were not officially announced, but the National Police Agency (equivalent to the U.S. Federal Bureau of Investigation) stated that the USSR paid *triple* Toshiba Machine's list price to obtain the milling machines.

- C. Itoh & Co. (one of Japan's Big Three general trading companies, or sogo shosha), the trading firm that arranged the deal for the Soviet Union, was asked in a letter from MITI to "refrain" from selling machine tools to Soviet-bloc countries and China for three months.
- Wako Koeki (a small Tokyo trading company devoted exclusively to trade with communist countries), which reportedly served as an intermediary between Soviet KGB agents (representing the trading firm Techmashimport) and Toshiba Machine, received a written reprimand from MITI.[3]
- Toshiba Corporation, the owner of Toshiba Machine, was not penalized.
- The president of Toshiba Machine voluntarily resigned. Meanwhile, it remains to be seen whether the employees of Toshiba Machine who are legally culpable will be convicted.

American congressmen regarded the penalties as exceptionally mild. After all, barely a month after MITI imposed its sanctions on Toshiba, the U.S. Securities and Exchange Commission (SEC) extracted a $25 million fine from Kidder Peabody, an investment banking firm responsible for several insider trading infractions. From the U.S. perspective, the Japanese punishments did not fit the severity of the crimes. Perhaps as a result, the Senate Banking Committee, led by Senator Jake Garn, prepared an amendment to an impending bill

---

[3]In December 1985, a former employee of Wako Koeki informed officials at Cocom's Paris headquarters that the firm had illegally exported equipment. Although Cocom notified MITI officials, the ministry either did not investigate the allegations or failed to discover information about Toshiba Machine's actions. Six months later, the Pentagon provided MITI with similar information. Yet, MITI again failed to uncover or disclose information regarding Toshiba Machine.

intended to prohibit the entire Toshiba group (and the Norwegian Kongsberg group) from participating in the U.S. market for two to five years. In addition, the United States was authorized by a new bill to demand compensation from Japan (and Norway) for the enormous cost of developing methods to detect the quieter Soviet submarines.

Anger over the episode mounted steadily in the Senate and the House of Representatives. Toshiba Corporation's failure to acknowledge culpability and the Japanese government's light-handed response added fuel to the fires of resentment in Washington. On July 1, 1987, two months after the initial revelations, 10 congressmen assembled on the lawn of the Capitol and flattened a Toshiba radio with sledgehammers.

That same day, the Senate, by an overwhelming majority (92 to 5), approved an amendment to the Omnibus Trade Bill that required import penalties against Toshiba Corporation and Norway's Kongsberg Vaapenfabrikk. Under the terms of the bill, Toshiba and its Norwegian accomplice would be prohibited from exporting their products to the United States for a period ranging from two to five years. The import ban, applying to the entire Toshiba group, would result in estimated lost sales of more than ¥400 billion ($2.75 billion) per year, substantially reducing (or eliminating) the firm's pretax profits for fiscal 1988.

In addition, the legislation would require the U.S. government to seek civil damages. Estimates of the cost of regaining U.S. antisubmarine capability range from $20–40 billion. Meanwhile, the U.S. Commerce Department temporarily suspended Toshiba Corporation's license to buy American high-technology products in bulk.

Less than 24 hours after the Senate bill was approved, Prime Minister Nakasone sharply criticized Toshiba Machine for exacerbating trade tensions between Japan and the United States. Although the criticisms were directed at the culprit, they also applied to the parent. In Japan as elsewhere, a parent corporation must take responsibility for the delicts of its subsidiaries. In Japan, however, the form of such responsibility is often amorphous.

Shortly after Nakasone's statement, the president and chairman of Toshiba Corporation resigned because they felt "gravely responsible for straining the already strained Japan-U.S. relations further." They carefully noted, however, that Toshiba Corporation had no role in its unit's illegal sale of machinery and that their resignation was not a response to the Senate vote. Toshiba Machine, they pointed out, was an independent subsidiary and not a division of Toshiba Corporation. Nonetheless, their resignation was viewed by the Senate as a positive, though merely cosmetic, gesture.

By way of partial compensation, Toshiba officials offered to assist the Defense Department in its efforts to develop new technologies to counter the Soviet advantage. In addition, Toshiba engaged Price Waterhouse, one of the Big Eight U.S. accounting firms, and several U.S. law firms to establish the exact relationship between Toshiba and Toshiba Machine. In this way, Toshiba Corporation hoped to demonstrate to the United States that it could not have known about or prevented Toshiba Machine's illegal sales and thus should not be held accountable by the United States for the independent subsidiary's actions. At about the same time, Toshiba Corporation initiated a massive advertising campaign intended to apologize for damage caused by its subsidiary.

Released in September 1987, the Price Waterhouse report confirmed Toshiba Corporation's claim that it had no prior knowledge of Toshiba Machine's shipments to the USSR. Simultaneously, Toshiba Corporation announced a detailed Strategic Products Control Program, under which a separate management group would monitor exports by the parent firm and its subsidiaries. In addition, Toshiba's export compliance program would verify the authenticity of prospective buyers and would conduct spot inspections of the subsidiaries. Employees guilty of any infraction (including unreported knowledge of infractions) would be severely punished. In this way, Toshiba hoped to prove its determination to assure that future breaches of Cocom regulations by any part of the Toshiba group would be impossible.

Concurrently with the Toshiba announcements, the upper house of the Japanese Diet rubber-stamped an export control law that had already been approved by the lower house. This law increased from three to five years the maximum prison term for violators and recognized intent as a crime. Intended to tighten controls on Japan's strategic exports to communist countries, the new law and its various provisions were designed primarily to dilute American anger and encourage the U.S. Senate to modify its sanctions against Toshiba Corporation. Nonetheless, the law was vague regarding necessary arrangements for cooperation among the ministries to ensure full enforcement.

However, not all U.S. interest groups were prepared to tar and feather Toshiba. A group of the biggest and most politically powerful

American companies (including IBM, Honeywell, Motorola, General Electric, AT&T, Hewlett-Packard, Rockwell, United Technologies, and Xerox) began lobbying against the congressional efforts to exclude Toshiba from U.S. markets. These companies were supported by the American Electronics Association, the Computer and Business Equipment Manufacturers Association, the Business Roundtable, and the National Association of Manufacturers.[4] Toshiba's electronic components, these companies and associations announced, were so vital that without them billions of dollars of corporate profits and many jobs would be endangered.

In support of these lobbying efforts, Toshiba brought the general manager (an American) of the company's facility in Lebanon, Tennessee, to Washington. There, he argued that sanctions against Toshiba would "cripple" all of Toshiba's American operations, including its plans to export U.S.-made products to Japan. Thus, Toshiba's 4,200 American workers could find their jobs at risk and potential U.S. exports to Japan (which, of course, would contribute to a reduction of the trade imbalance) could be lost.

American dependence on Japan's second largest electric machinery producer was revealed to be complex and considerable. Lobbyists announced that without imports from Toshiba many U.S. companies would be obliged to abandon product lines or market areas. Toshiba Corporation—with $17.8 billion in annual sales and more than 200 overseas subsidiaries—maintained supply contracts (including sole source arrangements involving custom-made components) with virtually every major electronics concern in the United States. Many U.S. companies were engaged in original equipment arrangements whereby Toshiba made products that were marketed under the labels of the U.S. importer. Thus, for example, some televisions sold under the Sears label are produced by Toshiba. A *New York Times* editorial observed that "when Congressional grandstanders lash out at Japan, they lash out at America too."[5]

* * *

Although the U.S. Senate was appalled by the Japanese government's mild punitive response to Toshiba Corporation, the limited

---

[4]As reported by *The New York Times*, September 14, 1987.
[5]"Bashing Toshiba, Hurting America," *The New York Times*, September 15, 1987.

export bans imposed on Toshiba Machine and C. Itoh were *the strongest ever given* to Japanese companies guilty of violating foreign trade control laws. Indeed, the imposition of such bans has been so rare that many who followed the case had no doubt that the relatively harsh penalties were designed to appease American anger. Thus, when the public memory of the case begins to wane, the two arrested Toshiba executives may receive mild sentences.

What can we learn from this case? That the Japanese government is a mild disciplinarian and a lackadaisical overseer of corporate international trade practices? That Japan has little concern for the strategic interests of its allies? That ultimately Japan's regulators turn a blind left eye to its exports and direct a sharp right eye to its imports? That only American anger can prompt the Japanese government to investigate or remedy trade infractions?

All of these marginal assumptions have become part of Western folklore: a beast, Japan, Inc., inhabits Japan. A pragmatic union of government and industry, the beast uses its corporate arm to satisfy government interests and its government arm to fulfill corporate aspirations. Meanwhile, a single institutional brain weighs alternatives and makes decisions. Foreign businesses that fall prey to this beast are faced with decline and obsolescence. Free market economies are no match for the synergy of Japanese government and business.

With a ruthless gleam in its eye, the beast goes out and eats foreign markets for lunch. While this is happening, terrified foreign businesses ask what the beast is planning to eat for dinner.

THE BEAST

Chalmers Johnson, in his insightful book *MITI and the Japanese Miracle,* writes that the Ministry of Commerce and Industry (MCI) and the Ministry of Munitions (MM) "were once such fearsome agencies that it was said the mere mention of their names would stop a child from crying."[6] The MCI became the MM in November 1943, and two years later, under the guidance of Occupation experts, the MM became MITI

---

[6]Chalmers Johnson, *MITI and the Japanese Miracle* (Stanford, Calif.: Stanford University Press, 1982), p. 33.

(the Ministry of International Trade and Industry). Although the "mere mention" of the name MITI, the Munitions Ministry's contemporary form, is no longer able to stop Japanese children from crying, it has occasionally been known to cause foreign adults to begin to cry.

MITI has been termed "the 'reincarnation' of the wartime MCI and MM."[7] Indeed, a majority of the prewar bureaucrats in the Ministry of Commerce and Industry continued to work in the Munitions Ministry and were not purged during the reorganizations instituted by the Occupation.[8] As a result, the same officials who dictated Japan's controlled wartime industrial policies formulated and implemented Japan's postwar industrial policies. *Not until 1976 did MITI have a vice minister who had not worked in the Munitions Ministry.* The importance of this smooth administrative continuity cannot be underestimated.

The economic and political orientation of the bureaucrats who determined Japan's industrial policies did not change significantly after World War II. Thus, *wartime* industrial policies, which entailed the systematic development of strategic industries concurrently with the careful protection of key domestic industries, continued to be MITI's primary *postwar* focus. In a nutshell, Japan's wartime economic nationalism became the philosophy of its postwar economic recovery.

The fundamental principles of Japan's economic nationalism during the Munitions Ministry's heyday (1943–45) entailed, of course, the absence of free trade. Japanese technology, currency, and labor were rarely permitted to move out of Japan. In addition, various industries were forced into mergers that resulted in the concentration of entities into monolithic agglomerations. Thus, for example, the MM demanded that the Mitsui Bank merge with the Dai Ichi Bank to form the Teikoku Bank, one of four large bankholding companies that controlled corporate lending in Japan. The Munitions Ministry also decided which corporations would receive massive funding from the banks.

During the decades that followed the end of the Occupation and the realization of Japan's "economic miracle," MITI played the vital role of determining which industries would receive favored government support

---

[7]Ibid.

[8]A notable exception was wartime Prime Minister Tojo, who simultaneously served as the minister of the Munitions Ministry, the minister of the army, and the chief of the General Staff.

and subsidies. Thus, MITI, a political entity, became the central actor in the development of Japan's postwar economy.

In assessing the role of MITI in Japan's postwar economic development, Johnson concluded that "the real equivalent of the Japanese Ministry of International Trade and Industry in the United States is not the Department of Commerce but the Department of Defense, which by its very nature and functions shares MITI's strategic, goal-oriented outlook."[9] However, MITI's influence and powers have been far more wide ranging than those of the U.S. Defense Department. Unlike the U.S. Defense Department, MITI has the authority to influence (through "administrative guidance" and other means) the development of entire industrial sectors. In addition, many ministers of MITI (including such well-known politicians as Kakuei Tanaka, Masayoshi Ohira, Yasuhiro Nakasone, and Noboru Takeshita) became prime ministers.

The power exercised by MITI during the postwar era was the outcome of Japan's state-controlled economic development, which began under the auspices of the Meiji Restoration in 1868. Japan emerged from feudalism in the late 19th century, not as a free market economy, but rather as a unique instance of centrally planned capitalist development. This union of the central planning now associated with communist-bloc countries with the elements of a free market system was extraordinarily successful.

Strategic industries (mining, chemicals, shipbuilding) were carefully nourished and directed by the central government. Financial institutions were especially created to function as conduits of funds from individual savers to vital industrial sectors. The MCI wielded the power to determine not only which industries would grow most rapidly but also which corporate entities would thrive. Thus, for instance, the government gave Mitsubishi ships to ensure that it would grow strong.

The economic history of modern Japan (excluding the war years) reveals the integration of the political and economic systems in such a way that neither the political nor the economic sectors have controlled the nation. In this unique political economy—a product of modern economic and political constraints—ultimate authority to dictate national policies is not possessed by politicians or bureaucrats or corporations.

---

[9]Johnson, *MITI and the Japanese Miracle*, p. 21.

All of Japan's institutions, industries, and organizations support the Japanese political economy as delicately as the surface of water can support a floating needle. Just as water molecules provide a cohesive skin that can sustain the weight of a carefully placed needle so too do Japanese groups, ranging from politicians to gangsters, *through their cohesion,* support a precisely balanced political economy that denies any individual institution or group a firm grasp.

From this system to the fallacious concept of Japan, Inc. is just a short step. The term Japan, Inc. is intended to evoke an image of unfair (and somehow illicit) collusion between the Japanese government and Japanese business. Viewed as a secret conspiracy by Japan's most extreme opponents in the United States, Japan, Inc. is believed to embody the applied consensus of Japan's political factions, ministries, industrialists, and special interest groups. All of these are believed to band together in order to employ all methods necessary to promote Japan's interests at the expense of its trading partners. This degree of cooperation, which surpasses the worst nightmares of antitrust regulators, is perceived as the secret of Japan's economic power. As is often the case, the reality is less complex but more profound than the myth.

The legacy of the totalitarian Munitions Ministry, which frightened away children's tears, was inherited by MITI. MITI has wielded exceptional power, and its close relationship with political factions has been evinced time and again (for example, by the electoral successes of its retired ministers). Nonetheless, throughout the postwar era, neither MITI nor the prime minister (nor any faction) has possessed the power to command particular industries to take actions. MITI can strenuously suggest mergers, but the industries that choose to reject its suggestions can do so—and flourish. Thus, for instance, MITI's attempts to force a series of mergers in the automotive industry (see below) were systematically ignored by all of Japan's automakers. Similarly, Prime Minister Nakasone was powerless to enforce the details of the semiconductor agreement that Japan signed with the United States in 1986 (see discussion below).

No segment of the Japanese political, economic, and financial systems has ultimate judicial authority over other segments. Of course, enforceable laws exist and actions are occasionally taken against individuals or corporations guilty of legal breaches. However, the power to flout official orders and demands is found at every level of the Japanese social and political system. As a result, all of Japan's major groups (the Diet, the ministries, the industrial organizations) can insidiously weaken the nation.[10] In this sense, Japan is the precise inversion of a totalitarian state. Its inverted structure, however, is perpetually teetering on the edge of instability. Consensus is the gyroscope that enables the nation's navigational system to work.

IS ALL OF JAPAN A STAGE FOR A PUPPET SHOW?

Bunraku, a traditional Japanese performing art, can be illuminating to anyone interested in Japan. Dating back hundreds of years, bunraku is a theater in which puppets enact great human dramas written for them by some of Japan's finest literary figures.

Each puppet, half life-size, is manipulated by the movements of three puppeteers. The process of manufacturing the puppets is an art requiring years of apprenticeship. The training of the puppeteers is an even longer process, requiring 30 years for full mastery.

The heads of bunraku puppets are painted with lifelike colors, possess eyes that move in all directions, eyebrows that move up and down, and noses capable of subtle motion. The puppeteers appear on stage dressed entirely in black and wearing translucent black hoods as they control the movements of the head, arms, and legs of the puppet (in order of expertise). These shrouded puppeteers are ignored by the audience, which chooses to see only the colorful puppets.

Devotees of bunraku insist that when the three puppeteers work in perfect synchrony, the puppets seem to mystically acquire an existence and a reality independent of the puppeteers. Thus, each bunraku puppet, pulsating with life and independent will, appears to transcend the triad of shadowy puppeteers that determines its actions.

Group consensus, which Americans believe to be the keystone of Japanese organizational behavior and corporate structure, is not fully understood in the West. It is a very simple concept, however, and it can be illustrated by means of bunraku. Like a bunraku puppet, the collective agreement of a corporate or bureaucratic entity is a well-crafted fabrication.

---

[10]Karel G. van Wolferen argues this point eloquently in his article "Japan Problem," *Foreign Affairs*, Winter 1986, pp. 288–303.

Japanese institutions, like institutions elsewhere, are composed of individuals who are committed to differing objectives and opposing strategies. Those individuals are often more concerned with their personal careers than with corporate objectives. The common view, which sees Japanese employees as working together toward a common goal with no regard for their self-interest, is a fiction.

Consensus is manufactured through guided discussion and socially imposed compromise. To be implemented, the group consensus, like the bunraku puppet, must be skillfully manipulated. Bunraku is the only puppet theater in which each puppet is controlled by more than one puppeteer. The tension created by different puppeteers pulling limbs in different but complementary directions gives the vibrancy of life to the puppet. Similarly, group consensus gains its strength and effectiveness from the balanced resolution of opposing forces.

Because few individuals can have their precise wishes implemented by corporate policy, all individuals are forever striving to achieve a consensus that maximizes the realization of their personal goals. In this way, group consensus becomes an artful compromise among a group of individuals with disparate desires and objectives. When directed perfectly, the group consensus, an artificial construct, achieves a compelling autonomy. Although it does not represent any individual idea or aspiration, it reflects a consolidation of individual perspectives and goals.

The bunraku puppet theater is a telling metaphor for many other aspects of Japanese business. Japan, Inc. is also aptly illustrated by bunraku. Japan, Inc. is a magnificent puppet, dressed and outfitted for economic battle. However, just as a bunraku puppet is devoid of activity without its puppeteers, Japan, Inc. has no existence outside the sphere of particular regulatory and corporate activity.

Japan, Inc. has neither an office nor a staff. Three puppeteers, shrouded but visible, use masterful and harmonious manipulations to give it the illusion of life. MITI, the Chief Handler, controls the head and right arm, while corporate presidents, the Left Handler, control the left arm; and macroeconomic constraints, a key determinant of industrial policy, function as the Leg Handler and help set the rhythm of movement.

Through "administrative guidance," MITI (like all other Japanese ministries) has used its authority to issue directives, warnings, and suggestions to corporations within its jurisdiction. MITI has imposed mergers on declining or fledgling industries to promote strength. It has channeled considerable volumes of government funds into "strategic" industries to nurture growth. Finally, it has used administrative restrictions to limit the importation of goods that would compete with domestic products.

The careful orchestration of MITI policies and corporate actions with economic constraints has resulted in Western perceptions of a concrete entity: Japan, Inc. That entity, however, has the reality of a character portrayed by a bunraku puppet. The puppet's character and goals are a fiction. When the puppeteers are not busy manipulating the puppet's limbs, the puppet becomes an inert cultural artifact.

TRADE TENSIONS: SMILES ARE NOT ENOUGH

From soda ash to supercomputers, from steam coal to semiconductors, Japanese manufacturers and institutions have been reluctant to the point of unyielding resistance to import products from the United States and Europe. Japanese companies simply prefer to buy from those domestic vendors with which they have long-established relationships. Thus, for example, although no barriers prevent the importation of soda ash (used in making glass and ceramics), Japanese firms refuse to increase their foreign purchases of this mineral.

In hundreds of meetings during the 1980s, U.S. and European trade negotiators attempted to persuade MITI that it must force Japan's companies to stop favoring other Japanese companies. Despite repeated assurances of cooperation, MITI delivered few concessions.

In 1986, mounting anger in Britain and the United States led to open threats of retaliation. Margaret Thatcher threatened to revoke the licenses of Japanese financial institutions in London unless Japan opened its financial markets to British institutions. In the United States, the Senate prepared a trade bill involving mandatory retaliation against trading partners with large trade surpluses that did not meet demands to remove domestic barriers to imports. The Toshiba scandal served to burnish the impending protectionist trade bill to a luster.

Mutters of dissatisfaction became grumbles of discontent. Unequivocal signals were given that MITI's shilly-shallying could be tolerated no longer. In response, MITI sent Makoto Kuroda to London and

Washington. Vice minister of MITI, Kuroda was the ministry's top negotiator.

Using "an often condescending tone of voice, a cocky demeanor, and a mocking laugh,"[11] Kuroda expressed the view that "the Japanese market is more open than those of the U.S. and the European Community, and Japan continues to make efforts to approach a completely open market."[12] Speaking in London, he commented that "it is not the Japanese way to reciprocate by using the same level of nonsense to describe the [trade] situation."[13] Offering few conciliatory statements and no concessions, Kuroda confirmed views in Washington and London that Japan did not take its trading partners' problems seriously.

TIED AID AND TRADE

Japan's trade with the Third World has a predominantly complementary character. Usually, Third World nations export raw materials to Japan and import Japanese technology—from radios to rubber factories. Because Japanese exports do not compete directly with Third World products, trade friction between Japan and nonindustrial nations, such as India, Indonesia, and Ghana, is not intense.

The disputes between Japan and Third World countries usually arise from Japan's import controls, particularly those applied to agricultural products. Thus, for example, Philippine mangoes cannot be imported into Japan because they are treated with a banned pesticide. Some agricultural imports, such as rice, are banned on principle.

One issue that has inflamed Third World passions against Japan has been aid. Many Third World nations have insisted for years that although Japan's foreign aid is the third largest in the world (after the United States and France), the amount it gives is small in relation to its massive gross national product (GNP)—0.29 percent in 1986.

---

[11]Damon Darlin, "Japan's Trade Negotiator Irks Americans, His Pugnacious Style Takes Washington Aback," *The Wall Street Journal*, April 3, 1987, p. 24.

[12]Quoted from an April 15, 1987, editorial written by Makoto Kuroda and published in the *Financial Times*.

[13]Quoted in "Tokyo's Chief Negotiator Still Hopeful Trade Barriers Can Be Avoided," *Financial Times*, March 13, 1987.

In 1985, despite promises to the contrary, Japanese foreign aid declined by 12 percent. The following year, in response to a torrent of complaints from its Third World and other trading partners, Japan increased its official development assistance by 48 percent over the 1985 level. These statistics, however, are calculated on a dollar basis (the Organization for Economic Cooperation and Development measures official overseas development aid in terms of U.S. dollars). In yen terms, increases in Japan's bilateral aid have been far less impressive than the 1986 growth rate would suggest.

Furthermore, the geographic distribution of Japan's bilateral aid correlates with Japan's trading interests. Of Japan's government-to-government aid in 1986, 44 percent was directed to China and the Philippines, 34 percent was allocated to other nations in Asia, only a tiny 11 percent found its way to Africa, and just 8 percent went to Central and South America. Under outside pressure, this skewed pattern of allocation will be changed during the next several years.

Even more disturbing to the governments of developing nations than allocation has been Japan's widespread use of *tied aid*. A tied loan is a foreign loan whose proceeds are applied to purchases of goods or services in the lending nation. In 1986, for instance, Japan lent India roughly $75 million at 3.25 percent interest. The loan was to be used for a telecommunications project. However, the terms of the loan stipulated that the funds could be used only to buy equipment in Japanese or Third World markets. Needless to say, Third World markets are rarely capable of competing with Japan's technological suppliers. In any case, the loan terms also required that all consulting services be provided by Japanese firms.

Dozens of similar loans given by Japanese lending institutions to Third World governments have forced recipients to spend the borrowed funds on Japanese consultants and to buy Japanese products. In this way, tied loans have served to increase Japan's growing trade surpluses. To make matters worse, following the appreciation of the yen, recipients have often found themselves obliged to pay unnecessarily high prices for Japanese goods financed with Japanese loans.

All industrial nations extend low-interest tied loans to Third World borrowers and classify such loans as aid. Critics argue, however, that because Japan's interest rates are relatively low, Japanese tied loans are not aid at all. In addition, the close relationships among Japan's consultants, suppliers, and bureaucrats assure that Japanese loans to Third

World nations help fulfill the sales quotas of Japanese manufacturers.

The Japanese government's International Cooperation Agency (ICA) is responsible for coordinating technical assistance to developing nations. In 1986, two ICA officials were alleged to have accepted bribes from Japanese companies in exchange for arranging contracts on aid projects throughout the world. This scandal confirmed frequent allegations that Japanese foreign aid was intended only to promote the international business of Japanese corporations. In this way, Japanese foreign aid was used as a method of sweetening export financing rather than providing grants for development.

In March 1987, under strong U.S. pressure, the Organization for Economic Cooperation and Development (OECD) agreed to a set of rules that would limit the use of tied aid and other subsidized loans. Although Japan and Switzerland expressed considerable reluctance to adopt new rules that would increase the cost of their foreign aid programs, change was in the air.

Finally, in May 1987, yielding to pressure to recycle a portion of its growing surplus, the Japanese government announced plans to increase overseas development aid to more than $7.6 billion a year by 1990. Grant aid to the most impoverished developing countries (the "Fourth World") would reach $500 million during the three-year period preceding 1990, and $20 billion of Japan's payments surplus would be recycled to developing nations. All funds, it was promised, would be provided on an untied basis.

However, there was one catch: a large portion of the funds was to come from Japan's private sector (city banks), and the private sector had not been consulted.[14] Not surprisingly, Japanese banks balked at the suggestion of lending money to high-risk borrowers. Nonetheless, the vague silhouette of a new Japan, leading the world in multilateral lending if not bilateral loans, began to appear in late 1987. Whether the silhouette will be a fleeting shadow or a substantial presence remains to be seen. Meanwhile, developing countries continue to be wary of Japanese lending.

* * *

---

[14]Of the $20 billion, about 40 percent is to be provided through multilateral development banks. The balance will take the form of loans from Japanese financial institutions, including the city banks and Japan's Export-Import Bank.

The apprehensions of developing countries, however, have been small in comparison with the near hysteria that has characterized the response of leading industrial nations to Japan's massive exporting machine. Countries whose exports compete directly with, rather than complement, Japanese products are apt to perceive Japan as a threat to indigenous industry. They consider it Japan's responsibility to alter its trading practices with all nations. Their negotiators make strong demands that would be inappropriate if voiced by Third World diplomats.

In test cases, such as *telecommunications* and *semiconductors,* Japanese negotiators gracefully agreed with their trading partners that a "problem" existed but denied that Japan was responsible for implementing change. These cases—each has recently threatened to explode into an international controversy—exemplify the problems and frustrations encountered by Japan's trading partners.

The two cases are presented in this chapter in order to portray American and European views of trade with Japan. It is assumed that other Japanese trading partners have encountered similar problems and hold roughly similar views. There is certainly little evidence to dispute this assumption.

THE WORLD IS LISTENING:
THE CASE OF TELECOMMUNICATIONS

Telecommunications is one of the most protected industries in industrialized nations, accounting for a hefty portion of their gross domestic product (GDP). Telecommunications services and equipment account for an estimated 5 percent of total GDP in the United States, 3 percent in Europe, and 3 percent in Japan.[15]

State-owned telecommunications monopolies frequently operate or supply a small number of officially sanctioned producers. Foreign corporations are not welcome. In the United States, for example, where non-American firms are prohibited access to the airwaves, there are only three foreign competitors. In France, a state-owned monopoly controls every sector of the telecommunications industry. Similarly, telephone

---

[15]Michael Borrus, "Japanese Telecommunications: Reforms and Trade Implications," *California Management Review* 28 (Spring 1986), p. 44.

monopolies (one domestic and one international) have dominated the telecommunications sector in Japan.

For more than 30 years, Kokusai Denshin Denwa (KDD) was Japan's sole international telephone carrier. During the 1980s, the costs of international telephone calls in Japan have been more than double those of comparable calls in North America and Europe. Recognizing the need to modernize the industry and anticipating an enormous increase in demand, the Telecommunications Business Law of 1984 promised to open the market. In 1985, Japanese authorities authorized the establishment of a second international telecommunications carrier. Legislation permitted the "second KDD" to have foreign ownership of up to one third.

Japan's Ministry of Posts and Telecommunications (MPT), which regulates the telecommunications industry, has long maintained an intimate relationship with KDD. Retiring senior bureaucrats at the MPT have often been given jobs at KDD. This is common practice in Japan, where the institution of *amakudari* (descent from heaven) provides a means for government regulators to move (down) from their ministries into top positions in the industries that they formerly regulated. Thus, for example, the current president of KDD is a retired MPT bureaucrat. While recognizing that KDD's monopoly must inevitably be eroded, KDD and the MPT were strongly motivated to minimize future damage to its profitability.

Following Japan's 1985 legislation, Cable and Wireless (C&W), a medium-sized U.K. telecommunications firm that had been engaged in creating a global network based on fiber-optic technology (the "Global Digital Highway"), saw an opportunity to construct a transpacific cable linking Alaska with Japan. Although C&W was not a prominent international firm (it evolved by creating telephone networks in British colonies), the U.S. Defense Department and National Security Council supported this development of a new fiber-optic cable route, which they regarded as a possible component of the Strategic Defense Initiative plan ("Star Wars").

With this in the forefront of its strategy, Cable and Wireless organized International Digital Communications (IDC), a consortium consisting of Japanese and U.S. corporations and capitalized at ¥360 million ($2.5 million). The largest shareholders in IDC were the Japanese trading company C. Itoh (20 percent), Cable and Wireless (20 percent), Toyota Motor Company (10 percent), and California-based

Pacific Telesis International (10 percent). Additional participants in the consortium included Merrill Lynch and the Industrial Bank of Japan.

This consortium, which was initially the only bidder for the second KDD, gave sole ownership of the fiber optic cable linking Japan and the United States to Cable and Wireless and the U.S. firm Pacific Telesis. Furthermore, as a major shareholder, C&W would be assured a substantial management role. In addition to the transpacific cable, plans were made to construct a satellite air station with operational centers in Tokyo and Osaka.

Japan's Ministry of Posts and Telecommunications did not disguise its opposition to the presence of a foreign telecommunications carrier on the board of directors of the second KDD. Ignoring Japan's new legislation, the MPT pointed out that none of the industrialized countries permitted its international telecommunications companies to have foreign managing ownership. Therefore, Japan was simply conforming to established international practice.

The MPT officially argued that the construction of a new cable was superfluous in light of existing capacity and projected long-term demand. Furthermore, the MPT maintained that it was unacceptable that the second KDD become a part of C&W's independent international telecommunications system.

In this way, the ministry dismissed the practicality, the utility, and the acceptability of C&W's participation in a new Japanese telecommunications venture. Not surprisingly, the MPT quietly encouraged the creation of a *second* consortium to bid against IDC and the foreign presence it represented.

With the word *Japan* prominently in its name, the second consortium, International Telecommunications Japan (ITJ), was capitalized at ¥1.2 billion ($8.5 million) and consisted exclusively of Japanese companies (no foreign firms were allowed): Matsushita Electric Industrial Company, five big trading houses, the Bank of Tokyo, and 48 major firms (all representing potential customers). Instead of planning the creation of a new transpacific Cable, ITJ proposed renting existing cable and satellite capacity from KDD and AT&T—more money for KDD.

C&W responded to the ministry's rejection of the cable proposal by arguing that growth of the Japanese international telecommunications market had been stunted for years by KDD's exorbitant prices and that the proposed cable would be vital to Japan's communications infrastructure if it were permitted to expand in a new era of widespread deregulation. C&W also argued that liberalization of the financial sector would lead to a dramatic increase in the use of international communications. It forecast a threefold increase in Japan's telecommunications market during the next decade (from $1.5 billion in 1986 to $4.5 billion in 1995), while the Keidanren (Federation of Economic Organizations) forecast a nearly sixfold increase by 1995 (to about $9 billion). Led by Cable and Wireless, the IDC urged the Ministry of Posts and Telecommunications to approve licenses for both consortia.

In response, the MPT, insisting that the Japanese international telecommunications market could not support three companies ("excessive competition"), pressured the two consortia to merge. Using a negotiator from Keidanren, the MPT succeeded in persuading all Japanese members of the two consortia to consent to a merger. Furthermore, under MPT direction, the Japanese participants agreed that foreign participation in the new telecommunications company would be reduced to a maximum of 3 percent per company and that all foreign management participation in the second KDD would be prohibited.

Shunjiro Karasawa, the minister of posts and telecommunications, was quoted in the Japanese press as terming Cable and Wireless "greedy" for insisting upon a 20 percent share of the second KDD and a management role. Needless to say, the proposal for the construction of a new cable was quashed.

Cable and Wireless replied that if the new consortium used KDD satellite and cable capability, it would not be a legitimate competitor of KDD. The governments of Britain and the United States were infuriated by the merger agreement. They stated that there could be no doubt that the agreement, representing collusion between the Japanese government and private industry, was designed to exclude foreign companies from gaining legitimate entry to Japan's markets.

Vociferous letters of objection were sent to Prime Minister Nakasone from the British prime minister and the American president. The U.S. secretary of commerce (the late Malcolm Baldrige) sent a scathing letter to Karasawa. Five days later, the U.S. Senate passed a resolution demanding immediate and "appropriate" action.

The Japanese government responded that the promise to allow one-third foreign ownership of the new telecommunications company had not been broken since each of 11 foreign companies would be given a 3 percent share. Nonetheless, as a direct result of foreign complaints, the largest Japanese shareholders in the newly merged consortia agreed to grant Cable and Wireless as well as Pacific Telesis shares equal to those of the six top Japanese partners. In addition, the two foreign firms were granted a management role and were permitted the opportunity to conduct a study of the feasibility of building a transpacific cable.

British Prime Minister Margaret Thatcher announced that her government considered the C&W bid to be a *test case* demonstrating the degree of openness of the Japanese market. She asserted that the outcome of the dispute could strongly influence the future of British-Japanese trade relations. She also suggested that Japanese access to British financial markets would be severely curtailed unless the Japanese government honored its 1985 legislation providing for one-third foreign ownership of a new telecommunications company.

In this way, the issue of C&W's participation in the Japanese telecommunications market became the stage for a bitter trade dispute between the United Kingdom and Japan. Behind the discussions of C&W was the United Kingdom's £3.7-billion balance of trade deficit with Japan.

U.S. senator John Danforth, coauthor of legislation intended to penalize Japan for trade infractions, announced in March 1987 that "the Japanese by their actions are doing more to ensure passage of telecommunications reciprocity legislation than anything I could do."[16] The Danforth-Bentsen bill is designed to make U.S. retaliation mandatory against nations violating international telecommunications agreements.

Encouraged by the U.S. government, Cable and Wireless as well as Pacific Telesis rejected the Japanese proposal. Subsequently, at the Venice Summit, Prime Minister Nakasone stated that Japan had no objection to the granting of separate licenses to each of the two consortia. Despite this conciliatory gesture, the Ministry of Posts and Telecommunications continued its attempts to force a merger between the two consortia. By August 1987, roughly one year after the dispute began, the telecommunications issue promised to explode into a "three-continent trade dispute," embroiling Japan with both the United States and the United Kingdom.

---

[16]Quoted in "Plan to Limit Phone Venture in Japan Scored." *The Wall Street Journal*, March 19, 1987, p. 4.

Under these circumstances, the MPT finally yielded to the accumulated pressure of threatened punitive trade measures from the United Kingdom and the United States. In late September 1987, the ministry agreed to license the IDC to begin a new telecommunications service in Japan beginning in 1989. Thus, Cable and Wireless, with the vehement support of the British and American governments, won a major battle against the bias of a Japanese ministry.

C&W's 16.83 percent share of the IDC in conjunction with the creation of other segments of its Global Digital Highway will make it the first private sector company to control an independent global telecommunications system. It will be perfectly positioned to become a world leader in the telecommunications industry of the 21st century.

And so the tale ends. Foreign pressure saved the day. But the governments of the United States and Britain were not impressed by the MPT's final acquiescence to their demands. Industrial and political leaders in the West were given further evidence that opening Japan's domestic markets to foreign competition required enormous and prolonged political and economic pressure.

JAPAN ACCUSED: THE CASE OF THE U.S. SEMICONDUCTOR INDUSTRY

Forbidden Fruit: Fujitsu Tries to Eat Fairchild

In 1986, Fujitsu, Ltd., a major Japanese electronics firm and the world's largest producer of semiconductors, offered approximately $200 million to buy 80 percent of Fairchild Semiconductor, a Schlumberger, Ltd. subsidiary. Schlumberger accepted the offer and Fairchild executives were excited by the opportunities offered by Fujitsu. Fairchild, a founder and faded flower of the U.S. semiconductor industry, promised to greatly strengthen Fujitsu's presence (in both production and sales) in the U.S. semiconductor industry.

The U.S. Defense Department objected. Fairchild, the Pentagon export control office pointed out, was a major supplier to the Defense Department, with contracts worth about $150 million per year. The only producer of a chip central to the electronic guidance and firing systems of F−16 jets, Fairchild was vital to U.S. security. The takeover of Fairchild by Fujitsu would make America's best fighter aircraft dependent on Japan. The Pentagon maintained that permitting the U.S. Air Force to become dependent on an "economically aggressive power" was intolerable.

The term *economically aggressive* was key to the Pentagon's opposition. Schlumberger, the parent of Fairchild, was itself controlled by foreign (French) interests. Thus, the Defense Department expressed the view that of two U.S. allies, one was more trustworthy than the other.

Subsequently, the proposed merger was postponed by an unusually lengthy U.S. Justice Department antitrust investigation. Critics accused the government of obstructing the consummation of the deal.

The Fujitsu-Fairchild case revealed that there is no U.S. policy regarding foreign investment in strategically sensitive industries. Indeed, Japanese companies already own dozens of small Silicon Valley companies and many others receive research financing from leading Japanese electronics groups. Moreover, U.S. companies have not been prohibited from establishing foreign alliances designed to share in the development of potentially defense-sensitive technology. Thus, for example, National Semiconductor signed a long-term agreement for the development of advanced chips with NMB, a major Japanese producer of semiconductors. Similarly, Motorola and Toshiba have been cooperating in the development and manufacture of microprocessors.

The thorny problem of foreign involvement in defense-related technology was not addressed by the U.S. Department of Commerce. Instead, a House of Representatives committee proposed the establishment of presidential powers to block all foreign investments threatening national security. Meanwhile, it was rumored that in private meetings U.S. representatives pressured MITI to demand that Fujitsu withdraw its takeover bid.

On March 10, 1987, Fujitsu announced that it would not permit "emotional trade issues" to interfere with its acquisition plans. One week later, without explanation, it withdrew its bid. Opponents of Japanese acquisition of U.S. chip manufacturers exulted. "Fujitsu got the message that the U.S. government is not going to allow legal rape and pillage of the U.S. semiconductor industry," remarked Wilfred Corrigan, former president of Fairchild and current president of LSI Logic, a semiconductor producer.[17]

---

[17]Quoted in "Japan Voices Concern at Blow to Fujitsu," *Financial Times*, March 18, 1987.

Not to be thwarted in their determination to cooperate, Fujitsu and Fairchild formulated a cooperation agreement for the joint development of new technology, joint manufacturing in both the U.S. and Japan, and the exchange of rights for current and future products. This agreement differed little in consequence from the abandoned merger.

In early 1987, the Fairchild-Fujitsu merger was widely perceived as a test case of U.S. trade policy. Appropriately, the outcome mirrored U.S. policy regarding Japan. Vague and unresolved U.S. trade positions resulted in small modifications of Japanese plans. The lack of resolution paved the way for new misunderstandings and increased trade friction. The Fujitsu-Fairchild episode demonstrated that the establishment of limits on foreign investments could do little to reduce the flow abroad of critical U.S. technology.

The growing realization in the United States that Japan (and other allies) have access to specialized technology vital to U.S. defense promises to become a key and unresolvable issue in the burgeoning trade conflict. Six weeks after Fujitsu's takeover plans were aborted, the Toshiba Machine scandal was revealed to Congress by the CIA. It is probable that the Defense Department already knew of Toshiba's sale of computerized milling machines to the USSR when it opposed Fujitsu's purchase of Fairchild.

As this book is being written, in the summer of 1987, the semiconductor industry has risen to the forefront of the trade controversy between the United States and Japan. As a result of the "failure" of a semiconductor trade agreement signed by the two nations in 1986, 100 percent tariffs were imposed on selected Japanese imports in April 1987. Although many of those tariffs were lifted before the end of the year, the sting of that action will remain in Japan as a reminder that U.S. anger (though perceived as irrational) is like nitroglycerin: it explodes under pressure or upon exposure to sudden heat.[18]

In 1986 and 1987, when the 3 biggest semiconductor manufacturers were Japanese firms and another 3 Japanese firms were among the world's top 10 semiconductor manufacturers, concerns that the entire semiconductor industry would fall prey to Japan were widespread. In many respects, the controversy that has surrounded the production and sale of microchips is an expression of deep-seated fears in the United

---

[18]As this book goes to press in the fall of 1987, $164 million of the original $300 million in sanctions remain in effect.

States (and Europe) that Japanese competition will destroy crucial industries at will. The development of the semiconductor industry in the United States and Japan and the subsequent Japanese market dominance provide a case in which current Western views of Japanese industrial production and international negotiations can be explored.

From Chip Leader to Chip Underdog

The integrated circuit (IC) was invented in 1959 by Jack Kilby, an American working for Texas Instruments. This discovery roughly coincided with the Soviet launching of the first man-made satellite, *Sputnik*. Partly as a result of U.S. fears of lagging behind the Soviet Union in the key defense-related technologies, Texas Instruments was given government contracts to develop ICs for the Minuteman missile program. The highest priority was placed on the development of production techniques that could yield large numbers of reliable ICs.

Not long afterward, Jean Hoenni of Fairchild Industries developed a photolithographic method (the planar process) for etching IC designs on specially treated silicon wafers. NASA subsequently gave Fairchild contracts to develop computer facilities for the Apollo spacecraft. In this way, the novel inventions of American engineers conjoined with the needs of the U.S. government (defense and space programs) led to the birth and rapid growth of the American semiconductor industry. Subsequent American developments, including the invention of the microprocessor and electron beam lithography, resulted in exceptional technological advances. By 1970, the United States was the unrivaled leader of a multibillion-dollar semiconductor industry.

Although the Japanese corporation NEC licensed the use of planar technology from Fairchild throughout the 1960s, the Japanese semiconductor industry lagged behind that of the United States. Because Japan did not have a significant defense industry or space program, Japanese corporations were not given the vital infusions of research funding received by their U.S. counterparts.

Through administrative guidance in the mid-1970s, however, MITI directed a number of Japan's leading electronics corporations to produce dynamic random-access memory chips (D-rams). Special funding and procurement contracts assured that the fledgling production sector would flourish.

During the decade 1977–86, a steadily growing and highly competitive Japanese semiconductor industry emerged. Japan's leading electronics firms cooperated in research projects funded by MITI while competing in domestic and international markets. One product of the collaborative research and keen competition was a reduction in production costs. This in turn led to a widening of Japan's total share of the world's semiconductor market.

By 1980, Japanese electronics firms held 40 percent of world market share in D-rams. During the next few years, this market share more than doubled, reaching 90 percent in 1986.

In 1984, with semiconductor demand exceeding supply, it became apparent to MITI that an impending world slump in computer sales would lead to a glut of semiconductors in global markets and thus to a decline of prices and profit margins. Fearing that Japan's semiconductor industry would be damaged, MITI advised the nine leading Japanese semiconductor manufacturers to increase their capital spending by 80 percent (to $2.7 billion) over the 1983 level. Increased spending was subsidized by MITI and by Japanese banks, which extended loans at rates far below those prevalent in the United States.

As a direct result, Japan surpassed the chip-making investment of U.S. commercial producers for the first time. During the next three years, Japan's chip makers invested more than 25 percent of sales in new plant and equipment, compared with less than 15 percent spent by their U.S. counterparts. Thus, as world demand for semiconductors declined, Japan's production of chips increased. Japanese manufacturers, determined to corner a larger market share during this critical period, raised production levels.

The strategy worked. Japanese manufacturers successfully *expanded* their total share of world IC markets from 33 percent in 1980 to 48 percent in 1987. During the same period, the U.S. share of world IC markets *contracted* from 52 percent to 39 percent.

Meanwhile, the unit cost of 256-kilobit D-rams (which are used in virtually all computers) plummeted from an average of $10 in 1984 to less than $2 at the end of 1986. Despite the decline in cost and the parallel decline in profit margins, Japan's semiconductor manufacturers continued to increase production, dumping excess supply in Asian markets. Losses (an estimated aggregate total of $1 billion in 1986) accrued by these manufacturers were easily absorbed by their parent corporations, some of the biggest electronics firms in the world.

During the period 1985–86, four of the six U.S. producers of

256-kilobit D-rams discontinued producing the chips for commercial sales. As a result of stagnant world demand, declining prices, and Japanese dumping, the U.S. semiconductor industry lost more than $1 billion in 1986 alone. Layoffs resulted in the loss of 60,000 jobs during the period 1984–86. Meanwhile, U.S. world market share of 256-kilobit D-rams declined to 10 percent, compared to more than 80 percent for Japan.

In 1986, imports from Japan represented 14 percent of the total U.S. semiconductor market. The lion's share of this $1.2 billion piece of America's semiconductor pie was purchased by IBM, which found it more cost effective to import 256-kilobit D-rams than to assume the cost of manufacture. (It is noteworthy that a portion of the Japanese imports were in fact produced by Texas Instruments' highly successful Japanese facilities.) In this way, Japan's chip makers (which were *losing* money) helped IBM to reduce the cost of its computers and to increase its revenue. Thus, while Japanese semiconductor manufacturers seized nearly one seventh of the U.S. market, the U.S. electronics firms that purchased Japanese semiconductors benefited from doing so.

Not surprisingly, U.S. semiconductor producers objected to Japanese encroachment in their territory. They quickly pointed out that "once again" Japanese manufacturers were using predatory pricing to increase their market share in Europe and Asia. It is by no means novel for U.S. manufacturers of all types of products to object to imports and to contend that dumping in third markets undermines their fair competitive advantage. In this case, however, the semiconductor companies had a strong ally: the Pentagon.

Sematech: "A Response to the Japanese Challenge"

Because semiconductors are intrinsic to all advanced weapons and detection systems, the U.S. Defense Department feared that U.S. defense strategies would become dependent on foreign suppliers. A Defense Department task force warned that "U.S. producers are increasingly becoming incapable of producing the highest technology products with sufficient quality in high volumes and with the timeliness required to achieve profitability by American capital market standards."[19]

---

[19]Quoted in Louise Kehoe, "Pentagon Takes Initiative in War against Chip Imports," *Financial Times*, January 27, 1987.

In mid-1986, the U.S. Defense Department proposed a "defense semiconductor initiative" intended to restore U.S. chip-making capability to its former preeminence. In grandiose terms, the new initiative was claimed to be designed to prevent a Japanese "takeover" of the entire U.S. semiconductor market. Curiously, the initiative bore a striking resemblance to methods traditionally used by MITI.

The Defense Department suggested the creation of a semiconductor industry cooperative manufacturing project—named Sematech by the Semiconductor Association. In addition, the establishment of a semiconductor manufacturing technology institute run by Sematech was seen as vital. The proposed project called for special government research funding, with $50 million earmarked for defense applications of new technology and $1.3 billion available to Sematech over a six-year period. Special antitrust exemptions were also proposed so that Sematech would not become an illegal monopoly.

The Defense Department also suggested that various Japanese competitive advantages (such as the lower cost of capital and the freedom from shareholder pressures that facilitated long-term planning) be equaled by special U.S. government protective policies. Charles Sporck, the president of National Semiconductor, told congressional representatives that Sematech "represented a response to the Japanese challenge, a recognition that, in order to remain competitive internationally, we need to achieve a far higher degree of cooperation among ourselves."

The idea behind the Defense Department's proposal is that Sematech would create and manufacture future generations of memory chips tailored to the needs of both U.S. defense strategy and commercial technology. In this way, Sematech would assure that foreign semiconductor producers and scientists would have as little role as possible in the U.S. defense system.

At the time of writing, it is not known to what extent the U.S. judiciary will find the creation of a government-sponsored cartel an acceptable method of rescuing America's semiconductor industry from foreign competition. Nonetheless, in the spring of 1987 the Semiconductor Industry Association, strongly supported by IBM, unanimously approved the creation of Sematech. "Sematech plans to produce its first chips by the second half of 1988 and to achieve parity with Japanese manufacturing technology by 1990," Sporck forecast.

The future of Sematech aside, however, the Pentagon firmly believed that without immediate government intervention, America's chip business would soon collapse. This catastrophe would leave the entire U.S. defense establishment at the mercy of foreign chip purveyors. In such a case, it was argued, the U.S. defense system could swiftly lose the technological edge upon which its superiority depends. This bleak scenario was whispered into ears located in the White House. The ears listened.

Semiconductor Accord or Discord?

Like the Pentagon, many U.S. congressmen believed that Japan stood poised, like an executioner with rifle aimed, to destroy a strategic U.S. industry. Such leading Japanese electronics firms as Toshiba, Fujitsu, and NEC were named by U.S. officials as culprits involved in the widespread dumping of integrated circuits in Hong Kong and Southeast Asia.

U.S. trade representatives negotiated, cajoled, and threatened. Finally, on July 31, 1986, the United States signed a semiconductor trade agreement with MITI. This agreement was intended to stop all of the perceived inequities in the pricing of Japanese chips outside Japan and to help U.S. chip makers gain a larger share of Japan's domestic chip market.

The agreement specified minimum prices, set by the Commerce Department, for D-rams and erasable programmable read only memory chips (Eproms) sold outside Japan.[20] U.S. trade representatives hoped that these minimum prices would eliminate the dumping of semiconductors in third country markets at prices less than half of the producers' manufacturing costs. In return for signing the agreement, the United States agreed to waive punitive duties against Japanese producers for dumping semiconductors in the United States.

President Reagan praised the agreement as a "landmark pact" that would serve as a model for trade cooperation between the United States and Japan. Just six months later, in early 1987, the agreement became the platform for U.S. protectionist legislation. Indeed a "landmark pact," the semiconductor agreement epitomized U.S. convictions that Japan could not be trusted to abide by agreements.

---

[20]Termed "fair market value," the minimum prices were intended to reflect each Japanese manufacturer's cost of production plus an 8 percent profit margin.

For their part, Japanese industrialists and bureaucrats expressed the unofficial view that the United States was a heavy-handed, bumbling producer outrageously demanding that Japan compensate for its inadequacies. Officials at MITI responded to U.S. accusations that the agreement had been breached with denials ("we are implementing the agreement in good faith") *and* counterallegations that U.S. chip makers were themselves dumping chips in third markets, thus discounting the minimum price levels set by the agreement.

It was scarcely a surprise that the semiconductor agreement did not work. The agreement was unworkable before the ink was dry on it.

The Agreement Fails

The minimum prices which the semiconductor agreement demanded were more than double those prevalent in the Japanese domestic market. As a result, American computer manufacturers were required to pay substantially higher prices for their chip supplies than were paid by Japanese manufacturers producing chips in-house. U.S. electronics firms objected to the semiconductor accord.

Furthermore, the price requirement obliged Japanese semiconductor producers to sell their chips at prices far above production costs. The actual production cost, for example, for a 256-kilobit D-ram was roughly $1.15 in early 1987, compared to a sales price of $1.50. However, the agreement compelled Japanese manufacturers to sell such chips for $2.50. Although this resulted in a reduction in their share of some markets, their overall profits increased.

Japanese producers were forced to dispose of their rapidly accumulating chip inventories. The largest producers (NEC Corporation, Hitachi, Ltd., and Fujitsu, Ltd.) ignored MITI's administrative guidance and continued dumping their excess chips in the familiar Asian markets. Soon, other Japanese chip producers followed the example set by the industry leaders.

Japan did not increase its imports of U.S. chips. In fact, Japanese imports of U.S.-made semiconductors declined. According to the terms of the agreement, Japan recognized U.S. demands that by 1991 chip imports should be doubled to 20 percent of domestic consumption (from 9.5 percent in 1986). This provision, even more than other terms of the agreement, was unenforceable. Because the same Japanese corporations that manufacture chips use chips, the need for imports in the Japanese electronics market is slight.

The semiconductor agreement may have been contrary to the principles of free trade. Nonetheless, U.S. trade representatives and congressmen fumed at the failure of Japan to fulfill its provisions. Such phrases as "flagrant disregard" and "continued and intentional violations" filled the Washington air, and "protectionism" became a buzzword. Punitive legislation was on the way.

Congress Retaliates

On March 30, 1987, in a move generally acknowledged as symbolic, President Reagan unilaterally imposed 100 percent tariffs (to become effective two weeks later) on selected Japanese electronic products valued at $300 million.[21] The products chosen either used semiconductors as component parts or were produced by the same firms alleged to be dumping chips. Designed to compensate the United States for business lost through Japanese violations, the tariffs were based on administration calculations of aggregate annual losses. Representing a mere 0.1 percent of total Japanese electronics sales in the United States in 1986, the $300 million of imports covered by the tariffs were a minuscule portion of Japan's total exports to the United States.

This was the first time that the Reagan administration formally retaliated against Japan on a trade issue. It was hoped that the tariffs would shock Japan into enforcing the semiconductor agreement and allay congressional demands for protectionism.

MITI Strikes Back . . . Indirectly

Following the announcement of U.S. sanctions, MITI ordered Japanese chip makers to reduce their output. Subsequently, Japanese firms reduced the production of 256-kilobit and 1-megabyte D-rams by roughly one third.

MITI claimed that the production cut was intended to address U.S. allegations that Japan was flooding world markets. However, Japan

---

[21]The companies affected included Hitachi, Ltd., Toshiba Corporation, Fujitsu, Ltd., NEC Corporation, and Oki Corporation.

controlled 90 percent of the global market in 256-kilobit computer memories and a major portion of 1-megabyte global production. As a result of the production cuts, U.S. computer manufacturers found it difficult to fulfill their production quotas. This forced them to turn to gray markets for semiconductors. These manufacturers (including IBM and Hewlett-Packard) lodged complaints with MITI. (Later, following President Reagan's partial removal of the tariffs, MITI allowed Japanese chip makers to increase their output.)

The MITI cut was perceived by U.S. computer manufacturers as *retaliation* against the U.S. sanctions. They believed that MITI's intention was to motivate them to pressure Congress for a repeal of the sanctions

History and Destiny

Japan's semiconductor producers are vertically integrated with electronics groups (Fujitsu, Toshiba, NEC, Hitachi) and exist primarily as providers to the equipment divisions of their parent companies. The profits or losses of the semiconductor units are not stated in the annual reports of their parent companies.

The massive capital of the parent companies permits the semiconductor subsidiaries to manufacture product lines and to implement plans *independently of short-term market conditions*. The parent companies subsidize losses, invest capital for research, and advise the subsidiaries regarding world market conditions.

The funding provided by the parent companies is likely to become increasingly vital. As a result of the decline in world semiconductor demand, 40 percent of global semiconductor production capacity and more than half of U.S. production capacity was not used in 1986 and will rapidly become obsolete. Furthermore, while the cost of a semiconductor plant was $100 million in 1986, it is predicted to rise to $650 million within a decade.[22] Japan's rich electronics groups are well positioned to fund costly semiconductor production—particularly because the lion's share of their semiconductor output is used in-house.

---

[22]Louise Kehoe, "Semiconductors, Facing Hard Realities," *Financial Times*, December 18, 1986, p. 17.

This is in sharp contrast to the position of the liquidity-starved, small U.S. semiconductor manufacturers.

Although supplying the parent company is the *raison d'être* of Japanese semiconductor operations, Japan's semiconductor producers also aggressively pursue sales throughout the world. The competition for international market share forces them to maximize cost effectiveness, to stay on the leading edge of technology, and, most important perhaps, to maintain a constant level of production.

In the United States, by contrast, most semiconductor producers are not subsidiaries of highly diversified electronic conglomerates. Those that are (such as the semiconductor subsidiaries of IBM and AT&T) produce exclusively for in-house consumption. Consequently, America's chip makers are obliged to shape product lines, marketing, and long-term strategy on the basis of short-term profits.

Because the U.S. semiconductor industry was molded by the needs of the defense and space programs, it focused on the production of high-grade chips. The production of these expensive and specialized chips required an all-industry focus far different from the focus required by the mass-produced commercial chips that spawned Japan's semiconductor industry. Japan's chip producers, driven by commercial forces, succeeded in mass-producing chips of a quality equal to or better than those of their U.S. competitors—and at lower prices.

As a result, U.S. chip makers were destined to fall victim to Japan's subsidized and aggressively marketed mass-produced chips. Nonetheless, America's weakness may very well prove to be its strength. Many market insiders believe that custom-made chips, particularly a category termed application-specific integrated circuits (ASICS) are the chip market of the future. The fastest-growing sector of the chip industry, ASICS promise U.S. semiconductor firms a field in which they are strongly suited to competition with their Japanese counterparts.

The tale is not over, of course. Trade conflicts about microchips will continue to add discord to U.S.-Japanese relations. It still remains to be seen whether or not growing Japanese dominance of the semiconductor industry will emerge as one expression of Japan's economic influence. By virtue of their predominant market share, will Japanese corporations control vital segments of the American defense and aerospace industries? Will Sematech save the day?

NEGOTIATIONS, THREATS, AND LEGISLATION

There are three techniques, often used concurrently, for persuading a trading partner to alter a trade policy or activity. *Negotiations* involving political pressure can offer incentives or disincentives for change. *Threats* to close a market through tariff or nontariff barriers can coerce private firms or sovereign bodies to alter policies. *Legislation* can establish regulations and tariffs capable of altering the flow of goods and capital.

Negotiating with Japan has been a confusing and often frustrating undertaking for many of its trading partners, especially those from the West. Japanese government negotiators offer candidly phrased conciliatory statements in fluent English, French, and German. These urbane high-ranking negotiators (often vice ministers) usually express a deep understanding of U.S. and EEC (European Economic Community) trade problems with Japan. They agree with their foreign counterparts that Japan's markets require deregulation and internationalization.

Having met with these foreign trade representatives, Japan's trading partners initially believe that their positions have been accepted and that change is imminent. Later, when no change of policy occurs, disappointment with Japan increases. Have the high-ranking Japanese negotiators deliberately misrepresented Japan's trade policies? No.

Westerners believe that statements and policy are causally linked. They assume that an official statement that a system requires change and will be changed means that change will be implemented. In Japan, that is not the case.

In Japan, words are words. They are exchanged to express sympathy and understanding, to promote goodwill, and to demonstrate a relationship. For the Japanese, the exchange of words, like the exchange of diplomatic gifts, is important to international relations. However, they do not regard policy as a matter of diplomacy. They see it as an expression of complex internal relationships, traditions, and exigencies that cannot be affected by the words of negotiators. Thus, the job of Japan's sophisticated and articulate representatives is to lubricate Japan's relationships with its allies. It is not to institute policy or to justify policy.

This makes negotiating with the Japanese a difficult task. Governments frustrated by the ineffectiveness of their negotiations with Japan have resorted to threats in order to induce change. As briefly mentioned above, in April 1987 Prime Minister Margaret Thatcher threatened to revoke the licenses of Japanese financial institutions in London unless Japan immediately opened its financial markets and its telecommunications market to British firms.

Had her threats been implemented, the roughly 5,000 British citizens employed by Japanese financial institutions would have faced unemployment. Indeed, the *Financial Times* reported that two British traders who were about to accept jobs with Daiwa Securities Company in London refused the offer for fear that Daiwa's London operations might be closed. Thus, the implementation of Thatcher's threats meant throwing out the baby with the bathwater. Had Thatcher actually sent Japan's banks packing, British nationals would have suffered as the price of protectionism.

Protectionism is a double-edged sword that moves in two directions at the same time. The wielder of this impractical political weapon is destined to stab himself as well as his victim. Then, while both parties lie bleeding, the cause of the problem remains unscathed.

While not oblivious to the problems of launching protectionist legislation, U.S. lawmakers in 1987 perceived no other avenue of communication with Japan. Convinced that the Japanese government was refusing to consider American problems, they decided that the only meaningful message that they could send to Tokyo had to involve economic hardship. They believed that through the infliction of deprivation Japan could be forced to change its closed and nonreciprocal policies. Thus, the Omnibus Trade Bill was based on the assumption that Japan had to be given the punishment of a recalcitrant child. The child who won't share his toys is sent to bed without dinner.

"BLAMING IS NOT ENOUGH: WE MUST ACT OR PERISH"

American legislation is often based on the views of constituents rather than sound economic considerations, rendering trade bills political rather than economic devices. In this way, international political statements are often hidden beneath the mask of economic policies.

The U.S. Congress has the power to launch a trade war through its legislation. Ironically, it does not desire that outcome. By unspoken consensus, U.S. senators and congressmen do not want to damage the prospects of American companies. Nevertheless, a full-scale trade war with America's biggest trading partner (namely Japan) could have no other effect. Thus, it is tragic that trade legislation has become the medium for the expession of American anger and frustration.

CHAPTER 2

JAPAN VIEWS THE WORLD

A HOT SUMMER

It was a hot July day in 1987. I was talking with a Japanese government official in a bustling bar near Dupont Circle in Washington, D.C. He was speaking with vehemence, and as he spoke, he rattled the ice in his glass for emphasis.

"In Japan, subsidiaries are not liable for defaults on loans by the parent company and parent companies exercise little control over subsidiaries. That is the Japanese system.

"Toshiba Machine is an *independent company,* with its own listing on the Tokyo Stock Exchange. It happens to be half owned by Toshiba Corporation. That does not mean that Toshiba Corporation participates in the daily business of Toshiba Machine. To hold Toshiba Corporation culpable for the crimes of a few employees at Toshiba Machine is like holding an umbrella responsible for the rain.

"The Senate and congressional response to Toshiba Corporation is just one more instance of 'Japan bashing.' Vengeful American politicians with little understanding of Japanese corporate structure are interested only in impressing their constituents with bold anti-Japanese statements. By acting this way, they antagonize the Japanese people and increase anti-American sentiment in Japan.

"Over and over again, the U.S. Senate has held a gun to our head and made demands. When we ask what we get in return, they say, 'We won't pull the trigger if you accede to our terms.'

"Now congressmen, *representatives of the American people,* pulverize a Japanese radio while parading a hangman's noose in front of television cameras on Capitol Hill. What are we Japanese to think?

America wants to fan the occasional sparks of trade friction into the flames of trade war."

"Well," I said, "Americans think that the Japanese care so little about the United States that they're willing to endanger U.S. national security just to make some extra money. The Toshiba sales involved the most serious leak of technology to the Soviet Union in decades."

He appeared to be unconvinced. "The technology loss," he said, "is deplorable, and those guilty of breaking the law will be punished. But the U.S. response is equally deplorable and misguided."

I attempted to be diplomatic. "If Japan had a tough espionage law that would result in harsh punishment for the culprits," I pointed out, "then perhaps U.S. anger would not have been as great."

"It was the United States that eliminated Japanese espionage laws!"[1] he replied indignantly. "And can we even be certain that Toshiba's technology *was* used to manufacture acoustically superior submarine propeller blades? Where is the evidence? It's quite possible that European companies sold multiaxis milling machines to the Russians long before Toshiba Machine."

A waitress brought us a fresh round of drinks and then disappeared behind a throng of customers. Mopping his brow with a handkerchief, the government official continued.

"A strong argument could be made that the sale of VAX computers to the communist bloc by a number of European companies was a technology loss of far graver importance. Yet, there was no popular outcry. No protectionist trade bills were drafted in order to retaliate against those countries.

"The same is true today. American senators and congressmen are not using Norwegian sardine cans for their primitive rituals of public destruction. If Toshiba Corporation is seen as responsible for the actions of Toshiba Machine, why isn't the Norwegian government, which owns Kongsberg Vaapenfabrikk, also ridiculed in the same way?"

I had no reply and my interlocutor nodded. We both knew that Washington was angry with Japan and that the episode we were discussing was a catalyst, not a cause. We left the bar and walked out into the sweltering heat of the Washington summer.

"Americans do not like to be surpassed in any activity." The

---

[1] During the American Occupation.

bureaucrat smiled grimly and continued. "The United States wants to punish Japan because Japan has succeeded where America has failed. While the Japanese fund profligate American spending, the Senate blames the entire U.S. budget deficit on Japan."

He hailed a cab, which pulled to the curb. "It is that kind of economic nonsense that angers us Japanese." With these words, he got into the taxi and disappeared.

JAPAN VIEWS THE WEST

For more than two and a half centuries (1603–1868), Japan was ruled by the Tokugawa shogunate. Under a harsh and inflexible policy of seclusion (*sakoku*) initiated in 1634, foreign visitors to the Japanese archipelago were prohibited and travel abroad by Japanese was a capital crime.

By 1639, Japan had been so successfully isolated from the world that even European missionaries abandoned attempts to visit and proselytize. Western ships rarely came within the vicinity of the islands— with a single exception: once each year, a Dutch trading vessel, traveling from the East Indies, would anchor at Deshima, an island in Nagasaki Harbor.[2] Throughout most of the 17th and 18th centuries, Japan was regarded, by those few Europeans who knew it existed, as an impoverished and insignificant group of islands in the general area of China.

In the late 18th and early 19th centuries, Western ships began to visit Japanese territorial waters with increasing frequency. A number of unsuccessful attempts to negotiate trade agreements in Japan were followed in 1853 by Commodore Matthew Perry's forceful delivery of a letter from the president of the United States to the Japanese emperor (the "emperor" to whom he delivered the letter was actually the shogun). This initiated a period in Japanese history termed *bakumatsu*, the end of the shogunate.

* * *

Ever since the hot summer days of 1853, when Perry arrived in Japan to propose "that the United States and Japan should live together

---

[2]Chinese traders also anchored at Deshima.

in friendship and have commercial intercourse with each other," foreigners have been hammering at the doors of Japan. "Unfair treaties" signed with France, Germany, and Holland during the 19th century were humiliating reminders that as a nation among nations, Japan was not in a position of strength.

Fourteen years before Perry landed in Japan, the first Anglo-Chinese war began. The example of neighboring China was a compelling warning to the Japanese. Great Britain, capitalizing on the degeneracy of the Ch'ing dynasty, forced China to permit the importation of opium. Widespread opium addiction came to symbolize the effects of dealing with the West.

Like an addict with glazed eyes, an emaciated body, and a mind focused solely on the infusion of a drug, China became a frail victim of Western power. Chinese wealth (in the form of silver coinage) was drained as inevitably as the vitality of a drug abuser. Not surprisingly, Japan was suspicious of the suggestion that it could "live together in friendship" with the United States. Western nations were dangerous "friends."

Unlike China, Japan was small and homogeneous and had a militarist tradition that had not been diluted by intellectual elitism. Japan could arm itself with advanced weapons and deflect the Western aggression that was driven by delusions of "manifest destiny." The new Meiji regime (which replaced the Tokugawa shogunate in 1868) recognized the urgent need to study and adopt European manufacturing techniques. Only with European technology could Japan replicate European weapons.

In 1870, the Ministry of Industry was born. The new ministry encouraged (through subsidies and credit) the development of all private enterprises with military application. A half century after the signing of unequal treaties, the Ministry of Industry had achieved its goals.

No longer was Japan a sword-wielding, agriculture-based country cringing at the sound of foreign cannon. Japan was able to arm itself and become a world-class military power strong enough to smash Russian forces in a war.

In just one generation, Japan mastered diverse Western technologies—from arms manufacture to mining, from telegraphy to textiles. As a result of Japanese ingenuity, organization, and collective concentration, Japan became the only Asian power in a world dominated by the West.

The stories of Japan's birth as an industrial nation in the early 20th century and of its phoenixlike emergence from the ashes of World War II have justifiably become present-day folktales. During the 1960s and 1970s, Japanese manufacturers applied to radios and automobiles the same skills that had previously produced outstanding military hardware. In this way, it carried the peaceful application of technological research and production to unprecedented heights.

Despite its industrial strength, Japan remained vulnerable. Japan is a nation poorly endowed with natural resources. As the Japanese economy modernized and the 20th century advanced, Japan necessarily became ever more dependent on the use of a wide range of mineral and agricultural resources.

During the 1980s, Japan imported 100 percent of its aluminum, nickel, wool, raw cotton, and corn. It also imported more than 95 percent of its oil, iron ore, copper, tin, and soybeans. Furthermore, it had to purchase the bulk of such products as natural gas, lead, wheat, coal, zinc, and lumber from Western and Asian trading partners. Thus, by becoming a part of the modern world, Japan became dependent on the world's supplies.

Because Japan is an island nation with a strategic dependence on mineral resources, the specter of blockade and tariffs perpetually floats above its political relations with its trading partners. Indeed, were it not for the pressure to procure oil, perhaps Japan would never have annexed Manchuria in 1932.

In 1970, Japan's most important trading partner was the United States, which then bought 31 percent of all Japanese exports. However, American attitudes toward Japan were subtle, complex, and potentially theatening. Although the American occupation of Japan had ended in 1952, the United States still held Okinawa (which it had annexed in 1945) in 1970.

During the late 1960s and early 1970s, U.S. government representatives complained increasingly about the degree of Japanese government protection of industry. They claimed that competition was allowed only in those areas in which U.S. (or European) corporations could not compete with Japanese industries. In a high-handed manner, oblivious to Japan's unique problems, U.S. trade representatives publicly blamed Japan for its trade surplus with the United States.

In 1971, Japan was rocked by the two "Nixon Shocks," which showed its leaders that the United States could not be trusted to act in

Japan's best interests. The Nixon Shocks served as a crude reminder that Japan prospered under the economic and military umbrella of the United States.

The first Nixon Shock was economic. The United States placed 10 percent tariffs on all imports and permitted the dollar to float in the international exchange markets. It also demanded that Japan revalue the yen and demolish so-called protectionist barriers in order to open its market to American trade.

These actions and demands of the United States were outrageous. America's unfavorable trade balance was the result of inflation: the Federal Reserve System had printed too much money so that the U.S. government could pay for the Vietnam War. As a result of the inflation, American products were not cost competitive in world markets. To compound this problem, American businessmen were too parochial. Only by learning the intricacies of marketing in Japan could U.S. corporations hope to find a niche in the Japanese economy. While Japanese businessmen conducted business in English in the United States, American businessmen did not even attempt to learn Japanese.

The second Nixon Shock was political. In July 1971, President Nixon announced that he would visit Peking the following year. This decision, though not in itself harmful to Japanese interests, stunned the Japanese Diet and foreign ministry. The United States, Japan's major ally, had announced a reversal of a critical aspect of its Asian foreign policy without informing or forewarning the prime minister of Japan. This move was insulting and potentially dangerous. What would be the new design of U.S. foreign policy? How would Japan be affected? Apparently, the U.S. government was indifferent to the effects of its actions on Japan.

The Nixon Shocks raised the perennial postwar question: Could Japan depend on the United States for military protection in the event of a global crisis? If forced to choose, would the U.S. government endanger U.S. cities in order to protect Japan? It seemed unlikely. Thus, President Nixon provided proof that Western nations could not be trusted.

More evidence of Japan's immediate susceptibility to foreign whims soon followed. The "Oil Shock" of 1973 further stimulated consciousness of the vulnerability of Japan's economy. The United States, Japan's so-called protector, could do nothing to alleviate Japan's oil deficiencies, which led to the bleeding of its economy and a decline in its gross national product (GNP). That fickle nations such as the United States and Saudi Arabia could dictate, through trade practices, the growth and health of Japan was unacceptable. The Japanese must hold their destiny in their own hands.

Easier said than done. The desire to maintain an autonomous political economy within the expanding nexus of global interdependencies became ever more difficult to realize during the 1970s and 1980s.

Fifteen years after the Nixon Shocks, in 1986, the intensity of Western pressure to change Japanese trade and monetary policies had not decreased. Political pressure (particularly American and British) urging Japan to instantly eliminate "barriers" to foreign participation in all of its markets ignored the unique features of Japan's regulatory structure.

The arguments that the United States and the European Economic Community (EEC) advanced regarding market "reciprocity" were oblivious to the fact that Japanese domestic institutions were no more free than foreign institutions to do as they pleased. For example, the number of institutions authorized to conduct trust banking in Japan was limited to eight. Japan could not be expected to grant a trust banking license to every foreign financial institution that demanded one.

When Japanese institutions seek overseas opportunities, they readily conform to the customs of the localities in which they conduct business. Japan does not demand that foreign legal and political systems grant it special treatment. It expects similar conformity to Japanese law and tradition from foreign institutions seeking access to Japan's markets.

Today, foreign governments threaten retaliation unless Japan burns its regulations and invites immediate access to every market sector. Are these threats any different from Perry's gunboat diplomacy? The more things change, the more they remain the same.

MADE IN JAPAN

How can a resource-poor nation with no military strength other than a small self-defense force hope to control its future in a bellicose world? Is there more than one answer? The solution of the postwar era has been the *power of exports*.

Japan's only hope of being an independent world power was to trade its exports for vital resources and foreign exchange. It would not be correct to suggest that conscious government decisions dictated the direction of growth. There was no master plan for the nurturing of a modern Japanese industrial economy. However, MITI encouraged the resuscitation and subsequent cultivation of choice industrial sectors.

The first products manufactured in the bombed-out shells of buildings in Osaka and Tokyo were crude consumer items intended for Japanese customers. As the nation was rebuilt, factories multiplied like rabbits.

Japan's earliest exported products were not a shining success. Although they were price competitive, their reliability was often questionable. "Made in Japan" became a phrase of ridicule in the United States and elsewhere.

The first Japanese product to gain international recognition as an example of unsurpassed quality was the Nikon camera, which reached the West via American soldiers returning home from the Korean War. In 1958, the development of the single-lens reflex camera ultimately catapulted the Japanese camera industry far ahead of West German producers.

Fifteen years after the war, Japanese products ranging from inexpensive transistor radios to colorful Hawaiian shirts flooded global markets. "Total quality control" was an American concept (invented by W. Edwards Deming) that the Occupation authorities introduced during the late 1940s. Japanese manufacturers developed this concept into an art. Blue-collar workers voluntarily formed "circles" devoted to improving the quality of the products that they helped make.

Twenty years later, the phrase "Made in Japan" acquired an altogether different connotation. Japanese products rivaled the finest in the world. By the late 1970s, the Japanese watch industry, for example, surpassed its famous Swiss competitor.

Akio Morita, the chairman and cofounder of the Sony Corporation, titled his memoir *Made in Japan*. For him, and for the other Japanese industrialists of his generation, the success of Japanese exports was the realization and the proof of Japanese superiority.

It is significant that Morita's autobiography begins with World War II and not with his own birth or the birth of Sony. Japan at the end of World War II was a country in disarray whose only asset was its people. The war marked a great turning point for the people of Japan. A martial tradition that dated back to prehistoric times had ended. The bitterness of defeat was tasted by every Japanese individual.

Like a caterpillar concealed in a cocoon, Japan during the late

1940s and 1950s appeared to the West to be accomplishing little. However, under the leadership of a prescient bureaucracy and devoted industrialists, the country was quietly developing a new form. The outside world was stunned when the butterfly emerged from its cocoon.

At last, Japan was able to show its true colors. By the late 1960s, Japan had become an awesome producer and exporter of all types of manufactured products of superb quality and rare ingenuity. The 1970s saw the consolidation and confirmation of Japanese manufacturing prowess. By the late 1980s, Japan had become too successful for its own good, inspiring severe trade friction with other nations.

Japan's trade problems in the 1980s were bittersweet to Japanese industrial leaders. Although trade conflicts were to be avoided at almost all costs, the existence of such conflicts was proof that Japan was the world's paramount producer. Superior ingenuity and competence were alone responsible for Japan's economic success. Could there have been a better comeback?

THE GREAT TRADE IMBALANCE

The West has become vulnerable to the superiority and low price of Japanese products. Japanese manufacturers have precipitated bankruptcies and industrial restructuring in the United States and the EEC. Not all foreign producers can compete with Japanese products. However, in a capitalist world where free trade flourishes, the best man wins.

Many countries now have balance of trade deficits with Japan. The United States, however, has the largest deficit and the worst attitude. It blames Japan for its massive balance of trade deficit. Such blame is misplaced.

The United States alone is responsible for its deficits. The $60 billion 1986 U.S. trade deficit with Japan is not the result of Japanese trade restrictions or pricing. If Japan demolished every alleged barrier and were completely open (more open than any nation in the world has ever been), the United States would not seize much new market share in Japan and the U.S. overall $170 billion trade deficit would be adjusted by no more than $10 billion.

For instance, if the Japanese market in meat were deregulated, Australia would underprice American beef, depriving U.S. farmers of that market. Would the United States then accuse Australia of dumping meat in Japan? If the Japanese rice ban were abolished, China and other Asian producers would underprice American rice. Would Washington then demand that Japanese consumers buy more expensive American rice in order to satisfy U.S. farmers?

Japanese financial and trade policies have not been the causes of the more than $100 billion rise in U.S. trade deficits during the period 1980–86. The U.S. trade deficit has mushroomed against all of its major trading partners in Europe, Latin America, and Asia. Indeed, the ratio of the U.S. trade deficit with Japan to the aggregate U.S. trade deficit was roughly the same in 1987 as it was in 1980.

The cause of the expansion in magnitude of the U.S. trade deficit is to be found in America's domestic policies and in the patterns of private sector savings and spending. If the United States wants to shrink its deficit with Japan and the world, it must reduce the domestic gap between savings and investment while maintaining a stable dollar.

Rather than considering these concrete actions, American legislators ignore macroeconomic fundamentals and blame their woes on Japan. Legislation that should focus on methods to resolve America's domestic problems is instead aimed against Japan, the modern-day scapegoat for Western failure.

RIDING THE OMNIBUS

The Omnibus Trade Act of 1987 (approved by the Senate on July 21) was intended to give American legislators the opportunity to take public action against Japan and other countries perceived as "adversarial" partners in U.S. trade. Through its more than 100 amendments filling a thousand pages, the bill offered American politicians broad scope to retaliate against alleged inequities in Japan's trade practices. The bill was designed to limit presidential discretion in trade issues because the administration had usually failed to retaliate against Japan and other nations.

For example, a telecommunications amendment[3] would authorize negotiations to open foreign telecommunications markets to U.S.

---

[3]Originally the Danforth telecommunications bill—S 596.

products and would require retaliation if the negotiations failed. Such a requirement promised the potential to pry open global telecommunications markets that are, in any case, deregulating of their own accord.

Prominent among the trade bill's amendments was a two–five-year import ban to be imposed on all products manufactured by Toshiba Corporation and Kongsberg Vaapenfabrikk. In addition, the bill contained a series of proposals intended to force Japan to open its markets or buy more American products. Among these proposals was a move to investigate restrictions preventing American construction companies from participating fully in the construction of the proposed Kansai International Airport (discussed in a later section of this chapter).

Other amendments required presidential corrective measures. Thus, if oil imports were to exceed 50 percent of demand, then an oil import fee (or tax incentives) would be established to stimulate domestic drilling activity. The authority to ban foreign investment if it threatens national security would, for example, enable the president to prohibit Japanese investors from purchasing U.S. real estate. An amendment that would have required disclosure of foreign investment was rejected, however.

The Omnibus Trade Act was fashioned by American lawmakers into a Pandora's box containing every protectionist demon and troll that legislative imaginations could contrive. Not since the Smoot-Hawley tariff of 1930 had American lawmakers participated in such antiforeign mass hysteria.

Ignoring the hard fact that Japanese imports of American products rose dramatically during the first half of 1987 and that Japanese exports to the United States decreased, Washington withdrew into a delusion. Refusing to examine real macroeconomic evidence, legislators instead invented their own microeconomic world and in so doing responded only to their own misconceptions.

HOW TO CUT THE TAIL OFF A DOG

Imagine the highest-ranking representatives of the U.S. Treasury visiting a sovereign nation and a vital American ally to forcefully demand in public that the nation's financial system be restructured instantly. Seem farfetched? Imagine further that the nation they visit has the second largest economy in the free world and that the U.S. secretary of the

Treasury himself calls a press conference in its capital in order to slam his fist on a table and declare that if no action is taken, the forces of protectionism in the United States will get the upper hand.

It happened in March 1984. U.S. Treasury Secretary Donald Regan and Treasury Undersecretary for Monetary Affairs Beryl W. Sprinkel made a trip to Tokyo. They did not visit Japan in order to view the cherry blossoms. Indeed, by arriving during the first several days of spring, they missed the full blossoming of the cherry trees. They did, however, arrive during the final days of the Japanese government's fiscal year. They had traveled halfway around the world in order to meet with their counterparts at the Japanese Ministry of Finance and to demand that Japan expand its tiny Euroyen market and swiftly deregulate all of its financial markets.

In Tokyo later that year, Sprinkel virtually commanded that Japan deregulate its financial system immediately and totally. "The only way to cut the tail off a dog is with a single chop," he informed the director general of the Banking Bureau of the Ministry of Finance.

Why should the structure of Japanese financial markets prompt such harsh and pressing U.S. demands? What was at issue for the United States and Japan?

THE IRON GRIP OF THE REGULATORS: THE CASE OF FINANCE

It is not possible to fully comprehend and appreciate the unique regulatory structure of the Japanese financial markets without some idea of the historical conditions that influenced their development. Although it is impossible to present an adequate survey of Japanese financial history in a dozen pages, a brief sketch can provide an indication of the unusual conditions that preceded the emergence of Japan's financial markets.

A Thumbnail Sketch of Japanese Financial History, 1603–1960

Little is known about Japan's early currency. The evolution of a monetized economy based on universally accepted exchange developed as the result of obligatory population movements. During the Tokugawa era, the feudal lords (*daimyo*) were required to live in Edo (Tokyo) with their families in alternate years. This requirement was invented by the shogunate to reduce the likelihood of insurrection or revolution. Throughout the 17th and 18th centuries, Edo was probably the most populous city in the world, with a population of from 1 million to 1.5 million. The continuous migrations in and out of Edo by the elite contributed to the development of a monetized economy. By the late 18th and 19th centuries, most transactions were conducted in currency.

Gold, silver, and copper coins of varying weights and issuance circulated throughout the Japanese archipelago. Exchange brokers, specializing in coin dealing, provided the populace with an easy means of conversion from one medium to another. In Osaka, 10 large currency-dealing firms (known as the Big Ten) became so powerful that they functioned as what may have been Japan's first monetary authority. By the end of the Tokugawa era, debased metallic currency circulated freely in the national markets and paper money (*hansatsu*) issued by the daimyo circulated regionally.

Although Tokugawa Japan was devoid of modern financial institutions such as securities firms, savings banks, life insurance companies, and long-term credit banks, rudimentary financial institutions did exist. Exchange brokers and credit cooperatives (*mujin*) as well as organized guilds of moneylenders constituted the precursors of modern financial institutions. There were no securities, and except for simple short-term bills of exchange, there were no fungible financial instruments. Most financing existed to provide loans to the extremes of the social strata: the ruling elite and small rural farmers.

The Emergence of the Yen

In Japan at the beginning of the Meiji era, the price of gold was below international market levels and the price of silver was above those levels. As a result, gold poured out of Japan and silver flowed in. At this time, the Mexican silver dollar circulated widely in Japan as a trading currency. When the "yen" was introduced in 1871, it was set at parity with the Mexican silver dollar. (The Mexican silver dollar was equal to one U.S. dollar, and as a result an exchange rate of ¥1 = US$1 obtained.) The difference between domestic and world prices of gold and silver did not at first result in problems of valuation between the yen and the currencies of other nations, nor did it lead to other obvious disparities. Why this should have been the case is a mystery.

By the late 1890s, however, the yen had steadily depreciated against world currencies because of its linkage to the price of silver. In 1897, Japan adopted the gold standard. During the first decade of the 20th century, the first significant sales of Japanese securities to foreigners occurred. These securities consisted largely of bonds to finance the Russo-Japanese War (1904–5) and small quantities of corporate stock.

The Emergence of the Modern Financial Structure

The Japan of 1860 was divided into 262 autonomous feudal domains, each ruled by a feudal lord (termed *daimyo*). The power of the shogunate, which had loosely united these domains through a central government based in Edo, was rapidly eroding. In 1868, following a series of small civil wars (the Choshu Wars), the shogunate collapsed. A revolutionary government with the emperor (Meiji) as its figurehead established a new regime in 1868. The era inaugurated by the new government, which is known as the Meiji Restoration (1868–1912), was characterized by processes of modernization and industrialization of unprecedented rapidity.

The new government was immediately faced with the critical problem of quickly establishing total centralized control of the 262 feudal domains, since each daimyo represented a potential source of rebellion. The successful solution of this problem assured the development of modern Japanese finance.

In 1869, each daimyo was made governor of his former domain and allotted an income consisting of 10 percent of the taxes (paid in rice) collected from the domain. Meanwhile, the central government assumed the debt burden and financing of all local governments. The stipends that the *samurai* class (about 6 percent of the total population) had formerly received from the daimyo were initially maintained by the central government and then substantially reduced.

In 1876, the Japanese government terminated the tithing of taxes to the daimyo and instead commuted their annual payments into onetime monetary pensions in the form of government bonds. This single reform had a profound effect on Japan's financial structure. Virtually overnight, the government had created a new financial instrument that dwarfed all of the existing nonmonetary financial vehicles. This was its intention. Faced with the unique problem of creating a modern financial and industrial infrastructure able to compete with the West, the government arrived at perhaps the only solution possible. In a time when foreign loans, if available, were onerous and indigenous banking capital was small, it was necessary to establish a group of investors who (1) possessed great nonliquid wealth in the form of government paper, (2) had little immediate or direct means of liquidating the government-issued debt, (3) were accustomed to wielding vast political power, (4) had been stripped of de facto political power, and (5) had little means of acquiring political power through government. The government hoped that the major recipients would use the bonds as capital to create financial and industrial enterprises.

Several types of bonds were issued, all salable after September 1878. Most of the bonds bore interest at 7 percent. Subsequently, the government made a vast distribution of bonds, representing an estimated 5 percent of the national wealth, to roughly 400,000 samurai.[4]

The government's intention was partially realized. National banks were capitalized with ex-daimyo and some former samurai owning blocks of stock that they acquired by tendering their bonds. The promulgation of the National Bank Act in 1872 led to the establishment of five national banks between 1873 and 1876, all of which were authorized to issue notes (redeemable in silver or gold) with government bonds as collateral. Some bonds were effectively monetized through acquisition by the banks.

The National Bank Act was a failure. Few bank notes were issued, and most recipients of bank notes immediately chose to convert them to metal. In April 1876, a revision of the National Bank Act rendered bank notes inconvertible. As a result, the Japanese banking system (modeled on the U.S. system) was firmly established by the end of the 1870s. When, in 1879, the government halted the creation of national banks, 151, all note-issuing institutions, had opened their doors in Japan and filled the nation with paper yen. In 1882, the Bank of Japan, a central bank based on the structure of the Banque Nationale de Belgique, was created. It became the sole note-issuing body. By this time, inflation was rampant.

In 1885, the national banks had assets equal to an estimated 15 percent of the national product.[5] At first, former daimyo and samurai

---

[4]See Raymond W. Goldsmith, *The Financial Development of Japan, 1868–1977* (New Haven: Yale University Press, 1983), p. 23.

[5]Ibid., p. 25.

contributed the bulk of banking capital. Eventually, however, the deposits of landowners and small entrepreneurs represented a large portion of national banking assets. Following American and European models, a variety of financial institutions, ranging from commercial banks to insurance companies to a postal savings system, were opened. Thus, during the first two decades of the Meiji era, the entire rudimentary structure of modern Japan's financial system was created.

Yet, the established families were reluctant to gamble their capital by investing in expensive and risky industrial ventures. The enormous expense of funding the formation of factories and the training of laborers had no appeal to merchant families accustomed to a long risk-averse tradition. Instead, the government was forced to borrow from the same former feudal lords whose wealth it had increased through the issuance of bonds. Meanwhile, privately held capital was invested in trade and banking—including the extension of loans to the government—and not in industry.

The Emergence of the Modern Corporate Structure

Leading families, which had been given the special honor of extending loans to the shogun under the Tokugawa shogunate, became directors of banks and the founders of industry under the Meiji regime. These families, the holders of the largest privately owned wealth, wielded a burgeoning economic power. It was a power linked with the central government and inseparable from it: much of the wealth of these families took the form of government debt, either direct loans or bonds. Thus, the financial power of the former feudal nobility moved firmly into the banking sector, favoring lending above industrial investment. In this way, bank capital far exceeded industrial capital.

This posed a serious dilemma for the Japanese government. Vast and populous neighboring China had been overrun by European occupiers. Western military might had recently pressured the former shogun to capitulate to foreign trade demands. That Japan could suffer the same fate as China was an imminent possibility in the world of the late 19th century. The solution to the problem was obvious but not easily obtainable: an army and navy capable of defeating a Western invasion force. The creation and continued support of modern armed forces required the immediate development of such key areas as shipbuilding, heavy industries, and mining.

Merchant families were unwilling to invest in untried, capital-intensive, and risky industrial ventures. The new government was in no position to force powerful financial figures in Japan to cooperate. Thus, the central government was obliged to undertake the task of funding a rapid industrialization that would ensure Japan's security against foreign military invasion (and the more insidious invasion of imported industrial goods).

The Rise of the Zaibatsu

Virtually overnight, the Meiji government became the biggest and most diversified entrepreneur in the world. The government nationalized all shipyards and iron foundries and hired foreign instructors to train personnel in the latest techniques. Technical institutes were established and staffed with foreign specialists. Japanese students were sent abroad for technical training. Similarly, transportation, communication, mining, and engineering were nurtured and developed with state funds and foreign instructors.

Japan entered the modern industrial world in accordance with a master plan whose paramount purpose was the maximization of military advantage. Strategic industries, targeted by the government as most crucial, developed so rapidly that in less than 30 years many of them were on a par with those of the West.

During the 1870s, the Ministry of Industry became involved in all key military industries from the production of weapons and shipbuilding to railroads and telegraphs. Factories producing machine tools, bricks, cement, glass, and other materials were built in Tokyo. Railroads linking key centers and opening domestic markets were constructed, and telephone and telegraph lines were rapidly erected.

To ensure the success of the few private strategic industries in Japan, the government heavily subsidized necessary ventures. In 1874, for example, it gave Iwasaki Yataro, the founder of the Mitsubishi Company, 13 ships and this gift was gratis, followed by the sale of more government ships to his company at a price far below cost. The Mitsubishi Company also was given a substantial annual cash subsidy. Similarly, the Mitsui Company was given a portion of the textile mills and mines that had been confiscated from the shogun by the new state. Through government gifts and subsidies, four large "houses" (Mitsui, Mitsubishi, Sumitomo, and Yasuda) and five lesser ones (Dai-Ichi,

Kawasaki, Furukawa, Tanaka, and Asano) acquired, at formidable discounts, vast holdings that were to become the core of Japan's military-industrial complex.

During the 1880s, Japan's industrialization began to consolidate and became increasingly profitable. The handful of speculators who had purchased industries at extraordinarily low prices controlled a major portion of Japan's new industrial structure. Mitsui, Mitsubishi, Sumitomo, Yasuda, and Dai-Ichi, having accumulated a range of crucial industries grouped like satellites around private banking enterprises, emerged as giant conglomerates, termed *zaibatsu* (financial cliques).

Mitsui and Sumitomo, the two largest zaibatsu, developed from merchant families that had risen to prominence during the Tokugawa era. Other major zaibatsu, such as Mitsubishi, Yasuda, and Dai-Ichi, were created by entrepreneurs during the first 20 years of the Meiji Restoration. By the turn of the century, the zaibatsu had become predominant in Japan's domestic and international trade. In 1900, for example, Mitsui alone accounted for an estimated 10 percent of all Japanese imports and 20 percent of all Japanese exports.[6]

The zaibatsu and other business concerns were not the evolutionary result of a capitalist tradition. Instead, they materialized in a new state whose business past had been based on a system not unlike that of Europe's medieval guilds. In Tokugawa Japan, businessmen cooperated in associations that fixed prices and set production limits. The style of monopolistic cooperation that had characterized Tokugawa enterprise persisted in Meiji Japan. Thus, for example, in 1885 Mitsubishi and Mitsui merged their competing steamship lines into a single corporation, the Japan Mail Line (Nippon Yusen Kaisha). Cartels were established in such industries as cotton spinning.

In addition, the zaibatsu structured their diversified industries as *interlocking combines in which the zaibatsu's own private bank became the "main" bank of member companies,* providing most of their financing, and the member companies in turn cooperated in all areas of manufacturing and sales. During the first decades of the 20th century, the zaibatsu grew through the vertical integration of manufacturing and raw materials acquisition and through horizontal expansion into new

---

[6]Ibid., p. 63.

areas. By the late 1930s, war with Russia and the Manchurian invasion had stimulated the growth of strategic industries, further strengthening the zaibatsu.

Keiretsu, the Reincarnation of the Zaibatsu

In August 1946, a special commission, created by the Occupation authorities, began the task of overseeing the dissolution of the zaibatsu combines, which were viewed as instrumental to Japan's involvement in World War II. In its attempt to fully democratize the Japanese industrial structure, the commission purged hundreds of corporate officers and prohibited all corporate officials from serving more than one corporation at a time.

During the Occupation, senior representatives from the former Big Three zaibatsu—Mitsui, Mitsubishi, and Sumitomo—met frequently in private restaurants. The content of the discussions among these executives is unknown, of course. It is well known, however, that they considered strategies of cooperation and consolidation that would facilitate the restructuring of the firms that had once been the core industries of the zaibatsu conglomerates.

The zaibatsu banks, which had not been dismantled, played a central role in the reorganizations that were to occur after the Occupation ended, in 1952. By becoming the center of new enterprise groupings based on the prewar holding company structures, the banks were able to adopt the role of primary lender to all member companies.

Following the reopening of the stock exchanges in 1949, the banks and the companies that clustered around them (in a loose postwar version of the holding company structure) purchased small volumes (from 0.5 percent to 3 percent) of each other's stock. The resulting interlocked cross-shareholding made the banks both creditors and shareholders in the member companies. It also sealed control of the corporations within the group. Termed *keiretsu,* these new conglomerate groupings became an intrinsic part of postwar Japanese business and finance.

By 1960, the four great prewar zaibatsu (Mitsubishi, Mitsui, Sumitomo, and Yasuda) had been reincarnated as postwar keiretsu. The three biggest maintained their former names, while Yasuda became Fuyo (Fuji). In addition, the Sanwa and Dai-Ichi banks each became the center of massive corporate groupings.

By 1980, 190 major Japanese corporations were core companies within the six groups. Together, the six giant keiretsu, including all of their related and dependent companies, accounted for an estimated 50 percent of all capital stock in Japan.

In the absence of holding companies, the keiretsu maintained "presidents' clubs." Thus, for example, the Mitsubishi keiretsu's Friday Club (Kinyo Kai) includes the presidents of 28 core companies, led by Mitsubishi Corporation, Mitsubishi Bank, and Mitsubishi Heavy Industries (see Table 3–1). In precisely the same way, the Monday Club (Nimoku Kai) of the Mitsui keiretsu consists of 3 leading companies (including the main bank and the trading company) and 20 other core companies. Much the same situation obtains for the White Waters Club (Hakusui Kai) of the Sumitomo keiretsu.

The major shareholders of each company belonging to a particular keiretsu are group members. For example, the five largest shareholders in Mitsubishi Oil are Mitsubishi Corporation (20 percent), Tokio Marine and Fire Insurance (5 percent), Mitsubishi Bank (5 percent), and Mitsubishi Trust & Banking (4 percent). This type of interlocked cross-shareholding (beneficial shareholding) is a characteristic component of keiretsu groupings and serves to insulate each company from outside control.

The chairmen, presidents, and directors of many companies within a keiretsu are the retired or seconded executives of the leading companies within the keiretsu. In addition, the main bank, at the core of the keiretsu, is the primary lender to each of its keiretsu colleagues. During the 1970s and particularly during the 1980s, the key role of the main bank began to break down. Nonetheless, the keiretsu remain strong.

The Death Knell

Working in conjunction with Japan's corporate structure, a highly segmented financial system fueled the extraordinary economic growth of postwar Japan. Large commercial banks based in cities ("city banks") provided short-term lending to Japan's leading corporations. These banks were prohibited from selling, issuing, and underwriting bonds. Long-term credit banks were allowed to issue debentures and were prohibited from taking deposits (other than from borrowers or the government). Small specialized financial institutions accepted deposits and channeled these deposits to the city banks. Trust banks and insurance companies managed pension funds, while securities companies

TABLE 3–1
Core Members of the Mitsubishi Keiretsu (the Kinyo Kai)

Leading Companies

Mitsubishi Corporation
Mitsubishi Bank
Mitsubishi Heavy Industries

Finance

Mitsubishi Trust & Banking
Meiji Mutual Life Insurance
Tokio Marine and Fire Insurance

Chemicals

Mitsubishi Gas Chemical
Mitsubishi Petrochemical
Mitsubishi Chemical Industries
Mitsubishi Plastic Industries
Mitsubishi Monsanto Chemical

Steel and Metals

Mitsubishi Metal
Mitsubishi Steel
Mitsubishi Aluminum

Electric and Machinery

Mitsubishi Electric
Mitsubishi Motors
Nippon Kogaku
Mitsubishi Kakoki

Real Estate and Construction

Mitsubishi Estate
Mitsubishi Construction
Mitsubishi Mining and Cement

Petroleum

Mitsubishi Oil

Transportation and Warehousing

Mitsubishi Warehouse & Transportation
Nippon Yusen

Others

Kirin Brewery
Mitsubishi Paper Mills
Mitsubishi Rayon
Asahi Glass

sold stocks and managed investment trusts. Thus, rigid distinctions were established between the banking and securities industries, between banking and trust business, and between long-term and short-term finance.

Stable interest rates and relatively low inflation helped the Japanese savings rate to become the world's highest. During the era of double-digit growth, Japan's specialized banking enclaves smoothly channeled bank deposits to those industrial sectors that were judged by the government to be the most vital to the national economy.

In 1964, Japan became a member of the Organization for Economic Cooperation and Development (OECD). This marked the incipient stage of Japan's gradual elimination of capital controls and financial regulations. As Japan's domestic and international direct investments increased, international financial transactions were slowly deregulated. The decline of Japan's economic growth rate led to a parallel decline in lending opportunities for domestic banking institutions, motivating them to look to overseas capital markets.

In December 1980, the Foreign Exchange and Foreign Trade Control Law was revised. The new foreign exchange law, which was free in principle, allowed Japanese funds to flow abroad without formal restriction. Long-term capital outflows grew from about $10 billion in 1981 to $86 billion in 1986. by 1984 Japan had become the world's largest single supplier of cash, and by 1985 it had surpassed the Organization of Petroleum Exporting Countries (OPEC) as the world's number one creditor.

Moreover, the unprecedented wealth of Japan's banks and securities companies gave them a strong voice at the Ministry of Finance when they articulated their demands for greater freedom in the financial markets. Meanwhile, domestic investors—particularly corporations —ceased to be satisfied with Japan's traditionally low interest rates and its narrow range of financial instruments.

Concurrently with these pressures, massive Japanese government debt—which had reached its considerable proportions partly as the result of the 1973–74 oil "shock"—was scheduled to come due in increasing volumes during the middle and late 1980s. The volume of outstanding government bonds grew from ¥10 trillion in 1974 to more than ¥134 trillion in 1985. Rolling over this mountain of maturing bonds promised to require vast leverage that would force up domestic interest rates.

The most myopic of regulatory authorities at the Ministry of Finance could read the handwriting on the wall. "Weighed, weighed, counted, and divided." Japan's segmented financial system could not continue in its current state. Internal pressures were shouting for systemic change. And to make matters even more pressing, U.S. financial markets were being liberalized and American authorities were howling for comparable changes in Japan.

The Weak Yen and the U.S. Budget Deficit

Modern Japanese finance originates with the Allied Occupation, when U.S. experts reorganized the Japanese industrial structure and introduced the concept of commercial banking. It is therefore not surprising that during the 1970s and 1980s deregulation in the United States was watched carefully in Japan. The abolition of interest rate ceilings and the disintegration of the Glass-Steagall Act (discussed in Chapter 4) served to introduce an intense competitiveness to American finance. These precedents were used to justify Treasury Secretary Regan's vociferous demands that Japan liberalize its financial sector. Regan's aim was twofold: to allow U.S. banks to participate in a broad range of financial services in Japan and, more important (from the U.S. perspective), to force the yen to become far more international.

The U.S. Treasury Department believed that the yen was substantially undervalued against the dollar. It regarded this undervaluation as the direct result of Japan's closed markets and the provincial character of the Japanese economy.

A weak yen gave Japanese products an unfair competitive advantage in world markets. This, in turn, served to increase the U.S. balance of trade deficit with Japan. In 1983, $22 billion of the $70 billion U.S. trade deficit was with Japan. The U.S. Treasury argued that strengthening the yen was the most effective way to shrink this trade imbalance.

Regan urged the Japanese government to "internationalize" its currency in order to strengthen the yen. In 1984, barely 3 percent of Japan's imports and 42 percent of its exports were priced in yen. The yen represented less than 4 percent of the reserves of the world's central banks, compared with roughly 71 percent held in dollars and nearly 12 percent held in deutsche marks. Although a massive market in Eurodollars had thrived for two decades, a market in Euroyen was virtually nonexistent.

Regan argued insistently that the deregulation of Japan's interest rate structure was imperative. From the American perspective, it was vital that foreign institutions be allowed to participate in Japan's domestic financial markets on an equal basis with domestic institutions. Regan also demanded that the tiny market in Euroyen bonds be expanded. American officials believed that if Japanese and foreign entities were permitted to issue yen-denominated bonds outside Japan, the global use of the yen would grow substantially.

Regan threatened that if Japan failed to open the Euroyen market, thus paving the way for a more international yen, then Japanese banks would be the targets of new U.S. trade sanctions. Regan and other U.S. negotiators referred to legislation proposed by Senator Jake Garn, then chairman of the Senate Banking Committee. If approved, the Garn bill would allow U.S. regulators to review the status of U.S. banks in particular foreign markets when evaluating banking applications. Thus, if Japanese regulators failed to give fair treatment to U.S. banks operating in Japan, then American regulators could retaliate by refusing to approve the applications of Japanese institutions to establish banking operations in the United States or to acquire U.S. banks.

American Confusion

Representatives at the Ministry of Finance flatly rejected the U.S. formulations regarding Japan's domestic financial controls. They dismissed as spurious any suggestion of a correlation between financial market regulation and the dollar's strength against the yen. Instead, they asserted that the U.S. Treasury was obfuscating the key influence of the U.S. budget deficit. The dollar's strength against the yen was the direct result of high U.S. interest rates, which, in turn, were the product of burgeoning U.S. government debt. The abolition of Japan's domestic financial market controls would have little impact on the international use of the yen. Ministry officials pointed out that key imports, such as oil, were denominated in dollars, not yen.

According to these officials, the U.S. government was deliberately confusing three distinct areas:

1. The relationship between the yen and the dollar on the exchange markets.
2. The provincial character of the yen.
3. Opportunities for foreign financial institutions in Japan.

In this way, American concerns regarding the overvaluation of the dollar against the yen were being intertwined with pressures to allow U.S. corporations to raise funds in the Euromarkets and to participate in Japan's promising domestic financial markets.

Furthermore, Japanese economists were quick to point out, there was no necessary correlation between reserve currency status and the appreciation of a particular currency. American demands that the yen become an international currency were irrelevant to American desires that the yen appreciate against the dollar. Japanese negotiators held their ground firmly, repeating a key point to their U.S. counterparts: high U.S. interest rates were *alone* responsible for the undervaluation of the yen against the dollar.

Japanese regulators feared that if the yen were allowed to be freely influenced by market forces, the result could be catastrophic. They maintained that strong appreciation of the yen against the dollar would lead to higher interest rates, increased domestic inflation, and dramatically slower economic growth. Japan's controlled interest rates and tightly maintained monetary policy were perceived as intrinsic to Japan's steady economic growth and low inflation.

American negotiators countered, of course, that U.S. interest rates were not high but that Japanese interest rates were too low. They accused the Japanese government of keeping interest rates artificially low in order to assist domestic corporations and, increasingly, to help finance its budget deficit. U.S. economists dismissed Japanese claims that a strong yen and higher interest rates would lead to inflation.

The Japanese perceived the issue differently. Ultimately, they believed, the Americans were cynically exploiting the issue of the U.S. balance of trade deficit with Japan in order to drive a wedge into Japan's closed domestic financial market system. The United States had become obsessed with the opening of Japan's markets to foreign institutions and was using heavy-handed threats to force dangerously rapid change. Privately, Japanese regulators noted that Secretary of the Treasury Regan had formerly been chairman of Merrill Lynch, the largest securities firm in the United States. Perhaps, they hinted, Regan had his own special interest in foreign participation in Japanese capital markets.

The Yen-Dollar Accord

Japan's financial deregulation, which had been moving at a snail's pace (but moving nonetheless) for 20 years, entered a new phase in May

1984, when two reports were issued in Tokyo: *The Current Status and Future Prospects for the Liberalization of Financial Markets and Internationalization of the Yen,* by the Ministry of Finance, and the *Report by the Working Group of Joint Japan-U.S. Ad Hoc Group on Yen/ Dollar Exchange Rate, Financial, and Capital Market Issues.* Concealed behind these dry and verbose bureaucratic titles was the possibility of a complete overhaul of Japan's financial market structure.

In March 1984, when Regan pounded his fist on a Tokyo table, Washington was frantic to achieve a high-profile agreement with Tokyo on the opening of Japan's capital markets. Such an agreement, it was believed, would lessen a host of domestic U.S. trade pressures. At that time, Japanese exports were flooding U.S. markets because, it was argued, the yen was simply too cheap in terms of the dollar.

The 66-page report released by the "Ad Hoc Group" of the U.S.-Japan Committee on the Yen and the Dollar expressed Japan's agreement to liberalize its domestic capital markets, to give foreign financial institutions the "opportunity to participate fully in Japan's domestic financial system," and to expand the Euroyen bond and banking markets. A key concession of the yen-dollar accord was Japan's agreement to steadily move toward market-determined interest rates. No mention, however, was made of small-deposit rates. The U.S. Treasury Department reciprocated these promises by agreeing to continue efforts to reduce the budget deficit. Thus, while adopting the guise of a mutual exchange of agreements, the yen-dollar accord was essentially a medium for documenting Japan's acquiescence to U.S. pressures.

Japan fulfilled its promises. Not only did it deregulate its financial markets in 1985–87, as specified in the accord; it also permitted foreign institutions wider opportunities for participation. Foreign securities firms joined the Tokyo Stock Exchange, and nine foreign banks were granted trust banking licenses. The Ministry of Finance granted dozens of foreign securities firms the four licenses necessary to qualify them as full securities companies in Japan. Foreign investment management companies were also granted licenses to manage domestic funds.

As a result of the many changes implemented in the financial sector, Tokyo slowly began to approach New York and London as a center for international finance. Widening foreign participation in Japanese financial markets thus provides proof that foreign companies are welcome to compete with domestic firms in their quest for business. Yet, they continue to complain.

THEY DON'T SPEAK OUR LANGUAGE: THE CASE OF THE KANSAI INTERNATIONAL AIRPORT

There is a Japanese proverb that says, "When you come to a place, follow its customs." In the West, the same sentiment is expressed by the maxim "When in Rome, do as the Romans do." Yet, foreign businesses have expected to walk into the Japanese marketplace and sell their products or services without regard for Japan's unique customs.

Foreign demands for participation in the construction of a planned new Kansai airport are illustrative of this insensitivity. The Kansai region is located in the center of Honshu, Japan's main island, and together with the Kanto region it holds more than 50 percent of Japan's population and the lion's share of Japan's industry. Tokyo is the capital of the Kanto region, and Osaka is the capital of the Kansai region.

When in 1968 planners first proposed building the Kansai International Airport (to replace the suburban Osaka International Airport), they never dreamed that two decades later the airport would become a symbol of the trade conflict between Japan and the United States. But it did.

The Kansai airport has propelled Japan's construction industry into the limelight of international news. The publicity has not been welcome. The Japanese construction industry is quite big, employing about 10 percent of Japan's work force and producing a substantial share of its GNP. There are more than half a million contractors in Japan, ranging from massive construction companies to tiny sub-subcontractors.

The linkages between many construction companies and organized crime are known to be close and complex. According to the *Far Eastern Economic Review*, the Japanese police "estimate that as many as 1,000 construction firms are under the control, or at least indirect influence, of gangster syndicates; and official police figures show that nearly 50 percent of all corruption cases . . . implicating national and local government officials are tied to the construction industry."[7]

The Japanese construction industry practices a limited bid-tendering system, termed *dango*. Dango is a form of bid rigging in which

---

[7]Bruce Roscoe, "The Tightest of Closed Shops Still Prospers . . . ," *Far Eastern Economic Review*, June 11, 1987, p. 71.

projects are parceled out in accordance with informal agreements. These agreements are an expression of the long-term relationships among construction firms, suppliers, and government bureaucrats. Only "authorized corporations" holding contractor's licenses are eligible to participate in the dango system.

With a price tag of ¥1 trillion, the proposed Kansai International Airport will be the most expensive airport ever built. About 75 percent of the cost will be consumed by the construction of an artificial island 511 hectares in area and located 5 kilometers out in Osaka Bay. Although the airport will be quite small (with a single runway 3,500 meters long), it is designed to handle nearly double the number of passengers and five times the volume of cargo that currently passes through the Osaka International Airport. Due to open in spring 1993, the airport would be operational 24 hours a day and would lead to the growth of business in the Kansai region.

Not surprisingly, foreign construction companies expressed a strong desire to bid for portions of the project. Their inability to procure major contracts ignited anger and indignation in the United States and Europe.[8] Incensed U.S. construction corporations voiced four objections:

1. From 1980 to 1985, the United States was the world's leading exporter of construction services, with contracts exceeding $225 billion. The comparable figure for Japan was less than $50 billion.
2. U.S. construction corporations were more experienced than the Japanese at building big airports.
3. While Japanese construction firms enjoyed open access to the United States, with $3 billion worth of contracts in 1986, no U.S. firm had won a major construction contract in Japan since 1965.
4. The strong appreciation of the yen against the dollar enabled U.S. construction companies to underprice their Japanese counterparts.

---

[8]The Bechtel Group, Inc. (the world's biggest construction/engineering firm) was given a small contract for the design and construction of an airport terminal.

Speaking on behalf of the U.S. construction industry, Senator Frank Murkowski suggested in 1986 that all federal airport and public works construction bids be closed to Japanese firms until American construction companies were allowed to participate in the construction of the new Kansai airport.

The president of the Kansai International Airport Company (KIAC) responded with perplexity to the foreign complaints. "Whether Americans are putting enough effort into entering the Japanese market is doubtful," he said.[9] Although the initial civil engineering work had been contracted to Japanese construction companies long ago, many opportunities for foreign participation in other portions of the project were still available.

A number of Japanese companies extended offers of collaboration to American companies. In any case, few (if any) American contractors had the land reclamation experience called for in a project of such exceptional magnitude. Furthermore, no foreign contractors held licenses qualifying them to do civil engineering jobs in Japan.[10]

American companies are not willing to make the necessary efforts to conform to the Japanese environment. The staff of foreign construction companies do not speak Japanese and cannot communicate adequately with Japanese workers. "Whether it's civil engineering or whatever, work cannot be done unless the workers understand," said the president of the Kansai International Airport.[11]

Foreign corporations seem to think that they can walk into Japan and conduct business on their own terms. Japan, however, is a sovereign nation with its own institutions and established traditions. Foreign construction firms can succeed in Japan only if they are willing to conform to Japanese expectations.

Japan is a unique country with traditions and characteristics that Westerners cannot appreciate. The issues connected with doing business in Japan are complex and misunderstood by special interest groups that use only trade statistics to support their limited concerns.

The long-term relationships that play a role in business are

---

[9]Quoted in "US Criticized for 'Failures' in Japan Deals," *Financial Times*, June 23, 1987, p. 6.

[10]In September 1987, the Construction Ministry appointed the Bechtel Group, Inc. as an authorized corporation eligible to receive a contractor's license.

[11]"US Criticized," p. 6.

grounded in deeply embedded institutions that cannot be dissolved. Japanese traditions include reciprocity and extend from the poorest farmer to the most eminent politicians. Other countries hoping to do business in Japan would like to reap the benefits that derive from a long-term relationship.

Foreign participation in domestic business is welcome. However, foreign businesses must play by Japanese rules in Japan. It goes without saying that the foreign businesses that come to Japan and are sensitive to the Japanese way of doing business are likely to find success.

Abrasive and tactless foreign demands that Japan dissolve its established structures in order to allot foreign competitors a share of its domestic markets are counterproductive. Japan will change at its own pace in its own way. Meanwhile, nothing good will come from foreign demands that are ignorant of Japanese values. This is exemplified by the case of agriculture.

JAPANESE AGRICULTURE: THE NEED TO BE SELF-SUFFICIENT

National Treasures

Japanese farmers, like masters of pottery or bunraku, are regarded as a national treasure. The farmer, like the pottery maker, may not use the most efficient methods, and his product is admittedly quite expensive. Nonetheless, farmers need to be nurtured and preserved lest their art disappear. If there were no Japanese farmers, the Japanese people would be obliged to eat only imported food. This not only would involve an even greater dependence on foreign sources, but in some elusive way it would entail a dilution of the link (discussed in Chapter 3) between the Japanese and the land that identifies them.

* * *

Japanese farms are, on average, the smallest to be found among the industrialized nations. Barely 1.2 hectares (2.471 acres) in size, the typical farm is too small to support a family. The average Japanese farm requires one person to tend it. This simple ratio of one person to one small farm does not seem surprising. By contrast, however, in the United States the average farmer tends an area of 45 hectares, or 37.5 times as much land as is tended by the average Japanese farmer.

Japanese agriculture is far less productive per capita than manufacturing and most other forms of economic activity. As a sector, agriculture produces less than 4 percent of Japan's GNP. Nevertheless, Japanese farmers are by far the most powerful political lobby in Japan.

How can farmers, Japan's most inefficient producers, who are for the most part incapable of achieving self-sufficiency from their profession, have become and remained kingmakers in a trillion-dollar economy based on financial services and manufacturing? The answer to that question is the key to understanding many of the barriers blocking Japan's trade doors.

* * *

Japanese agricultural products represent a special protected enclave. Of Japan's 27 import quotas, 22 apply to agricultural commodities. One of the most rigorous systems of import controls in the free world insulates Japan's food from global competition. Import quotas on products ranging from peanuts to steak have resulted in domestic prices that are from 3 to 10 times above the market levels of the United States and other free world nations. In addition, nontariff barriers are applied to agricultural imports, such as detailed customs evaluations stipulating stringent health standards. As a result, food prices absorb an estimated 30 percent of the average wage earner's disposable income, compared to 20 percent in Europe and 17 percent in the United States.

In a country renowned for the efficiency of its production techniques, Japan's agriculturalists stand out as a curious anomaly. Using inefficient and costly methods, protected by import barriers and expensive price support mechanisms, Japanese farmers are an odd bunch. Only 13 percent of the farming families in Japan are able to support themselves from their harvests.[12] Without the largest agricultural subsidizations in the free world, the percentage would be virtually zero.

Because the average Japanese farm is today too small to support a family, most Japanese farmers (and their family members) work in nonagricultural jobs to supplement their income.[13] Thus, weekend

---

[12]In 1980, Japan had 600,000 full-time farms and 4 million part-time farms. Thus, for the majority of Japan's farm population, farming is a subsidiary activity. See Jimmye S. Hillman and Robert A. Rothenberg, "Wider Implications of Protecting Japan's Rice Farmers," *World Economy* 8 (March 1985), pp. 43–62.

[13]Hillman and Rothenberg point out that because part-time farmers who enter the job force receive lower wages than other industrial workers, they have "helped to sustain the growth, profitability, and capital accumulation of secondary and tertiary industries in Japan" (ibid., p. 49).

farming has become common in Japan. The small farm size has forced neighboring farmers to pool their resources in order to buy automated equipment with which they farm their rice paddies communally.

While nontariff barriers keep out foreign agricultural produce, government subsidies ensure that farmers profit. Eighty percent of Japan's agricultural products are subject to subsidies that were expected to cost the government about $40 billion during fiscal year 1987. Moreover, government-mandated prices of Japan's agricultural products were expected to cost consumers an additional $20 billion. It has been estimated that if all protection were removed from the agricultural sector, permitting unrestricted imports, the cost of food for the average Japanese consumer would decrease by two thirds.

In terms of economic rationality, Japanese agriculture is a peculiar phenomenon. Indeed, if Adam Smith ruled Japan, there would not be a farmer in the archipelago.

How did this situation come about? How long will it last?

A Capitalist in His Own Right

One of the most successful and durable of the reforms introduced by MacArthur during the initial Occupation years was the Land Reform. Under the motto "land to the working farmer," pure land tenancy (in which farmers owned less than 10 percent of the land they cultivated) in Japan was reduced from more than 30 percent to about 5 percent in two years. To achieve this redistribution, land was taken from landlords and given, in small allotments, to the tenants who farmed it.[14] In his inimitable style, MacArthur summarized the effect of the reform: "Japan was transferred from a feudal economy of impoverished serfs and tenant farmers into a nation of free landholders. . . . Every farmer in the country was now a capitalist in his own right."[15]

Concurrently with the Land Reform, electoral districts were mapped out by the Occupation authorities. The apportionment of the districts was based on population. Thus, the number of representatives in the Diet to which a district was entitled was determined entirely by the district's population in proportion to the national population.

---

[14]Technically, the land was bought by the government. However, because preinflation prices were paid, the land was actually expropriated.

[15]Douglas MacArthur, *Reminiscences* (New York: McGraw-Hill, 1964), p. 359.

During the more than 30 years that the Liberal Democratic Party (LDP) has ruled Japan, farming families have successfully wielded their political clout. This has ensured the maintenance of the formidable barriers that have protected the farmers' produce from foreign encroachment and world market prices. As a result, the average household income of farming families (including income from nonagricultural sources) is more than 10 percent higher than that of urban "salarymen." Farmers pay less taxes, live in larger homes, and own more cars than urban workers.

As the effects of rural-urban migration became more pronounced during the 1970s, the population of Japan's rural farming areas declined drastically. Increasing numbers of farm children decided to move to the cities and abandon farming. Thus, the median age of farmers rose from 41 years in 1960 to 52 years in 1987.[16] Nonetheless, the representation of rural districts in the Diet was not modified in accordance with demographic changes, making farmers the primary base of support for the LDP. In 1987, although farmers represented only about 6 percent of Japan's population, they exercised an estimated 25 percent of its voting power. With roughly 60 percent of Diet members from rural or semi-rural districts, the Diet has been quick to respond to the farmers' demands.

The continuing decline in the size of the agricultural population during the 1980s caused a growing disparity between the number of votes required to elect a rural Diet member and the number required to elect an urban Diet member. As a result, the Japanese Supreme Court ruled that a population difference between urban and rural voting districts of more than three times was a breach of the constitution. This decision led to small adjustments in the size of a few electoral districts. The Supreme Court is likely to make additional decisions against the gerrymandering and to alter the ratio to two times in the near future, thus diminishing the political influence of farming districts and slightly increasing the power of urban districts.

Although changes in population distribution are shrinking the constituency of the farmers' union (Nokyo) and judicial decisions may

---

[16]After retiring from a full-time job, many part-time farmers become full-time farmers. Thus, farming is a retirement activity in Japan, providing fulfilling work and a vital supplement to a pension or an annuity.

reduce the farmers' voting power, it will be quite some time before Japan's farmers lose their crucial political influence. Nokyo, after all, contributes an estimated $110 million per year to its supporters in the Diet.

Nokyo's 8 million members are politically conservative and, almost without exception, support the LDP. Thus, for the present, farmers remain a consolidated and well-organized voting bloc capable of determining the outcome of national elections. Every faction in the LDP depends on the farm vote for the maintenance of its influence.

Urban voters believe that farmers reduce, by however slight a degree, Japan's dependence on the outside world. For this reason, there has not been a popular outcry condemning the farmers' disproportionate political influence. However, the release of the Maekawa report (in April 1986), which urged increased consumption, increased imports, and new housing, has helped legitimate urban concerns about the LDP's preference for rural rather than urban development.

Growing Rice and Growing Trade Disputes

Rice is the center and staple of Japanese cuisine, carrying powerful connotations similar to the connotations carried by bread ("the staff of life") in the West. Although the Japanese diet is rapidly changing, highly polished white rice represents the mainstay of Japanese meals. Thus, the food eaten with rice is considered secondary in importance to the rice itself. The word for cooked rice in Japanese (*gohan*) also means "meal." *Sake,* an alcoholic beverage made from fermented rice, is consumed in a variety of symbolic rituals.

Rice for consumption, for storage, and for secondary purposes (for use in rice cakes, sake, and other products) is Japan's key cash crop. Nearly all irrigable land in Japan has been devoted to wet rice agriculture, with other crops grown only in those fields that cannot easily be made into flooded paddies. As a result, about half of all Japanese farmland is used to grow wet rice.

Much of this farmland, representing roughly one quarter of *all* nonmountainous habitable land in Japan, has soared in value. Although a good deal of farmland is located in the Tokyo and Osaka metropolitan areas, where land prices are the highest in the world, farmland is rarely sold. Emotional attachments contribute to the reluctance of farmers to sell their small parcels, but of key importance is taxation. Farmland is virtually untaxed. But if a farmer sells his land, he would transfer most of the payment to the government in the form of taxes, thus gaining little money and losing government subsidies as well as his family heritage.[17]

* * *

Despite the attention that Japan devotes to rice agriculture, it is not by any means the world's biggest producer of rice. With rice production of about 11 million tons per year, it ranks eighth among the rice-producing nations, supplying just 3.1 percent of world rice production in 1983, compared to 37.7 percent for China and 16.5 percent for India.

The most costly government agricultural subsidy has been the support that has propped up Japan's rice farming. All rice imports are banned in Japan. To ensure that Japan produces sufficient rice to satisfy its domestic consumption, the government purchases the bulk of the rice harvest at a fixed price that is determined each year. (It was roughly $2,000 per ton in 1987, or nearly 10 times the average world price.) This price is intended to counterbalance the extremely high cost of Japan's rice production, which is about three times higher than that of the U.S. and six to eight times higher than that of Indonesia or Thailand. The price supports also ensure the solvency of Japanese farmers.

Most of the agricultural produce consumed in Japan is imported, and the agricultural sector accounts for roughly 14 percent of Japan's imports. Because most of Japan's grain consumption is imported (68 percent in 1983, compared to 36 percent for Britain and 20 percent for West Germany), Japanese consumers have felt strongly that Japan should at least be self-sufficient in the production of rice. After all, Japan imports 95 percent of its wheat and 99.5 percent of its corn. The dramatic increase in the world price of wheat and corn that occurred in 1979 served to reinforce Japan's determination not to depend on foreign suppliers for its rice.

---

[17]The situation in Japan's cities is similar to that in the countryside. In Tokyo, for example, 6 percent of the land area consists of small plots of farmland scattered throughout the city. Because taxes on *urban* farmland are negligible, urban "farmers" (who work in full-time city jobs and farm on weekends), like their rural counterparts, have little incentive to sell their tiny plots to developers. It has been estimated that Tokyo's residential area would increase by 10–15 percent if all the patches of farmland were converted to housing.

To avoid a national rice surplus, many Japanese farmers are paid subsidies to cultivate crops other than rice. After buying the national rice crop, the government sells the rice to distributors at a big discount. By the time the rice reaches the consumer, its price has risen substantially, resulting in the most expensive rice in the world. Meanwhile, the Japanese have been eating less rice as their diets have become increasingly Westernized. Rice consumption has declined by 34 percent since 1960, and it is likely to fall an additional 12 percent before 1990.

In 1986, the government reduced by 6.6 percent the price it paid farmers for rice. Subsequent "negotiations" resulted in a 50 percent reversal of the reduction. Dissatisfied with the resulting 3.3 percent compromise, Japan's influential Zenchu (the Central Union for Agricultural Cooperatives) and Nokyo (the farmers' union) systematically "lobbied" LDP representatives, reminding them of their dependence on rural electoral support. In less than a month, Prime Minister Nakasone announced that no reductions would be made in the price the government paid for rice. In 1987, however, mounting pressures led to a 5.95 percent reduction. Although the price cut will not reach consumers, it was the first such reduction in more than two decades. The price adjustment was an indication of a new government responsiveness to consumer dissatisfaction with high agricultural prices.

Japanese Farm Trade Reform?

Led by the United States, Japan's trading partners have been clamoring for the demolition of the regulatory structure that protects Japanese farmers from foreign competition. It is argued that abolition of the barriers that exclude agricultural imports could quickly lead to a reduction in Japan's trade surplus with the United States and the EEC.

American rice farmers have demanded that Washington pressure Japan to open its rice market to U.S. imports. American rice would cost Japanese consumers less than half as much as Japan's domestic crop. Nonetheless, the Japanese government, farmers, and consumers want to maintain the status quo. Japanese farmers enjoy their subsidized benefits, the LDP is dependent on the farm vote, and Japanese consumers believe that their country should be self-sufficient in rice.

Japanese farm trade negotiators have observed for years that Japan is the biggest export market for U.S. agricultural products and that U.S. farmers therefore have nothing to complain about. The Ministry of

Agriculture maintains that the complete opening of Japan's agricultural markets would affect the U.S. trade deficit with Japan only negligibly.

Japanese authorities have responded indignantly to foreign insistence that agricultural markets be deregulated. They point out that all industrial countries subsidize farming. U.S. farming subsidies through the Commodity Credit Corporation, for example, totaled $16 billion in 1984. Meanwhile, the United States imposes strict tariffs and import quotas on food products ranging from beef to sugar. Similarly, price supports combined with protectionist policies assure farmers in the EEC high prices independent of the world market. By virtue of protectionist policies, prices of such commodities as milk and butter have been so artificially buoyed that the EEC has gained a disproportionate world market share.

Privately, Japanese bureaucrats express exasperation at U.S. and other foreign demands that Japan relax all restrictions on agricultural imports. Japan, a nation with few natural resources, is obliged to import nearly all key staples, including 99.8 percent of its crude oil, 98 percent of its iron ore, and all of its wool and raw cotton. A major industrial nation cannot afford to depend on other nations for its food and thus render itself perpetually vulnerable to global commodity fluctuations and political risk.

Industrial nations that trade with Japan reply to these defensive arguments with the observation that many nontariff barriers in Japan are irrelevant to the emotive issues of food self-sufficiency. Take the case of wheat.

In fiscal year 1986, Japanese wheat consumption was about 4.7 million tons, of which 85 percent was imported from the United States, the EEC, or Australia. The Japanese government, acting as the exclusive agent in all wheat purchases and sales, paid ¥43,686 per ton for imported wheat and ¥184,867—4.2 times as much—for domestic wheat. The government then sold the wheat to flour millers at a fixed price of ¥85,524, or double the price it paid for the imported grain and less than half the price it paid for the domestic grain. In this way, the domestic wheat market has been supported by subsidies and price manipulations at the expense of Japanese consumers *and* foreign farmers.

Frustrated with Japan's regulations restricting agricultural trade, members of the EEC formally charged that, according to the General

Agreement on Tariffs and Trade (GATT), Japan's economic system was itself a trade barrier. From this perspective, the entire character and structure of the Japanese economy preclude open trade. The United States has concurred with this view and has sought more frequent GATT summits (every two years instead of every four) in order to pressure Japan to deregulate its agricultural sector.

In April 1987, U.S. Agriculture Secretary Richard Lyng visited Japan to initiate comprehensive bilateral trade discussions. He demanded that Japan import rice (under a quota system), eliminate quotas on the importation of beef and oranges, relax restrictions on a dozen other agricultural products, and lower import tariffs on chocolate from 20 percent to 7 percent. Mutsuki Kato, Japan's minister of agriculture, forestry, and fisheries, refused to let rice become an issue for bilateral trade negotiations and hedged the government's position on Lyng's other demands.

From the perspective of Japan's bureaucrats, farmers, and consumers, Japan has the right to determine what it will import and what it will produce at home. Japan, an island nation with few natural resources, depends on imports for its survival. That Japan's food supplies, particularly rice, should be controlled by foreign producers is anathema to the Japanese people. Thus, they consider it the fate of Japan's consumers to bear the high cost of national self-sufficiency in food.

If all Japanese government farm subsidies and import barriers were demolished, Japanese consumers would spend substantially less money on food. Some of the savings, argue U.S. trade representatives, would be spent on purchasing more imported products, thus relieving U.S. and EEC trade deficits. And some would be spent on various services and domestic products, stimulating an expansion of the Japanese economy.

It will be a long time, however, before Japan eliminates the densely woven web of subsidies and barriers that protect domestic agriculture from foreign competition. For Japan's trading partners, nothing could be more irrational, unfair, and opprobrious than the expensive shelter that the Japanese government has erected to protect farmers. Today, trade representatives from the United States and Europe are determined to demolish that shelter and open Japan's agricultural market to the world.

UNFAIR PLAY: THE CASE OF THE
U.S. SEMICONDUCTOR INDUSTRY

In mid-April 1987, while U.S. trade representatives accused Japan of ignoring the semiconductor agreement, MITI responded pointedly. In a 13-page paper, the ministry criticized the United States for failing to play fair in the negotiations, for concealing information, and for using accounting methods that had created arbitrary discrepancies between U.S. and Japanese statistics. Discounting American allegations to the contrary, MITI insisted that Japan had abided by the semiconductor agreement. The export prices of Japanese semiconductors had been raised, more U.S. chips were being imported, and the dumping of chips in third markets had been curtailed.

MITI argued that the U.S. Commerce Department based its allegations of Japanese infringements on questionable data. The refusal of the Commerce Department to reveal its statistics and analysis regarding Japanese chip dumping reinforced MITI's belief that there was no basis for the U.S. accusations. The paper stated: "Japan should not be charged with conduct which the U.S. is unwilling to document. . . . Japan has information of its own which demonstrates that the U.S. allegations are incorrect."[18]

A major cause of the misunderstanding was the accounting method used to determine the cost of chip production. The cost of chip production is a vital factor in calculating the "fair market value" of semiconductors. Japanese companies calculate the cost of chips at the date of shipment, whereas U.S. companies calculate the cost six months before shipment. The MITI paper commented that the U.S. method of determining the "fair market value" was "not a universal principle" and was "strictly an aberration."[19]

MITI and Japan's semiconductor manufacturers expressed the view that the United States was going too far in its attempt to impose tight controls on Japan's semiconductor prices. By doing so, the United States was attempting to impose its authority on other sovereign nations.

---

[18]Quoted by Carla Rapoport, "Japan Condemns 'Unfair Play' of U.S. in Chip Negotiations," *Financial Times*, April 13, 1987.
    [19]Ibid.

Japan's leading financial newspaper[20] editorialized that determining whether a firm is dumping should be "left to the government of the country where the product in question is sold—it is no business of the U.S. government."

Accusations of chip dumping incensed Japan's semiconductor manufacturers. They were persuaded that the dumping issue was blown out of proportion to justify anti-Japanese trade measures. In March 1987, in a letter to EEC government leaders, a group of leading Japanese executives responded to an EEC proposal to impose antidumping duties. The letter stated that if the proposed antidumping measures were established, the flow of Japanese investment in Europe would be reduced, eliminating prospects for thousands of new jobs. Japanese-owned factories would be shut down, thus leading to increased unemployment.

Japanese bureaucrats and industrialists cogently argued that retaliatory measures discouraged or directly penalized those in Japan who were determined to improve Japan's trade practices. When the United States threatened to impose punitive trade tariffs on Japan, in March 1987, angry Japanese officials said that such action would "pour cold water" on U.S.-Japan trade relations and in effect would "pick a fight" with Japan.[21]

Many in Japan readily acknowledge that a major cause of trade friction is Japan's unique administrative system. Open-minded Japanese regulators perceive this system as a complex and confusing labyrinth of bureaucratic regulations that are tacitly approved by most Japanese while being incomprehensible to foreigners. Although enlightened Japanese industrialists and officials are striving to change this system, the process is necessarily slow. Foreign measures taken against Japan can only delay or negate internal efforts to alter Japan's trade practices and policies.

In congressional testimony given in the spring of 1987, the late

---

[20]The *Nihon Keizai Shimbun* (Japan's equivalent of *The Wall Street Journal* and the largest circulation financial daily in the world). See "More Noise on Chips," *Japan Economic Journal,* March 14, 1987.

[21]Quoted in Stephen Kreider Yoder and Peter Waldman, "Japanese Say Figures Show Compliance on Chip Pact, but U.S. Data May Differ," *The Wall Street Journal,* March 19, 1987.

Malcolm Baldrige commented that he could "only conclude that the common objective of the Japanese Government and industry is to dominate the world electronics market. Given the importance of this market to United States industry in general and our defense base in particular, we cannot stand by idly."[22]

Japanese government officials perceived Baldrige's comment, and others like it, as intentionally inflammatory. The Japanese government and Japanese industry do not necessarily share common objectives. The United States was thus promulgating a "Japan, Inc." conspiracy to heighten U.S. fears about Japanese trade strategies and goals.

In his discussions of the proposed Fujitsu acquisition of Fairchild (mentioned in Chapter 1), Baldrige termed the deal a "national security risk." The Department of Commerce manufactured a "domino theory" that declared that if Fairchild fell to the Japanese, many other American manufacturers of vital technology would follow. In this way, it implied that Japan, though a U.S. ally, could not be trusted.

Furthermore, the American government resorted to tactics of intimidation to suppress routine Japanese trade activities with the United States. It was through such intimidation that Fujitsu was *forced* to drop its merger plans for Fairchild and Japanese semiconductor manufacturers were *pressured* to alter their legitimate trading practices.

Yuzuru Hatakeyama, MITI's director general of trade, commented that "if the fact that Japan is abiding by the [semiconductor] agreement is ignored, then the reaction of the Japanese people will be very anti-American."[23] The Japanese government, seeking to minimize trade friction with the United States, attempted to mollify heated American objectors. However, high Japanese unemployment combined with the devastating effects of the strong yen gave Japanese negotiators little room for maneuverability. Meanwhile, American insensitivity to how the Japanese political economy worked and American blindness to Japan's short-term constraints encouraged growing anti-American sentiment in Japan.

Japanese economists and bureaucrats recognize that Japan's current account surplus in general and with the United States in particular

---

[22]Quoted in Clyde H. Farnsworth, "U.S. Resentment Grows on Japan Trade Barriers," *The New York Times*, March 30, 1987, p. 30.

[23]Quoted in Ian Rodger, "Tokyo Digs In over Chip Dispute," *Financial Times*, April 2, 1987.

is too high. Virtually no one in Japan disputes this. The ratio of current account surplus to gross national product was 3.8 percent in late 19th-century Britain, when Britain's economy reached its zenith, and averaged 2.5 percent for the United States during the period between the world wars, when the United States posted relatively large trade surpluses. By contrast, in fiscal 1986 the ratio for Japan was about 4.27 percent—far higher than the ratio for Britain and the United States during their heydays as exporters.

Japan's unprecedented trade surpluses conjoined with a significant dependence on the United States are seen as the chief culprits responsible for the ominous trade friction between the two countries. Japan's dollar-based exports to the United States (on a customs clearance basis) accounted for 38.5 percent of its total exports in 1986, a 15 percent increase over the figure for 1976. Japan's investments in the United States have also increased sharply, as exemplified by a JETRO (Japan External Trade Organization) survey indicating that Japanese manufacturing plants in the United States doubled in number between 1980 and 1985 (from 200 in 1980 to 404 in March 1985).

U.S. and EEC responses to trade problems with Japan stress retaliation. Retaliatory strategies are perceived in Japan as gratuitous aggression deriving from resentment of Japanese success. In an April 1987 poll conducted in Japan by the Tokyo Broadcasting System, a majority of the respondents described U.S.-Japan relations as unfriendly. This was a major change from the results of a similar poll conducted a year earlier.[24] Of the respondents to the 1987 poll, 77 percent indicated that the United States was blaming Japan for its own economic problems. U.S. tariffs imposed on Japan because of alleged infractions of the semiconductor agreement are one expression of this phenomenon.

* * *

In early 1987, the U.S. Defense Department published a report stating that all of the memory chips in the department's supercomputers were produced by Japanese manufacturers. A key reason for Japanese dominance in the production of these memory chips is that Japan is virtually the exclusive supplier of gallium arsenide transistors. Gallium arsenide is indispensable to the production of advanced guidance sys-

---

[24]See Clyde Haberman, "Poll Reflects Trade Strife," *The New York Times*, June 5, 1987.

tems. The Defense Department's report expressed the concern that with U.S. military dependence on Japanese electronics ranging from 100 percent to 30 percent, the United States was becoming ever more vulnerable to Japanese supplies.

Later in 1987, the U.S. House of Representatives Subcommittee on International Trade issued a report warning that Japan must not be allowed to usurp dominance of the semiconductor industry from the United States. Were that to happen, Japan would become the Saudi Arabia of chip production. Thus, just as the Saudi Arabian–led OPEC could determine the price of a vital commodity and pressure the United States as a result, Japan too would assume power to exert pressure on American foreign policy.

Both the U.S. Defense Department and the House subcommittee used national security as an argument for maintaining and *protecting* an indigenous industry despite more economical foreign production. Why, then, do American trade representatives reject an identical Japanese argument when it is applied to agriculture? Just as Americans fear that Japan could someday decide to suspend exports of semiconductors or gallium arsenide transistors to the United States, the Japanese fear that the United States could halt exports of food to Japan.

Indeed, in 1973 President Nixon temporarily halted the export of soybeans to Japan. Because 98 percent of Japanese soybean consumption is imported, the brief effect of this ban has not been forgotten. Millions of Japanese housewives were forced to wait in long lines to buy their weekly supply of bean curd and bean paste (versatile ingredients in Japanese cuisine). Several years later, the United States used a ban on agricultural exports to express anger at the Soviet Union because of its invasion of Afghanistan. President Carter's ban on the export of wheat to the USSR was regarded with considerable concern by the Japanese people. In the event of war-caused shortages, could Japan depend on the United States for its food?

If the United States demands that Japan, its vital Pacific ally, should not worry about stable supplies of food, why does it worry about stable supplies of semiconductors from Japan? This apparent contradiction suggests muddled reasoning or hypocrisy.

WE DO NOT WANT A TRADE WAR

Japan's markets are not closed. Certain so-called nontariff barriers have caused misunderstandings with trading partners. To avoid trade friction, Japan's domestic labyrinth of regulations is being transformed into a straight and simple path.

Japanese tariff rates are by far the lowest in the industrial world. At the end of 1986, they averaged just 2.1 percent, compared with a U.S. average of 4.3 percent and an EEC average of 4.8 percent. All of Japan's import restrictions are compatible with the General Agreement on Tariffs and Trade (GATT).

Dozens of American and European companies have set up operations in Japan whose products have achieved massive domestic sales. Indeed, the sales of U.S. subsidiaries in Japan are quadruple the size of the U.S. trade deficit with Japan. Kenichi Ohmae and others have even suggested that these sales are *responsible* for the trade deficit.[25] They contend that because the domestic sales and exports of U.S. subsidiaries in Japan are not taken into account in the computation of U.S. trade statistics, American perceptions of a trade deficit with Japan are false.

A short-term solution to Japan's apparent trade surplus can be achieved by expanding the domestic economy. In 1987, the Diet approved a number of economic measures intended to stimulate domestic demand and thus increase imports. Japan is importing more foreign products than ever before, and trade imbalances will gradually resolve themselves.

Japan wants to avoid a trade war. However, if foreign governments introduce misconceived protectionist legislation, it may someday take countermeasures. Such countermeasures would exacerbate the antagonism between Japan and its trading partners, particularly the United States.

---

[25]Kenichi Ohmae, *Beyond National Borders* (Homewood, Ill.: Dow Jones-Irwin, 1987). Similarly, a study (cited in the *Economist,* April 11, 1987, p. 68) written by Enzio von Pfeil, an economist with Smith New Court, concluded that Japan's surplus could be accounted for entirely by the production of overseas (particularly American) companies in Japan. On average, over the period of von Pfeil's study, "the local sales of Japanese affiliates of American firms were four times larger than the two countries' trade balance."

Nonetheless, strong foreign opposition to now obsolete Japanese distribution and regulatory systems can be a positive force for change. Certain Japanese organizations (such as Nokyo) can go too far to satisfy their narrow interests. In such cases, foreign trade representatives can play an important role as catalysts.

Japanese politicians and bureaucrats who want to modernize regulations but are prevented from doing so by the inertia of a ponderous system can shift the responsibility for implementing change to the insistent demands of foreign forces. *Diplomatic* suggestions are always appreciated. Thank you.

CHAPTER 3

THE WORLD OF JAPAN

Having, by virtue of the glories of Our Ancestors,
ascended the Throne of a lineal succession
unbroken for ages eternal. . .

First words of the Meiji constitution

MY FATHER'S HOUSE

When I worked in Tokyo, my Japanese coworkers took me to a wide variety of restaurants and bars so that I could experience the "Japanese life." They introduced me to friends as well as business associates over sake or Suntory whiskey. Sometimes I would be taken to private clubs that had no more than two tables and a tiny bar. Here Japanese businessmen would relax in a convivial atmosphere in which drinking and singing songs were mandatory. It was a new experience for me to take a microphone and sing a duet with a bar hostess.

Perhaps because I was a foreigner, older drinking companions often delighted in ribbing me about "my role" in World War II. After fending off the remarks of a particularly vehement general manager one evening, I sighed to my friend in a casual expression of my feelings about the conversation. Instead of answering me with the laugh I expected, my friend took my arm and flagged down a taxi.

"I'll show you something that my father once showed me," he said. Minutes later we were standing on a narrow street like many others in neighborhoods throughout Tokyo.

"There," my friend said pointing upward. "That was my family house for generations."

My eyes scanned the six-story glass and concrete office structure in front of us. "Nice house," I said conversationally. "I didn't realize your family was so rich."

My friend shook his head. "This building (or its predecessor, to be precise) was built on the rubble left by your bombers. My great-great-grandfather built the house that was leveled in 1944. My family lost everything. Of course, I wasn't born until 1948, so I had no direct personal involvement in the events. But my cousin still has weak bones because of the milk shortage during the immediate postwar period. He broke his back in a minor accident in 1965 and was hospitalized for two years as a direct result of a systemic calcium deficiency. He remembers the war clearly, although he was an infant at the time. I'll introduce you soon."

"No hurry," I said, feeling uncomfortable.

* * *

This was not to be my last social blunder in Japan. One day, while I was walking down the street in the morning, I saw a new Lincoln Continental double-parked in front of an office building. Large American cars are a rarity in Japan, where their size and gasoline consumption make them impractical. This one caught my attention because it was carelessly blocking traffic and because its tinted-glass windows added an aura of mystery. I wondered whether the car belonged to a visiting dignitary or movie star.

As I surveyed the anomaly, three men wearing similar blue polyester pin-striped suits walked out of the office building and entered the car. All of them wore sunglasses despite the overcast day, and as they passed me, I made a mental note of their identical company pins. I memorized the pin design so that I could later ask my friend the identity of their company. I wondered what Japanese firm extravagantly used American limousines as corporate vehicles.

Later, in the office, I quickly sketched the pattern of the company pin I had seen earlier and asked what prestigious Japanese firm it represented.

"Yes, very prestigious," said my friend, while he laughed uproariously at my question. In fact, while he was still laughing, he began to show my sketch around the office, and soon at least a dozen people were giggling.

Somewhat nonplussed, I waited for the laughter to die down. "Well," I asked expectantly, "what's the joke?"

"The name of the company," my friend replied soberly, "is the Yamaguchigumi."

"It's not listed on the first section of the Tokyo Stock Exchange," I replied authoritatively, proud of my familiarity with the listed firms.

"No, it's not," my friend said.

"What does it produce?" I asked.

"Nothing," he answered with a poker face.

"Oh, it's a service company," I said, becoming impatient with the guessing game.

My friend laughed again. "Yes, it provides a range of special services, from extortion to prostitution," he answered. "It is also the primary source of amphetamines and heroin in Japan, and it imports illegal firearms."

"They wear company pins to announce all of this to the world?" I asked incredulously.

"It keeps people out of their way," my friend commented. "Unlike your American gangsters," he explained, "who are uncontrollable and violent, our yakuza are organized and generally cooperate with the police. The yakuza consist of various factions, some of them quite large, and each faction has its own company pins and business cards."

"Business cards?" I was perplexed. "Each gangster has a card with his name on it, his position, and the gangster group he belongs to? Does it say 'K. Watanabe, pimp, member of the Yamaguchigumi' or 'Yamada, senior dealer in illegal substances?'" I asked facetiously.

"That's right, although, as far as I know, the position of the gangster is not included on the card."

At this point during my stay in Japan, nothing the Japanese might do would have amazed me.

* * *

The longer I worked in the Japanese financial sector, the more aware I became of how Japanese finance differed from that of the United States or Europe. This did not surprise me, because everything about Japan differed greatly from the West.

Differences that at first seemed insignificant to me gained in importance and began to loom over me. For instance, wherever I went in Japan, there seemed to be an excessive number of employees milling about offices, ready to wait on me in restaurants, bowing to me at department store elevators, and ever present wherever services were provided. "Sunshine boys," so called because they had no assigned duties other than to sit in the sunlight in corporate offices reading newspapers, pretended to busy themselves in the office where I worked. The overstaffing, which seemed extravagant, inefficient, and irrational to me at first, gradually became intelligible as I grasped the Japanese orientation. When I first asked my friend about overemployment, I was mystified by his explanation.

"There is no welfare in Japan. Japanese corporations exist so that they can employ people," he said.

"What about profitability?" I inquired with a trace of sarcasm.

"Whereas Western companies exist for the bottom line, profits in Japan are a by-product and not an end," he replied.

At first, I thought that he was being evasive or humorous. Gradually, however, I came to appreciate the truth inherent in his glib observation. Contrary to Western views of labor utilization, the deployment of workers in Japan is not necessarily based on the assumption that good employees contribute the maximum of which they are capable at a given point in time. Instead, the white-collar employees of major Japanese corporations resemble in certain respects the recruits of armed forces in the United States and elsewhere.

Like the armed forces, Japanese companies accumulate the best recruits they can locate and attempt to keep them as long as possible, in the knowledge that their services, though perhaps unnecessary at present, could become vital in the future.

Thus, for example, each year a new crop of fresh college graduates is hired by each Japanese company. These graduates are hired with no fixed idea of how or where they will be employed within the corporate structure. This minor detail will be determined much later, after they have worked for a number of years in a variety of low-level tasks. These unchallenging responsibilities are designed not only to train them but also to reveal strengths and weaknesses to their superiors and, perhaps most important, to give them a sense of corporate identity.

In many ways, the early, tedious years resemble boot camp. Instead of receiving a private's stripe after boot camp training, Japanese recruits (after about two years of employment) receive a company pin. They wear the pin on the suit lapel every day of their working lives. Although my new perception of the system was fascinating to me, I did not understand its significance at that time. My goal was to get a company pin. I was not planning to spend the rest of my life working for a Tokyo securities firm. However, I thought that a company pin would be a unique souvenir of my stay in Japan.

Imagine my surprise when I was told by a senior officer of the company that I would never be qualified to receive a company pin. Until that time, everyone in the office had acceded to all of my requests with remarkable courtesy. The unyielding simplicity of his denial seemed incongruous. That afternoon, while sipping bean curd soup in the company cafeteria, I asked my friend for an explanation.

"Why did the director refuse to give me a company pin?" I inquired as I tossed some seaweed into my mouth.

"Why do you want a company pin?" my friend countered.

I could immediately sense that one of our baffling discussions was about to begin.

"For a souvenir?" I suggested tentatively.

"Company pins are not souvenirs," my friend replied matter-of-factly.

"What are they then?" I asked pointedly.

"They are like *hachimaki*," he explained.

I shook my head to indicate that I had no knowledge of hachimaki.

"Hachimaki," he explained patiently, "are headbands."

"Oh," I replied uncertainly.

"We Japanese, unlike you Americans, like to do things in groups. We know that the group is more powerful than the individual. When a group is facing a very difficult task, extra strength is needed. So, all of the group members wear identical hachimaki. The hachimaki focuses the power of their concentration on and dedication to the group goal. By wearing a hachimaki, a person abandons his selfish interests and insecurities. He devotes himself entirely to a single objective. Hachimaki can be worn by all kinds of people. Next time we go to a sushi restaurant, I'll point one out to you. Sushi makers wear them. Students at *juku*, special schools for exam preparation, also wear them. During the Pacific War, *kamikaze* pilots tied them on each other's foreheads before entering their planes."

"Well," I began firmly, returning to the subject of the pin. "I'm part of the company, so why can't I wear a company pin? Perhaps it would improve my work."

My friend shook his head, indicating pity. "You haven't understood anything I've said."

My perplexity increased because I thought that I had followed his argument quite well.

"Although you are an employee, you are not part of the company. You cannot wear a company pin."

"I'm not part of the company?" I repeated. "Who is paying my salary?"

"The situation is very simple. This is a Japanese company, and you are not Japanese. Therefore, you are not a part of the company, though you are an employee of the company. For example, we rent a mainframe computer. It is very expensive, and it is a valuable component of our corporate operations. The computer, of course, is not a part of the company. We use its services and pay for its availability accordingly. You are like the computer. Your abilities are valued, and we all appreciate having you with us."

"It sounds as though you are suggesting that I'm not human."

"No," he said, "I'm saying that you are a foreigner. You are human, but you aren't Japanese. Your heritage derives from the United States, so your goals belong to the United States. Your goals will never be Japanese. So, how can you truly be a part of a Japanese company?"

We sipped our green tea in silence as I pondered my origins. I wondered whether Kipling was right after all and "East is East and West is West and ne'er the twain shall meet."

THE RISING SUN

The rising sun is the symbol of Japan. The Japanese national flag has a white background on which the red orb of the sun is suspended as though it were floating in its own light. The sun is one of Japan's most ancient symbols. The Imperial family claims descent from the sun, and during World War II, when the emperor was considered a divinity, the rising sun symbolized Japan's emerging military power.

Although archaeologists can trace the origins of the Japanese people to successive waves of migration from the Asian continent (and possibly Southeast Asia), folklore indicates a different origin. During Japan's earliest history, the country was divided into clan groupings, termed *uji*. Each uji controlled a particular geographic area and worshiped its own god, which was defined as a founding ancestor. The uji battled each other for control of arable land until members of the Yamato uji, descendants of the sun line, consolidated power during the fifth century.

Today, the imperial family traces its descent directly to the Yamato and from the Yamato to the sun. In the absence of genealogical information, it is assumed that all Japanese can claim ancestry from the ancient gods of the uji. Thus, all of the Japanese people are descended from gods.

WE THE JAPANESE

The human heart is made up of cells. When separated and suspended in a sterile medium, the individual cells beat independently. If two cells are pushed together so that they are in contact, eventually they conform to the same rhythm, beating synchronously. In fact, if cells from different hearts of the same species are put together, they invariably beat together.[1]

The Japanese, like individual heart cells, combine into a unified entity that they term "we the Japanese."

"We the Japanese" is a category that conveys the shared culture, language, history, and location of one national group. The Japanese regard themselves as racially and linguistically homogeneous, despite some evidence to the contrary. The roots of "we the Japanese" are partially explained and justified by Shinto and its myths.[2]

Shinto, a tradition rather than a religion, combines Chinese and Buddhist influences with ancient animistic beliefs. In this tradition, the worship of natural forces and parts of nature itself, such as trees and rocks, is linked with ancestor worship. After death, ancestors become *kami*, which may be loosely translated as gods. These kami dwell within the land, giving the land a soul, the soul of Japan. The soul of Japan, the souls of the ancestors, and the souls of the living Japanese people are believed to be interlinked.

Thus, according to the Shinto beliefs that still permeate many aspects of Japanese culture, the Japanese people ("we the Japanese") cannot be separated from Japan the land. A Japanese person not resident in Japan is not fully Japanese. In this way, the Tokugawa ban on travel outside Japan can be understood in terms of Shinto.

Today, Japanese businessmen who return to Japan after long assignments abroad are not at first regarded as full members of their companies. A period of adjustment must mediate between the residence abroad (a period of enforced "non-Japaneseness") and residence in

---

[1]This is a necessarily simplified description. For more detail see N. Sperelakis, "Electrical Properties of Embryonic Heart Cells," in W. C. DeMello, ed., *Electrical Phenomena in the Heart* (New York: Academic Press, 1972).

[2]In addition to Shinto, Zen Buddhism subtly permeates Japanese culture. Zen, because of its complexity and elusiveness, will not be discussed here. However, the critical influence of Zen will be explored in my forthcoming book.

Japan. During this adjustment period, the Japanese businessmen gradually lose the "smell of the foreigners" that figuratively clings to their skin and their thoughts. Similarly, Japanese schoolchildren who return to Japan after a period of foreign residence are usually harassed by their peers because of actual or putative foreign influences. To be separated from the land for more than a brief period is to lose a component of Japanese identity.

IN-GROUPS AND OUT-GROUPS

In-Groups

From earliest childhood, each Japanese learns that he belongs to a group of peers. Incalculable importance is attributed to a primary loyalty to this immediate group. Both in folklore and in contemporary society, betrayal of the group is seen as the most heinous of acts. Children have beaten, almost to the point of death, other children who have been perceived as abandoning their group. A Japanese, like a single heart cell, is useless without the support of a group.

There are many types of groups in Japan. Indeed, within a single corporation one person may belong to a number of different but overlapping groups. Dedication to the group can be as strong in a school or a sports club as in the workplace. The primary group, of course, is "we the Japanese"—the entire nation.

Foreigners accustomed to cultural heterogeneity have difficulty in comprehending Japan's homogeneous society. Nearly all the residents of the archipelago share a common history and what is reputed to be a common racial heritage. Within this homogeneous society, considerable value is attached to conformity. Prime Minister Nakasone's comment in 1986 that the average level of intelligence in America is impeded by the presence of "quite a few black people, Puerto Ricans, and Mexicans" is indicative of the Japanese attitude toward racial and cultural mixing.

Out-Groups

"We the Japanese" does not include certain segments of Japan's population. Japan is one of the few countries in the world where place of birth does not assure citizenship. Second- and third-generation "residents" of

Japan, including 700,000 Koreans, are not entitled to citizenship and must submit to periodic fingerprinting as aliens. These formal barriers are small inconveniences compared to established discriminatory practices that exclude certain groups, such as Koreans, from many opportunities.

Unlike the Koreans, another out-group, the *burakumin*,[3] are Japanese citizens, free to live as ordinary Japanese. The burakumin have not existed as an official category since the Emperor Meiji declared them "new citizens" in 1871.

The burakumin, who are believed to be descendants of an ancient caste of leather workers, were originally shunned as polluted people dealing with carcasses. They were termed *eta* (meaning "much filth") because in a Buddhist society that prohibited the slaughter of animals, contact with the dead was defiling. The burakumin of pre-Meiji Japan were forced to live in specified sections of the cities or settlements (*buraku* means "community" and *min* simply means "people") and were prohibited from wearing shoes. They were required to use straw to tie their hair, and a patch of leather sewn to their clothes identified them as a separate polluted caste of nonhumans.

Today's officially nonexistent burakumin number from 1 million to 3 million and continue to live as a distinct group. They can rarely hope to marry ordinary Japanese, and their educational and employment opportunities are severely constrained. As in pre-Meiji Japan, they live in slum areas in Japan's cities. They are still an out-group.

Heart cells from different hearts beat together. Cells from other organs have no compatibility with heart cells.

In Japan, it was once believed that the burakumin carried an inherited physical stigma—a blue mark under each arm.[4] Like the smell of butter that is believed to cling to the skin of Europeans, the stigma was mythical.

---

[3]For further discussions of the burakumin, see Sueo Murakoshi, ed., *Discrimination against Buraku, Today* (Osaka: Burakumin Liberation Research Institute, 1987); and Hiroshi Wagatsuma, "Socialization, Self-Perception, and Burakumin Status," in George A. De Vos, *Socialization for Achievement: Essays on the Cultural Psychology of the Japanese* (Berkeley: University of California Press, 1975), pp. 391–419.

[4]Wagatsuma, "Socialization, Self-Perception, and Burakumin Status," p. 413.

OFFICE FURNITURE

Of all the changes and reforms introduced in Japan during the 20th century, none would seem to be more irrelevant to understanding Japan than office furniture. Yet, the decor and the use of space in Japanese offices provide a compelling example of the role of the individual in Japan's post-industrial society.

The standard narrow steel-gray desks and the uncomfortable gray swivel chairs used by the staff of the supreme commander for the Allied powers (SCAP) quickly found their way to the rebuilt and reorganized offices of Japan's various ministries—and from the ministries to Japan's postwar corporations.

Today, undersized gray metal office furniture is still *de rigueur* in Japanese corporate and government offices. The bureaucrats, managers, administrators, and other personnel who are the body and soul of every institution in Japan, work in offices packed with serried rows of gray desks.

Each desk supports a number of gray bins overflowing with stacks of paper. As in the military, most desks do not hold personal mementos, such as family photographs. And as in the army offices of the late 1940s, the desks rest on linoleum floors that are seldom maintained. Cigarette smoke fills the air, while uniformed women (who never smoke at the office) fulfill low-level secretarial and administrative tasks.

* * *

Long after the computer revolution transformed American offices, technology to facilitate the rapid use of the Japanese written language (which uses ideographs as well as several syllabic systems) had not been developed. By the mid-1980s, however, new software permitted a wide use of the Japanese language on computer screens and spreadsheets had advanced to remarkably high levels of refinement.

Nonetheless, in 1987 the ratio of Japanese office workers to desktop computers was 25 to 1, compared to a ratio of 7 to 1 in the United States. While accountants did their work with an abacus or a hand-held calculator, robots constructed automobiles. In contrast to the crowded and antiquated working conditions of Japan's offices, the manufacturing environments staffed by blue-collar workers were immaculately neat and manufacturing production employed the most advanced technological methods.

Why have Japanese offices lagged behind the modernization of all other areas of Japanese business and industry? The answer to this question has more to do with the concept of "we the Japanese" than with the cost of office improvements or technological ignorance.

* * *

In Japanese corporate organizations, fewer than six of the highest-ranking executive officers (including the chairman, the president, and the executive vice president) have private offices. Indeed, at certain institutions (e.g., the headquarters of Osaka-based Sanwa Bank, Japan's fifth largest) only the president and chairman are entitled to private offices. In Japan, accomplishments are regarded as the direct product of group effort. An individual alone, it is believed, can accomplish little. To isolate the individual in a private office is to negate his value as a contributor to the development of business.

Remove one cell from a human heart and the heart will be unaffected. Continue removing heart cells, however, and the organism will eventually cease to function. The life of an organization depends on the harmonious combination of its employees. The contribution of one employee, like that of a single heart cell, is incidental.

It follows, therefore, that individual employees do not require the luxurious indulgence characteristic of American offices, where a philosophy of individualism prevails. The carpeting, large wooden desks, and separate work units (offices or cubicles) of American offices are inappropriate to the design of a Japanese environment. A Japanese executive, regardless of his contribution to corporate progress, is not entitled to a personal computer or a personal secretary. Just as ideas are shared and developed through group participation, tools too are shared.

The Japanese office, derogatorily termed a "bull pen" by foreign visitors, is filled with dozens of desks much like those of the U.S. Army headquarters in the Tokyo of 1948. However, unlike the desks in a U.S. Army office, these desks are not separated from each other. They are pushed together so that the adjacent desks in each row of 3 to 15 desks are in contact with each other, and often the desk fronts are pushed against a facing row of desks. The physical contact of the desks symbolizes the social contact of the employees who spend much of their working lives seated at them *and* a portion of their leisure time interacting with employees seated at neighboring desks.

Japanese offices have been slow to modernize because, in a real sense, the individuals who would directly benefit from changes ranging from carpeting to desktop computers are unimportant. The group, however, is all-important.

Technology tends to separate people from each other. If each employee in a Japanese office had his own desktop computer, his concentration would be devoted too exclusively to the screen and his data. Thus, American developments in office technology would disrupt the group.

SWORDS, SAMURAI, AND RONIN

An unusual relationship exists between the samurai, the swords that symbolized their power, and the ronin of the Japanese past, on the one hand, and today's Japanese businessmen, the money that facilitates their business, and the contemporary Japanese gangsters (the yakuza), on the other hand. Just as a house of mirrors transforms the appearance of those who enter it, the Japanese present replicates the Japanese past without directly resembling it.

Like the sword that was the tool of the samurai and embodied their accomplishments, money is now the tool of Japanese businessmen, its accumulation facilitating their continued success. Of course, swords were not collected and deposited in banks or invested in fungible instruments. Likewise, money is not carefully made by master craftsmen. However, each—the sword of the samurai and the money of modern Japanese businessmen—has been the quintessential implement of power in its own time.

That businessmen are the contemporary version of the samurai is a popular image in Japanese culture. Japanese businessmen enjoy seeing themselves as a modern-day version of courageous samurai going out to battle in the business world. The accuracy of this comparison is less important than its widespread appeal.

Just as Japan's businessmen identify themselves with the samurai, Japan's gangsters, the yakuza, enjoy comparing themselves to the *ronin*. They believe that they are the direct descendants (through tradition) of ronin from villages who fought bandits during the Tokugawa era. A group of outcasts, the ronin were pursued and eventually destroyed by government authorities. Today's yakuza factions, like ronin groups, consist primarily of outcasts. For example, burakumin, the little-discussed outcast group, make up an estimated 70 percent of the Yamaguchigumi (the largest yakuza faction).[5] Most of the yakuza members who are not burakumin are of Korean descent and are also outcasts in Japanese society, deprived of citizenship and treated as aliens.

The line of descent of businessmen from samurai is often claimed in a more documented fashion by particular individuals who know their lineage and have inherited a great-grandfather's sword. Although Japan does not have a recognized class system derived from relationships that obtained during its feudal history, the descendants of leading Tokugawa-era samurai are not working in factory assembly lines or as waiters.

Swords

The great 14th-century swordsmith Muramasa spent weeks hammering a single sword. The sword would be pounded with a hammer, heated in the forge, and pounded again. The procedure would be repeated thousands of times. The process continued until the edge of the sword contained an estimated 4 million layers of perfectly forged steel. Although the edge of the sword was extraordinarily strong, the remainder of the blade was pounded far less, so that it would be softer. If an entire sword blade contained millions of layers, it would be hard but brittle. Such a blade would break on impact.

Japanese master swordsmiths perfected a method of varying the hardness of a single piece of forged steel. This technique was never developed in Europe. As a result, the steel of the finest Japanese swords was far stronger than any steel that could be produced in Europe. With a single blow, a samurai's sword could slice through an inch of European steel as though it were butter.

The long and short swords that were carried by samurai became their emblems. The craftsmanship of the finest swords transformed them into works of art that were displayed with great pride by their owners. Today, burnished sword blades glisten inside the glass cases of mu-

---

[5]According to unofficial police statistics cited by David E. Kaplan and Alec Dubro, *Yakuza: The Explosive Account of Japan's Criminal Underworld* (Reading, Mass.: Addison-Wesley Publishing, 1986), p. 145.

seums and are admired more for the graceful harmony of their lines than for their potential as weapons.

Unlike matchlocks and other antique implements of war, samurai swords have not been relegated to a nostalgic corner of obsolete technology of interest only to collectors. To the contrary, the samurai sword has remained a special symbol that embodies the combination of Japanese manufacturing skill with traditional Japanese values.

For the average Japanese, no object expresses traditional Japan better than the samurai sword. Some of these swords, like heirlooms, have been kept by the descendants of samurai. On rare occasions, they are removed from their velvet-lined boxes, unwrapped, and admired.

Although there are many other links with the past, a family sword exudes the vitality and confidence of the departed samurai who once carried it. Perhaps no other symbol expresses the potency and power of traditional Japan better than a samurai sword. Just as the sword rests quietly in the box where it is protectively stored, the spirit of the samurai rests in the hearts of all Japanese—quietly radiating strength.

Samurai

A thousand years ago, during Japan's Fujiwara Period (857–1160), the authority of the central government weakened to such an extent that the ruling family had little control over the provinces. Armed struggles between rival factions were common throughout the Japanese islands, and piracy became the scourge of many coastal areas. In order to exercise some control, provincial bureaucrats were given the power to maintain armed militia, and eventually they acquired military titles. In addition, the proprietors of rural estates assembled armed groups to protect *their* local interests. Throughout this period, amalgamation of local military groupings resulted in the development of fiefdoms bearing a strong resemblance to medieval kingdoms.

By the 10th century, the Fujiwara family and the imperial house had become too large to effectively delegate power to all qualified male members. As a result, excess family members were thrown out of the lineages and given new names (Minamoto and Taira). This prevented the dilution of political control through descent.

Excluded from the imperial court, the expelled men left Kyoto, the capital, and traveled to the provinces, where they became the managers of lands officially owned by the emperor. Although these men were no longer formally connected to the ruling or imperial families, their outstanding pedigree enabled them to create a rural aristocracy. Using their wealth as a tool for the accumulation of power, these disinherited aristocrats became the leaders of small rurally based armies.

Gradually, a warrior class termed *bushi* (warrior) or *samurai* (retainer) emerged. From the middle of the Fujiwara Period (about 950) until the beginning of Tokugawa rule (1603), the samurai, by virtue of their military activities, played a key role in Japan's political economy. Sporadic wars and skirmishes resulted in rearrangements in the deployment of political power.

Like the knights of Europe, the samurai were mounted and armored, fighting other samurai in individual encounters. Their weapons included the long bow and arrows as well as the sword.

The men who ruled the feudal domains were termed *daimyo*. Each daimyo employed an army of samurai who were totally dependent on him for financial support. Wars waged between rival daimyo for the control of land were fought by the samurai. Military defeat was considered a disgrace, and samurai were expected to die in battle rather than suffer the humiliation of failure. Often, however, the samurai of a defeated daimyo abandoned the battlefield and wandered, homeless and usually poor, through the countryside. Such leaderless samurai, called *ronin*, functioned as mercenaries and were often hired by daimyo planning a military undertaking. Some of the ronin became bandits and terrorized villages. Other ronin, often living as village workers, banded together and fought the bandits. Thus, in Japanese folklore two types of ronin, one bad and one good, battled in the countryside.

Ronin

In 1603, Ieyasu Tokugawa unified Japan and, ending centuries of civil war, inaugurated two centuries of peace. As a result, more than 500,000 samurai were rendered superfluous. Some became merchants, and the highest-ranking samurai entered the civil bureaucracy. Many poor samurai, however, having no capital to begin business and no avenue for bureaucratic success, drifted through the countryside.

These unemployed samurai resembled the ronin of earlier periods. Having no special skills other than martial training, many of them became bandits and plundered farming villages for a living. Termed *kabuki-mono*, these masterless samurai were wanderers who had renounced normal Japanese morality. Stories abound of how kabuki-mono randomly killed farmers in order to test a new sword.

* * *

One of the oldest and most popular Japanese stories is the tale of the 47 ronin. The daimyo Asano Naganori was insulted by a high official of the shogun. Because Naganori drew his sword, a forbidden act in the shogun's palace, he was ordered to commit ritual suicide.

The daimyo's loyal samurai Oishi, rendered a ronin by his master's death, vowed revenge. For seven years, he and 46 other former samurai of Naganori feigned abandonment of military life and led a drunken and dissolute existence in Edo (the capital city).

When the moment was right, during a blizzard, the 47 ronin seized the house of the offending official, killed his armed guard, and beheaded the official. The official's head, placed in a temple beside their master's ashes, symbolized the revenge of the daimyo's loyal retainers. Although the act of these ronin was considered exemplary, they were ordered by the shogun to commit suicide.

Modern Japanese regard the story of the 47 ronin as a tale expressing the irreconcilable conflict between loyalty to the master (the *group*) and loyalty to the shogun (the *state*). The 47 ronin committed the ultimate act of honor by choosing loyalty to their master above the rule of law and subsequently submitting to the rule of law and paying the price of their act. In this way, the 47 ronin honored both systems without compromising their integrity.

* * *

Although the contemporary Japanese is never forced to choose between his loyalty to the group and loyalty to the state, the potential conflict remains implicit. Ideally, loyalty to the group always takes precedence, but it does not justify neglect of the larger institution (the corporation, the school, the state).

The tale of the 47 ronin adds respectability to the wanderer who is deprived of his group affiliation by fate. Today, the term *ronin* is applied to high school students who fail their university entrance examinations and spend years working in odd jobs while studying to take the examinations again. These modern-day ronin are pitied and respected. Those among them who succeed and pass their exams become successful people, and their former status as ronin is forgotten. However, those who fail in their final attempt at redemption are relegated to a lifetime of employment in obscure, poorly paying jobs. There is no pity for the failed ronin.

MONEY, BUSINESSMEN, AND YAKUZA

Japan's position in world business and finance is the direct outcome of unique historical forces and conditions. Japan possesses a martial history spanning more than a millennium and ending with the Occupation in 1945. Martial traditions, exemplified by *bushido* (the credo of the samurai), are intrinsic to a wide range of cultural expression. Officially, all aspects of Japanese militarism and the glorification of martial activities were terminated by the new Japanese constitution drafted under the auspices of the supreme commander for the Allied powers. However, deeply embedded traditions in literate cultures cannot be obliterated by manifesto. If deprived of their historic outlets, such traditions are expressed in other ways. Thus, Japanese business entities have replaced military groupings in certain respects, allowing an outlet for national pride.

Money

Every day, the Japanese people save $1 billion and Japan's corporations accumulate $500 million. Japan has the highest savings rate in the world, about 350 percent more than the American savings rate. Japan's vast accumulation of savings has made Japanese banks the biggest in the world, and Japanese securities companies have waxed rich on the commissions generated by stock purchases.

Like the 4 million layers that made the samurai sword the strongest implement of its time, the layers of money that fill Japanese banks, securities companies, insurance companies, and corporations have made these financial institutions the strongest in the world. Just as the brittleness of the samurai sword was balanced by the soft steel in its center, the hollowing out of Japanese industry caused by the high yen is being balanced by growing Japanese investments in factories, real estate, and securities abroad. Such foreign investments will gradually help prevent trade friction and will protect the Japanese currency from becoming too strong.

The samurai sword was able to effortlessly slice through European steel. Will Japanese money be able to slice through foreign corporate ownership of assets in the same way? Will Japanese money be wielded with the same unshakable confidence as the samurai wielded his sword?

Businessmen

Japan's modern businessmen date back to the early Meiji period (the late 19th century). When the samurai were commanded by law to put away their swords, a new class of corporate leaders began to emerge. Dressed in Western suits and often living in Western-style homes, by the 20th century Japanese businessmen had become as distinctive a group as the samurai. Their uniform consisted of dark suits, Western ties, and black shoes. Easily recognizable, they staffed trading companies and filled the offices of Japan's developing industrial corporations and emerging financial institutions.

The samurai never contributed directly to the prosperity of Japan, but they assured its prosperity by protecting their daimyo from invasion. Similarly, by devoting their lives to the development of Japan's corporations and thus increasing Japan's export capability and wealth, modern businessmen have enhanced Japan's autonomy. The samurai were military defenders of Japan; Japanese businessmen are its economic defenders.

Yakuza

Japan has an enviably low crime rate. For example, every year more homicides occur in the city of Detroit than in all of Japan. Until recently, many Japanese city dwellers did not even lock their houses. Cases of murder, burglary, and mugging in Japan are more often the result of intrafamily disputes than of random crime. The yakuza take credit for Japan's peaceful streets.

At least 200 years old, the term *yakuza* is derived from the lowest losing combination in a card game and originally connoted uselessness. Today, the term refers to a collection of independent criminal factions or gangs.

The leaders of yakuza factions, unlike the leaders of organized crime elsewhere in the world, are popular figures. When the boss of Japan's largest yakuza faction, the Yamaguchigumi, died, famous Japanese politicians, businessmen, and movie stars attended his funeral. The ceremony in which the new boss was initiated was broadcast live on national television. Subsequently, NHK, the national broadcasting company, interviewed the top leaders of the Yamaguchigumi in a television program that was viewed by tens of millions of Japanese.

Japan's gangsters, the yakuza, perceive themselves as the honorable ronin of 20th-century Japan. Like the good ronin of the 18th-century who contained the banditry of the bad ronin, today's yakuza claim to control crime by ruling the streets. Petty criminals who are not affiliated with a yakuza gang cannot survive. The yakuza insist that Japan's low crime rate is the direct result of their vigilance. Consultation and collaboration with the police have developed over the years into a close working relationship between law enforcement officials and gangster leaders. Traditionally, the yakuza leaders have opposed the importation of heroin and have prohibited violence against ordinary Japanese citizens.

Politically aligned with the far right, all of Japan's yakuza factions are ultranationalist. They support virtually all of the extremist and militarist movements that call for Japanese rearmament and a strong Japan. Like the 47 ronin who sacrificed their lives to avenge the wrongful death of their leader, today's yakuza perceive themselves as devoted to avenging the wrongful death of Japan's military supremacy. Links among yakuza political extremism, certain industries (such as the construction industry), and Japan's political machine (leading factions of the Liberal Democratic Party) have been well documented.[6]

JAPAN THE INVINCIBLE

The myth of the kamikaze is one of the best-known myths of Japan. It derives from the 13th-century Japanese victory over Kublai Khan.

By the year 1259, Kublai Khan had conquered much of Asia and parts of Europe. Ruling the eastern section of the Mongol empire from Peking, he ordered Japan to submit to his rule in 1266. Although the royal court in Kyoto was ready to yield, the ruling Hojo family refused to become a tributary vassal of a foreign power. In 1274, Kublai sent an amphibious force, consisting of about 30,000 troops, to Hakata Bay in Kyushu, the southernmost of Japan's major islands.

Utilizing superior weaponry and massed cavalry tactics that had

---

[6]It is beyond the scope of this book to explore these interconnections. There are hundreds of books in the Japanese language that discuss various facets of these linkages. Clear documentation is provided for English-language readers in Kaplan and Dubro's *Yakuza*.

enabled them to overrun much of the civilized world, the Mongols were confident of a quick victory against Japan's defending forces. However, before a decisive battle could be fought, a severe storm forced the invaders to return to port with considerable losses. Kublai subsequently sent envoys to Japan demanding submission. The envoys were beheaded.

In anticipation of a new invasion, the Japanese built a wall around Hakata Bay. They lacked weaponry that could match the Mongols' catapults and gunpowder, but they trained troops in the use of Mongol mass cavalry tactics in order to combat the invaders with their own devices.

In 1281, Kublai Khan sent 140,000 troops back to Hakata Bay. For two months, the Japanese kept the invaders confined to a small beach-head below the defensive wall. It was only a matter of time, however, before the invading army, which had already smashed through the Great Wall of China, would penetrate the Japanese defenses. That time never arrived. A typhoon struck the coast of Kyushu, sinking more than half of the Mongol fleet. Some of the invaders were able to retreat; the rest were killed or enslaved. This was by far the biggest defeat ever suffered by the Mongols under Kublai Khan.

The Japanese referred to the typhoon as the *kamikaze*, the "divine wind," the wind sent by the protective *kami* (the Shinto divinities). With encouragement from the Shinto priests, the kamikaze quickly became a mythic symbol in Japanese folklore and tradition. During the course of the centuries, the kamikaze served to exemplify the divine singularity of Japan and of the Japanese people who were inseparable from its islands.

FROM IMPERIAL LIGHT TO THE DARKNESS OF WAR

The earliest Japanese word for government (*matsurigoto*) means religious observances or worship.[7] the leader of the ancient Yamato clan was above all else a religious functionary.[8]

Traditional Shinto beliefs did not establish a sharp distinction be-

---

[7]Robert N. Bellah, *Tokugawa Religion* (Boston: Beacon Press, 1970), p. 87.
[8]Ibid., p. 86.

tween nature and society. After death, society became nature and the souls of people were united with the land. This link between the ancestors and the land of Japan was simply the inversion of the evolution of society from the gods of nature. Furthermore, the distinctions between particular individuals and society, like the demarcations separating particular souls within the land, were hazy.

In the world of Shinto, the divine and the human, nature and society, are a totality. Not surprisingly, Japanese folklore is filled with entities that are part human and part god. It is a small step from this (necessarily oversimplified) cosmic model to the belief that the emperor is himself a divinity.

Throughout most of Japanese history, the emperor (a religious and sovereign symbol) has been sharply separated from the shogun (a political leader). The emperor symbolized absolute religious authority within the Shinto tradition but had no de facto political power. Even after the Meiji Restoration, when political power was officially "restored" to the imperial family, the emperor remained a symbol of national unity rather than an active participant in political decision making.

Japan's first constitution, drafted under the auspices of the Meiji regime, was promulgated in 1889. It established a bicameral parliament under the moral jurisdiction of the emperor. Although this constitution was based on a German model, central to it was the *kokutai* (the national entity—a harmonious totality), which radiated from the imperial family as beams of light radiate from a rising sun. The kokutai consisted of the emperor (and his lineage, which linked him with the sun goddess) and the unique Japanese people.

Long after the death of the Emperor Meiji, during the 1920s and 1930s, the concept of the kokutai was subtly reinterpreted. According to a vague sociopolitical ideology prevalent during the two decades that preceded the Pacific War, the kokutai could no longer be perceived as having two components: the emperor and the Japanese people. Instead, the kokutai was an absolute unity corresponding to the Japanese state, which itself was "a single great family" whose "main house" was the imperial family.[9]

---

[9]Of course, Japanese political philosophy between 1910 and 1945 was far more complex, consisting of different (and often opposing) views. However, this simplified summary conveys the predominant attitude during the period.

Japanese textbooks during the 1930s communicated this Shinto political and social cosmology. Not coincidentally, this view of history and Japanese society, which prevailed during the 1930s and the early 1940s, was not incompatible with the ultranationalism that the military used as a force to seduce Japan into war.

As is well known, one brand of German nationalism used a peculiar blend of philosophies to justify the claimed superiority of the Germanic (Aryan) race. Many of these philosophies, from the Volkism of Fichte to the doctrines of Nietzsche and Heidegger, were adopted in the 1930s by Japanese intellectuals.

More important, however, Germany had provided Japan with a model for its constitution. Thus, the subversion of the German constitution (and of all democratic principles) under Hitler had no little impact on Japan. The growth of fascism in Japan, the emergence of wartime orthodoxy during the late 1930s, and the tragedy of the Pacific War are well known.

DEFEAT

For 664 years following the "divine wind," no invader violated Japanese soil. In 1944 and 1945, facing inevitable defeat in the Pacific War, young Japanese pilots used their planes as missiles in massed attacks against U.S. naval vessels. Named *kamikaze*, these suicide planes were a final desperate attempt to destroy an implacable amphibious force that was about to invade Japanese territory. They failed.

Japan's defeat and occupation (1945–52) involved a great loss of pride for "we the Japanese." Not only was Japanese sovereignty held prisoner, but the sacred and mystical bond linking the people with the land was sullied by the presence of foreign authorities. Institutions were altered or liquidated, and traditional networks were destroyed or rechanneled. For those who lived through World War II and its aftermath, indelible scars served as lifelong reminders of the humiliation wrought by foreign power. The fundamental cause of the catastrophe —the fact that a war had been initiated and lost—was irrelevant to the emotive response to it.

Most of Japan's senior financial bureaucrats in the 1980s were children during the intense fire bombing of Japanese cities in 1944–45. At an impressionable age, they witnessed the national loss of face.

These men (they are nearly all men) are sophisticated specialists. Some of them are among the most urbane and refined diplomats in the world. Although they may harbor little or no bitterness toward the West, they remember the humiliation of defeat. Many of the speeches given by the doyens of Japan's financial sector make some reference, however oblique, to the war years. World War II is a remote memory or irrelevant knowledge for most Americans or Europeans currently engaged in international finance. But for their Japanese counterparts, regardless of age, it is one part, however small, of the definition of a Westerner.

* * *

Forty years after the Pacific War, in the Euromarkets, Japanese financial institutions competed with the biggest universal banks and investment banks of the West for underwriting business. Predatory pricing, an activity far more respectable in underwriting than in manufacturing, was used by Japanese securities houses. As a means of seizing market share, Japanese underwriters sold bonds at a loss. These bonds were referred to as "kamikaze issues."

The use of the term *kamikaze* to characterize a type of bond can easily be disregarded as a trivial linguistic means of emphasizing the "suicidal" aspect of selling at a loss. Nevertheless, the appearance of this term in the international financial world of the 1980s was not casual. Not surprisingly, the Japanese promoters of these bonds heatedly denied that the bonds were loss leaders and would have ridiculed any suggestion of an intended allusion to divine winds and suicide. Yet, the term had a purpose and it was illustrative of a collective world view.

MONSTER MOVIES

Monster movies were once a Japanese product. Although the genre was not invented in Japan, during the 1950s and 1960s such movies were produced in quantity in Japan, for both domestic consumption and export. We have all seen them.

A bizarre monster, of gigantic proportions and impervious to weapons, begins to destroy the metropolis. Buildings topple, trains are derailed, and people flee in terror. The nation itself is threatened with destruction. Heroes, usually fearlessly dedicated scientists, collaborate tirelessly against impossible odds. In the end, the monster is eliminated and peace returns. As the film concludes, the viewer knows that, although the damage will be repaired, the memory of the monster and the destruction it has caused will last forever. Often the film concludes with hints that the monster could return.

Mysterians, directed in 1958 by Inoshiro Honda, the creator of Godzilla, is one of the most famous examples of the Japanese monster movie. It tells the tale of alien superbeings who attempt to conquer Earth by first taking over Japan. The initial indications of the aliens' arrival are a range of localized phenomena similar to those that occurred in the vicinity of Hiroshima and Nagasaki after the atom bomb explosions. The ground becomes hot and dead fish float in the rivers. A metallic monster, exuding radioactivity, ravages the countryside. Subsequently, the aliens announce their presence by annexing a small circle of land (1 kilometer in radius) outside Tokyo. Later in the movie, the aliens demand the right to intermarry with Japanese women. Eventually, Japanese ingenuity, technology, and a hero's self-sacrifice (kamikaze style) defeat the aliens, enabling life to return to normal.

That dozens of monster movies were made in Japan and achieved great popularity among the Japanese during the era of post-Occupation recovery is significant. The wanton and mindless destruction wrought by the monster bears more than a coincidental resemblance to the wartime destruction of Japan's urban centers. Each monster movie provided not only a symbolic reenactment of wartime devastation but, more significant, also portrayed the victimization of the populace by irrational forces beyond its control. In the face of the terrifying threat of total annihilation, the populace unites to combat the danger. The destructive forces always die and life returns to normal.

Honda's Mysterians, like the Allied Occupation forces, were preceded by the devastation of radioactivity and later sometimes took (intermarried with) Japanese women. For the Japanese, whose country had never been occupied and who valued the myth of racial purity, the lost war and the subsequent Occupation were very much like an invasion of monsters.

Monster movies were not made for children, and they provided the adults who viewed them with a means of unconsciously coming to terms with the effects of World War II. Because the monster was unique, and therefore unclassifiable, it could symbolize both the attacks of a foreign military and the awesome danger of the indigenous political regime that held Japan hostage during the war years.

During the 1960s, when the postwar industrialization of Japan's economic miracle rendered the Japan of 1945 a remote world, monster movies faded from popularity. By 1985, Japan had become the world's preeminent manufacturer and trader, achieving a degree of success that stymied the West.

PEACE AND ARROGANCE

The American Occupation of Japan lasted seven years.[10] In those seven years, the course of Japanese history was directed along a course that would never have been taken otherwise.

In September 1945, Japan resembled a newborn child in one important way. The newborn's brain is waiting for environmental programming, and so too was Japan after the war. At that time, it consisted of cities without superstructure inhabited by people without leadership. Its cities were piles of rubble, few of its factories were left standing, its railroads were in disarray, and its people were malnourished. When the emperor's surrender speech was broadcast to the nation, the entire population lost its direction. Instead of a final and devastating "battle for Japan," civilians and the military were faced with unexpected peace.

The American Occupation authorities filled this void in a manner that took the Japanese people by surprise. Expecting vindictive and merciless rule, the Japanese encountered something quite different. The American government, foreseeing the need for a strong U.S. ally in the Pacific and aware of Japan's strategic location between the United States and the Soviet Union, was determined to transform Japan-the-totalitarian-enemy into Japan-the-democratic-ally.

In 1945, the Japanese political system contained both democratic and totalitarian characteristics. Wartime mobilization had entailed a controlled and highly centralized economy. These features were reinforced by institutions for national planning and a close integration between industrial combines (the zaibatsu) and government entities. Such institutions as secret police and severe censorship resulted in a

---

[10]Officially, the Occupation of Japan was international, consisting of a 13-nation Far Eastern Commission based in Washington and an Allied Council based in Tokyo. In reality, however, the Occupation was entirely American, directed by General Douglas MacArthur, who had the title of supreme commander for the Allied powers.

system resembling that of the Soviet Union. Indeed, if Japan had been occupied by the Soviet Union instead of the United States, there can be little doubt that Japan would now be a communist nation.

To establish Japan as a durable democratic state, the American Occupation authorities instituted comprehensive reforms. Decentralization was one of the guiding principles of these reforms. Like Alexis de Tocqueville, the 19th-century French philosopher, American Occupation experts were persuaded that centralized institutions provide totalitarian rulers with a key to power. Therefore, Occupation reforms were devoted to decentralizing every sector of Japan's institutional structure, from the police to the universities.

Eighty-three so-called merchants of death (zaibatsu holding companies) were dismantled, and antimonopoly laws were drafted to prevent their reestablishment. Corporate leaders were purged, and zaibatsu families were stripped of their wealth. Corporate stock was transferred from zaibatsu ownership to individual ownership. Many government financial institutions were transformed into private institutions. Overall, a comprehensive program for economic deconcentration was designed and implemented by the Occupation authorities.

The Japanese empire was formally dissolved. *All* ultranationalist organizations were disbanded and made illegal. *All* Japanese soldiers and civilians scattered throughout East and Southeast Asia were sent back to Japan. The entire Japanese armament industry was abolished.

Meanwhile, a new constitution, drafted by Occupation specialists in 1947, renounced war and permitted the maintenance of only a small "self-defense force." Japan's martial traditions were officially gone forever.

* * *

After the Occupation ended, some reforms were reversed. The zaibatsu, for example, regrouped around banks, forming the contemporary keiretsu. Thus, the antimonopoly legislation imposed by the Occupation was short-circuited. Private ownership of stock fell from 69.1 percent in 1949 to 46.3 percent in 1960 (today it stands at 23 percent).

Although certain sectors reverted to former patterns during the post-Occupation years, on the whole Japan remained decentralized, deconcentrated, and demilitarized. Moreover, as a result of the massive and enduring changes established by MacArthur and his entourage, its outlets for national pride were rechanneled. The military and all symbols of military strength were gone. In their place were new postwar industries. Japan's postwar generals were industrialists whose activities were guided by the long-term plans of MITI.

* * *

Yet, could the changes established by the Occupation have truly succeeded in destroying a deeply embedded martial tradition? More pointedly, did Japan's parochial nationalism simply evaporate in 1945? Did the abolition of ultranationalist organizations mean that ultranationalism disappeared? The answers to these questions are obvious, but they are also complex.

During the late 1960s and 1970s, Japan became the free world's second largest economy. At the same time, ultranationalist organizations, banned by the Occupation, reappeared. Together with the development of Japan's strong economy, there occurred a resurgence of the same arrogance that had led the Japanese military of the 1940s to believe that the nations of Southeast Asia would welcome Japan's invasions.

During the postwar era, Japanese industries exported their products and expanded their market share in Asia and Europe. The riots that greeted Prime Minister Tanaka's visit to Thailand in 1974 were an early symptom of the powerful resentment of Japanese exports that was expressed globally a decade later. Many Japanese industrialists and bureaucrats (exemplified by MITI's Kuroda—discussed in Chapter 1) responded aggressively to the foreign complaints.

In 1987, with trade friction approaching a flash point, Japan's Ministry of Foreign Affairs in its annual policy statement published an unprecedented critique of Japanese attitudes. It urged Japanese industry to gain "the humility needed to accept other cultures and values." It also warned that nationalism could result in Japan's isolation from the world community.[11]

The criticisms presented by the foreign ministry indirectly recognized that Japan had become a major economic power in large part by exporting to the United States and Europe and that it could not afford to neglect the welfare of its trading partners. "It is imperative in today's increasingly interdependent international community that we share in

---

[11]Foreign Ministry, *Blue Book* (Tokyo, 1987).

both the pain and the gain, and it is unacceptable that any one country should selfishly seek to profit at others' expense," the policy statement lectured Japanese industry.[12]

Although approved by the Japanese cabinet, the policy statement did not necessarily reflect the views of Japanese industry and government, nor was its reprimand likely to be taken to heart by all of Japan's trade negotiators. Japanese bureaucrats who are too young to remember World War II are now approaching senior levels within their ministries. A new generation of corporate executives who know little about the war will soon qualify for senior positions. By the end of the century, Japanese politics and industry will be directed by people who have known only a strong Japan.

Perhaps with this knowledge in mind, the Foreign Ministry pointed out that

> there have been some people who say that the Japanese have recently become more arrogant in their perceptions and behavior. It is impossible either to improve ourselves or to win the trust of other nations unless we have the humility needed to accept other cultures and values and to respect diversity. Should parochial nationalism take hold, Japan could well find itself isolated in the international community.[13]

The samurai placed no value on humility; nor have Japan's ultranationalists of the past and present. Will Japan's industrial, financial, and bureaucratic community abandon its arrogance and acquire "the humility needed to accept other cultures and values"?

---

[12]Ibid.
[13]Ibid.

CHAPTER 4

THE WORLD OF
INTERNATIONAL FINANCE

THE YELLOW RIVER

Despite its dauntless title, this brief chapter will not provide a voyage to the exotic and arcane world of international finance. The colorful jargon and abstruse formulas, the deals, the rumors, and the other paraphernalia that have made this world a remote planet for the average layman must be sought elsewhere. Instead, this chapter, like a telescope, directs its gaze to a few selected points in order to draw them closer. Although the distant world cannot be seen in its entirety, the points chosen suggest the whole.

* * *

Many financial markets have been international for a long time—at least since sovereign European territorial states began their official existence following the Peace of Westphalia, in 1648. Nevertheless, during the past 25 years, and particularly during the past 3 years, a new pattern of global investment in the world's major financial markets has been altering the character of international finance.

There is nothing subtle about the changes that are taking place. Just as the Yellow River periodically shifts its location by hundreds of kilometers, altering the topography of China, today the world's capital flows are changing their course. As in China, the floodwaters will recede, leaving many casualties and a permanently changed environment.

GLASS-STEAGALL AND OTHER
AMERICAN ANTIQUES

Contemporary finance relies on electronic and telecommunications technologies undreamed of a short time ago. Meanwhile, the Euro-markets (discussed below) have taken on a life of their own, while new and complex financial instruments sired by investment bankers have been born in New York and London. In this new world, American financial institutions are governed by regulations written in 1927 and 1933.

American commercial banks and securities firms conduct their domestic business under the guidance of archaic laws that could not have anticipated the creation of the high-capacity computers and the satellite communications that have facilitated the awesomely competitive global finance of the late 20th century.

The Banking Act of 1933, best known as the Glass-Steagall Act, was a child of the New Deal. Its proponents assumed that the dominance of the securities industry by banks during the 1920s led to widespread conflicts of interest that precipitated the Great Depression. Intended to exterminate corrupt self-dealing by the banking industry, the act created a Chinese Wall between commercial banking (taking deposits and lending money) and investment banking (underwriting and dealing in nongovernment securities). Thus, most banks cannot be affiliated with securities companies and banks are prohibited from owning or being owned by an entity that is not part of the banking industry.

As a result of Glass-Steagall, American commercial banks are prohibited from issuing, underwriting, selling, or distributing new corporate securities offerings as well as most municipal revenue bonds. Securities companies cannot take deposits or extend loans. By separating the issuance of new securities from investment in those securities in fiduciary accounts, the act denied commercial banks virtually all access to the securities industry. One consequence is that today, unlike Japanese banks, which are both primary shareholders (limited to 5 percent) and creditors of domestic corporations, U.S. banks do not buy corporate stock for their own accounts. They do not own a piece of corporate America.

The decline of the Glass-Steagall Act is already under way, as evidenced by a number of regulatory and judicial decisions in 1986 and 1987. In 1986, for example, a federal court of appeals ruled that

Bankers Trust was entitled to sell commercial paper (uncollateralized short-term corporate debt). A 1987 decision permitted the subsidiaries of bankholding companies to provide investment advice. Later in 1987, the Federal Reserve Bank authorized seven bankholding companies to underwrite consumer-related receivables.

At about the same time, several major American Banks bought stakes in Canadian securities dealers (for example, Security Pacific's acquisition of Burns and Fry). Although a few U.S. banks already owned British stockbrokers (Security Pacific bought London-based Hoare Govett in 1982), a move into the securities industry so close to home indicated conviction that Glass-Steagall would eventually be abrogated.

In the fall of 1987, William Proxmire, chairman of the Senate Banking Committee, announced plans to introduce legislation that would repeal Glass-Steagall. At that time, a report from a House committee recommended a restructuring of U.S. financial services laws that would permit an amalgamation of commercial and investment banking as well as ownership of banks by nonbanking companies. Nevertheless, although the letter of the law will be liberally interpreted, the *total* elimination of Glass-Steagall—which would pave the way for the establishment of large multiservice U.S. bankholding companies—is not likely to occur soon.

Meanwhile, U.S. stockbrokers have long offered domestic customers "cash management accounts" (pioneered by Merrill Lynch) that bear a striking resemblance to savings accounts. Brokers also provide other services that are paving the way for the union of broking and banking. Since 1985, for example, Advest Group, Inc. (a diversified financial services holding company based in Hartford, Connecticut) has offered clients a system that connects banks and brokerage firms by computer. The system enables money deposited in a brokerage account to be transferred to the client's bank account.

While Glass-Steagall remains a topic of debate, the McFadden Act of 1927, which (along with the Douglas Amendment of 1956) bans interstate banking, is disintegrating. As big regional banks merge with banks in other states, America's embedded banking tradition of geographic segmentation is fading away. This trend is exemplified by the 1987 merger of First Fidelity of New Jersey and Fidelcor of Pennsylvania, which created the 17th largest bank (in terms of assets) in the United States.

As a result of interregional banking, commercial bank deposits in particular states will increasingly be owned by out-of-state institutions. The five largest commercial banks in Maine are owned by banks located in other New England states.

Not all of America's more than 14,000 regional banks and the hordes of "thrifts" (savings and loan associations and credit unions) will evaporate in a new torrid financial climate, nor will monster "superbanks" (or "megabanks") raise their heads above the financial jungle.

Nonetheless, major bankholding companies in the United States will significantly expand the parameters of their national and international business. Mergers of large commercial banks and even hostile takeovers within the banking sector (initiated by the Bank of New York in September 1987) will become common. Furthermore, mergers will produce larger and better-capitalized "superregional" banks. Facing declining profitability, the regionals and thrifts will be forced to experiment with new financial products.

Concurrently with the emergence of interstate banking, American banks will enter areas that have been the exclusive preserve of the securities industry. Such sectors of securities underwriting as commercial paper, mortgage-backed securities, mutual funds, and municipal revenue bonds will eventually fall firmly into banking territory. In the process, Glass-Steagall, like a piece of old furniture, will be relegated to an attic corner. It will not be destroyed, however, and in the event of a banking crisis it could be restored and modernized. Today's discard becomes tomorrow's antique.

ARTICLE 65, JAPAN'S FINANCIAL CONSTITUTION

Japanese securities companies were born in Japan's unique financial world of the late 19th and early 20th centuries. During the Meiji Restoration (1868–1912), Japanese finance was transformed from unregulated medieval transactions into a modern system.

Giant banks blossomed as the center of the zaibatsu holding companies. Mutual loan companies (termed *mujin*) provided funding to small businesses and brokers traded securities (primarily bonds) in Japan's small but proliferating stock exchanges. During the half century from the establishment of the Bank of Japan (1882) to the maturing of

Japan's economy in the 1930s, Japan's securities companies plied their trade as small financial institutions devoted primarily to the sale of bonds.

In their efforts to "democratize" Japan, the Occupation authorities attempted to create a modified Japanese financial system based on an American model. Just as U.S. experts wrote a democratic constitution for Japan, U.S. experts also prepared parallel legislation for the financial sector.

Article 65 of the Securities and Exchange Act of 1948 was designed as a Japanese version of the Glass-Steagall Banking Act. Its formulators believed that Japan's big banks would be prevented from consolidating new power if a separate securities industry were permitted to develop.

Article 65 separates the Japanese banking and securities industries. It prohibits banks from selling equity or underwriting primary securities issues. Under this article, Japanese securities companies, like their U.S. counterparts, are not allowed to accept deposits or extend loans in their domestic market.

By assuring that the major banks—with their national networks of branches and their established corporate relationships—could not compete with securities firms, Article 65 enabled the Big Four securities companies (Nomura, Daiwa, Nikko, and Yamaichi) to grow rapidly and become Asia's biggest investment bankers and brokers.

As with Glass-Steagall, which has been eroded by the financial deregulation and liberalization of the 1980s, holes have appeared in the edifice of Article 65. The substantial budget deficits resulting from the two oil "shocks" led the Ministry of Finance to allow Japanese banks to sell government bonds in the secondary market. Beginning in 1980, the Big Four began to sell government bond funds that functioned as virtual savings accounts.

Article 65, like Glass-Steagall, was domestic legislation and not intended to regulate the foreign financial activities of domestic institutions. Japanese securities firms set up banking operations first in Luxembourg and Amsterdam and subsequently in London. Japan's overseas banking branches engaged in the underwriting of foreign corporate securities and financial subsidiaries participated in a wide range of activities denied to the banks in their home market. London and other foreign financial centers became the testing grounds for financial activities that could not be attempted in Japan.

At home, however, Japanese banks have been completely excluded from stock market business. Nonetheless, foreign banks have been allowed to set up securities branches in Tokyo. Beginning with the universal banks of Germany and Switzerland in 1985–86 and continuing with American banks in June 1987, more than two dozen foreign banking institutions now conduct brokerage business in Japan. As a result, foreign banks are now able to underwrite corporate securities in Japan while Japanese banks are denied that opportunity by Article 65.

The Ministry of Finance does not customarily favor foreign institutions at the expense of the domestic firms that it is designed to protect and regulate. A radical modification of Article 65 is likely to occur by 1990. Thus it is only a matter of time before Japanese banks receive authorization to establish partially owned securities branches in Japan. When that happens, Article 65 will have become an amalgamation of regulatory tension and deregulatory relaxation.

MERGING, ACQUIRING, AND DIVERSIFYING

Carlo de Benedetti (the chief executive officer of Olivetti and a leading European entrepreneur) has commented that "the traditional multinational approach [to business] is *dépassé*. Corporations with international ambitions must turn to a new strategy of agreements, alliances, and mergers with other companies."[1] This observation is becoming ever more apparent in the financial world.

Manufacturers, for example, have been joining the financial services industry through acquisition and structural change. American Can Company, which owns the investment bank Smith Barney, transformed itself into Primerica, a financial services conglomerate. Volvo has an in-house bank and a stockbroking subsidiary.

Similarly, the old-line retailer Sears Roebuck has used more than the stars to plot its special route to the securities industry and banking. The largest retailer of financial services in the United States, Sears provides brokerage (through its Dean Witter subsidiary), property and life insurance (through its Allstate subsidiary), savings (through the Sears Savings Bank and other facilities), and real estate (through Coldwell

---

[1]Quoted in *Business Week*, August 24, 1987, p. 42.

Banker) services. In 1986, Xerox Corporation derived 47 percent of its operating profits from financial services sold by leading financial boutiques that it had acquired.

The Japanese Ministry of Finance has not permitted nonfinancial corporations to merge with banking or nonbank financial institutions at home or abroad. However, Japanese corporations have been free to set up financial subsidiaries outside Japan. During the 1980s, more than 50 major Japanese corporations, from Nippon Steel to Sony, created new financial businesses in Europe and the United States. In 1986, for example, Sumitomo Corporation, one of Japan's leading trading companies, created three foreign subsidiaries: Sumitomo Corporation Overseas Capital, Ltd., incorporated in the Cayman Islands; Sumitomo Finance International SA, incorporated in Panama; and Sumicorp Finance, Ltd., incorporated in London. These financial subsidiaries are designed to increase corporate profits by participating in international financial arbitrage, termed *zaitek* in Japan (*zaitak* is discussed further in Chapter 5).

STOCK MARKET GROWTH AND TURMOIL

At the end of 1986, total global stock market capitalization reached $5.616 trillion. The fastest-growing stock markets have been in Japan. From 1975 to 1986, when the U.S. share of global equity capitalization fell from 61.2 percent to 39.2 percent, Japan's share grew from 12.3 percent to 31.8 percent.

Many of the world's major equity markets doubled in value between mid-1985 and mid-1987. During one 18-month period (December 31, 1985 to July 31, 1987), the world's major stock markets performed outstandingly. Curiously, the countries famous for bullfighting had the most astounding stock market growth. Mexico led the world's top-performing equity markets with an index gain of 1,722 percent (in pesos)—a gain of 544 percent in U.S. dollar terms. At the same time, Spain, the runner-up, gained 133 percent.

While the New York Stock Exchange reached record highs in the summer of 1987, the leading Pacific Basin markets (Tokyo, Hong Kong, Singapore, and Australia) gave investors roughly a 100 percent local currency return. Because of the opportunity to reap handsome profits combined with the promise for foreign exchange gains, American investors increased foreign investments in 1986 to $1.068 trillion (up 13 percent from 1985).

Many causes account for this period of outstanding global stock market performance. In addition to such causes as low interest rates and stable oil supplies, other causes with less precedent stimulated equity market growth. *Financial innovation* conjoined with positive *supply-demand factors* was instrumental in spurring the world's equity markets to heights that would have been considered beyond reason several years ago. The ongoing *deregulation* of most of the world's financial markets and the concurrent *privatization of government assets* also stimulated equity market growth.

On "Black Monday," October 19, 1987, the "crash of 87" wiped out a sizable portion of world stock market growth. On that day, the Dow Jones Industrial Average fell 508 points, a decline of 22.6 percent. European stock prices plummeted and Asian equity markets followed. The Hong Stock Exchange was closed and, when the Exchange reopened the following week, the Hang Seng Index lost one third of its value.

Portfolio insurance (a hedging technique that involves the sale of stock index futures to protect an equity portfolio from the effects of a declining market) was widely regarded as a primary cause of the U.S. crash. Another potent catalyst was a growing fear of a sharp rise in U.S. interest rates. By the early fall of 1987, substantial central bank intervention to support the dollar was believed to be the inevitable precursor of tightening U.S. monetary policy.

When, by year end, the dust had begun to settle, the U.S. equity market had lost virtually all of its 1987 growth (down 30 percent from its peak) and Britain had grown a modest 3.6 percent for the year. Meanwhile, France and Switzerland each lost 30 percent, West Germany 40 percent, and Italy 33 percent. Alone among the world's major stock markets, Japan had *risen* significantly for the year—up 8.2 percent in yen terms.

While foreign investors in the Japanese stock market frenetically liquidated their holdings during the week of Black Monday, Japanese investors were net buyers of stock. Thus, although price volatility increased, the Japanese stock market remained remarkably stable. Good economic growth, growing domestic demand, and expanding domestic liquidity promise to maintain the Japanese stock market for some time to come.

Throughout the free world, from Tokyo to Turkey, shares in government-owned companies have been sold to the public. Pension funds, mutual funds, and individuals hungry for a high return feverishly purchased these shares in 1985–87. Significantly, a sizable portion of these purchases were foreign investments.

International U.S. mutual funds, for example, tripled in size in three years, rising from $5 billion in 1984 to nearly $16 billion in 1986. Because international investment improves overall risk adjusted returns, institutional investors often sought to diversify their portfolios by purchasing issues from the world's major markets.

The most international of these markets is the Euromarket, where traders study screens to learn the latest prices and use telephones or telexes to execute their buy or sell orders. In the Euromarket, the market design of the future, exchange floors where traders excitedly buy or sell shares are as obsolete as slide rules.

STATELESS (BUT NOT HOMELESS) MARKETS

The Emergence of the Euromarket

In the summer of 1944, much of Europe lay in ruins and the decisive Battle of the Bulge had not yet been fought. Japan would not surrender for another year. At this time, Allied meetings were usually conducted by generals and their agenda was usually concerned with the war effort. In these respects, the July 1944 meeting of Allied representatives in Bretton Woods, New Hampshire, was unusual. Economists from the United States, Great Britain (John Maynard Keynes was there), and other Allied nations met in this quiet place to reach an agreement regarding the structure of the postwar international monetary system.

The Bretton Woods Agreement had one goal: the establishment of stable, mutually convertible currencies. The International Monetary Fund (IMF) was created as an international agency. It was designed to facilitate cooperation among nations within the postwar international monetary system. This was to be achieved through the stabilization of exchange rates and the establishment of a multilateral payments system among member countries. The Bretton Woods Agreement also resulted in the creation of the World Bank (officially known as the International Bank for Reconstruction and Development), which was intended to assure capital adjustments among member countries to promote postwar reconstruction and the development of remote areas.

By means of the IMF, member nations submitted a par value of their currencies expressed in terms of gold (or of the U.S. dollar). Subsequently, all exchange transactions were conducted at a rate permitted to diverge by no more than 1 percent from the par value. Overall, the Bretton Woods Agreement created the foundation for the postwar international monetary system.

During the 1950s, virtually all of the nations in the free world maintained (directly or indirectly) a stable relationship between the dollar and their own currencies. Officially, within this system, the U.S. dollar was the only currency that was directly convertible into gold. As a result, the reserves of most central banks became predominantly dollars (rather than gold).

During the late 1950s and 1960s, the growth of the U.S. balance of payments deficit gradually threatened to destabilize the system based on the Bretton Woods Agreement. To prevent, or at least forestall, the inevitable demise of the agreement, the U.S. government took a number of actions that were to have an unforeseen and profound effect on the world of international finance.

In 1963, to prevent the outflow of private capital from the United States, the Kennedy administration imposed an Interest Equalization Tax (IET) on the value of all foreign securities purchased by U.S. residents. The 18.75 percent tax[2] forced foreign borrowers to raise funds outside the United States and compelled most American investors to abandon the purchase of foreign securities.

Although the tax reduced the outflow of funds for foreign investment, the desired effect was not achieved, because American banks increased their lending to foreign borrowers, while U.S. corporations increased their foreign direct investments. Consequently, in 1965 the Johnson administration applied the IET to bank loans to foreigners and encouraged U.S. banks to voluntarily curb overseas lending. Three years later, this "voluntary restraint program" was replaced by "mandatory investment controls," which required that the overseas subsidiaries of American corporations raise their funds outside the United States.

The IET and the investment controls stimulated the swift growth of

---

[2]Later reduced to 11.25 percent and finally repealed in 1974.

Eurocurrencies, particularly Eurodollars. A Eurocurrency is simply a bank deposit in a European bank located outside the country that issued the currency. Thus, for example, a dollar deposit in a London bank creates Eurodollars. Eurocurrencies were made possible by the Bretton Woods Agreement, which assured the free convertibility of currencies.

Financial markets based on Eurocurrencies grew rapidly during the 1960s as a direct result of the IET and the investment controls of 1968. Because of these restrictions, the overseas operations of American corporations needed Eurodollar funds and fulfilled their borrowing needs by issuing dollar debt in Europe. Eurocurrency banking developed during this period as a wholesale banking sector serving corporations, governments, and supranational organizations such as the World Bank.

Because the Euromarket was free from government regulation, it provided an avenue for the rapid mobilization and allocation of funds. A corporation wishing to raise capital in a hurry could go to the Euromarkets and issue debt without waiting for government approval.

During the 1960s, the U.S. government's balance of payments deficit continued to increase and international confidence in the dollar plummeted. Finally, the Bretton Woods Agreement collapsed on August 15, 1971, when President Nixon halted the gold convertibility of the dollar, permitting the currency to float in the foreign exchange markets. This action, which in Japan was termed the Nixon Shock (mentioned in Chapter 2), caused the yen to appreciate by nearly 17 percent in less than a year.

During this period of currency crisis, the Eurodollar bond market thrived, growing from $17.4 billion in 1966 to $65 billion in 1971, a growth rate of about 28 percent per year. This market continued to grow, reaching $575 billion in 1980 and then doubling in size by 1985. Meanwhile, securities markets and money markets in a range of Eurocurrencies (e.g., yen, deutsche marks, Swiss francs) slowly blossomed.

In 1979, major European countries eliminated foreign exchange controls. A year later, under international pressure, Japan enacted a new free-in-principle foreign exchange law. During the 1980s, most of the major economies in the noncommunist world established liberal foreign exchange laws. Taiwan, one of the newly industrialized countries of East Asia, was an exception to this trend and maintained strict foreign exchange laws. As a result, by June 1987 it had amassed $60 billion in foreign exchange reserves, the second largest reserves in the world after West Germany.

During the 1980s, U.S. corporations borrowed funds in the Eurodollar market in order to get interest rates below those available at home. Concurrently, the United States was forced to pay out more in dollars for imported goods than it received for U.S. exports. As a result, expanding U.S. balance of payment deficits caused Eurodollars to become the largest short-term pool of funds in the world, exceeding $2 trillion in 1986.

International Markets for International Investors

During the 1980s, the world's financial institutions were able to freely move funds among most countries and currencies. This new freedom encouraged the creation of new products that would protect investors from currency and interest rate volatility. While bonds with fixed interest rates did not become extinct, new vehicles providing interest rates that floated with the market were introduced.

In 1979, before the removal of foreign exchange controls, about 5 percent of British pension funds were invested in foreign stock; by 1986, more than 16 percent were. Similarly, U.S. investors increased their holdings of foreign equity from $19 billion in 1982 to $41 billion at the end of 1985.

New technologies facilitated the invention of novel and complex market instruments that thrived in the unregulated Euromarkets. During the 1980s, developments in electronics and telecommunications made it possible to trade unprecedented blocks of securities via video screens and on exchange trading floors.

Although the first Eurobond issued in yen was floated in 1977, it was not until December 1984 that the Japanese Ministry of Finance authorized foreign corporations to float yen-denominated debt in the Euromarkets. In 1986, Euroyen issues totaled $18.66 billion, making the yen the most popular currency of issue in the Euromarkets after the dollar.

By 1987, the Eurobond market had become the third largest securities market in the world (after New York and Tokyo) in terms of total debt and the second largest in terms of volume traded. Thus, in just 15 years the Euromarket became an intrinsic part of the global financial system, representing a vital source of financing for international trade and investment.

Yet, no sooner did the Euromarket achieve its remarkable size and liquidity than it began to show signs of old age and decrepitude. At the end of 1986, the market in perpetual floating rate notes collapsed, leaving bankers and investors with an estimated $18 billion worth of useless paper. Perpetual debt, a Euromarket "innovation" is undated, which means that its holder is never paid back. (Semiannual interest, indexed to a money market rate, is paid out, but the debt can only be traded, not redeemed.) The demise of this new Euromarket sector damaged the market's reputation, bringing into question its capacity to maintain long-term liquidity.

Asian Markets

Dollar and yen deposits in Singapore and Hong Kong, led to the emergence of "Asia dollar" and "Asia yen" markets that constituted a smaller-scale parallel of the Eurocurrency markets. During the 1980s, Asia dollar bonds and Asia yen bonds were underwritten by Japanese securities firms for East and Southeast Asian borrowers.

Also during the 1980s, markets in Asian certificates of deposit emerged in Tokyo, Hong Kong, and Singapore. Most of these "Asian CDs" were denominated in dollars or yen. In Japan, bonds denominated in foreign currency (shogun issues) were floated on the domestic market. Due to regulatory constraints, the shogun bond market was not able to compete with the Euromarket. Offshore banking in Singapore, Hong Kong, and, most recently, Tokyo, will assure the continuance of markets in Asian currencies.

Euroequities

In 1985, Nestlé, the Swiss food company, raised the equivalent of $425 million from three equity issues. For each of these issues, Crédit Suisse First Boston assembled a syndicate of U.S. and European banks that underwrote and sold the Nestlé shares directly to investors. In this way, the stock exchanges were bypassed.

Thus, like the Eurobond market, the emerging market in primary Euroequity issues is international and has no trading floor, employing Eurobond syndication techniques. The international Euroequity market enables corporations to raise more capital more quickly than can be done by means of particular domestic equity markets. In 1986, Euro-equity issues of all types reached roughly $12 billion, compared to $1 billion in 1983.

Uniformity

As deregulation makes global capital markets increasingly interdependent and prone to move together, instruments and prices will become ever more uniform. As a result, the Euromarket will lose its central role as the international market par excellence. Investors intending to buy bonds denominated in a range of currencies will find it easy and economical to do so in their home markets. Thus, a measure of deregulation among the world's major economies and the parallel globalization of securities markets signify the decline in importance of the Euromarket.

THE ROLE OF TECHNOLOGY

The Euromarket, a product of financial pressures in the world of the 1960s, became the outstanding example of the application of high technology to finance during the 1980s. The simultaneous distribution of information and the virtually instantaneous processing of orders created a remarkably efficient marketplace.

Because all borrowers and lenders in the market had access to virtually identical information, intermediaries found it necessary to offer new instruments in order to increase their market share. Of course, financial instruments could be swiftly copied by competitors. Therefore, the need to constantly innovate forced financial institutions to attempt to devise new products—or products that seemed to be new. Investment instruments with such exotic acronyms as LYONS, COLTS, TIGRS, and CATS appeared.

Computer programs designed to hedge complex chains of risk were devised, and new financial instruments proliferated like rabbits. Among these financial instruments were Nomura Security Company's "Heaven and Hell" bond, which involved three interest rate swaps as well as five currency swaps. Hybrid creatures such as "stock performance exchange-linked bonds" enabled investors to obtain unique exposure to equity and fixed income components in a single product. In their efforts to differentiate identical products, underwriters contrived ever more imaginative special features intended to enhance appeal without necessarily improving yields.

Meanwhile, new financial technology improved the ability of commercial banks to "securitize" their loans by repackaging them as debt instruments (issuing negotiable securities backed by them). The securitization of mortgages, bank loans, auto loans, and credit card receivables became standard procedure. In the United States, public issues of securities collateralized by mortgages and other assets surpassed $60 billion in 1986, a threefold increase from the preceding year. Meanwhile, bonds were routinely "stripped" to enable buyers to invest in either principal or interest coupons.

Thus, technological developments began to transform long-term credit risks into market risks. This, in turn, has been gradually changing the character of commercial banking. When Glass-Steagall has been transformed from a hulking, fearsome guardian of the border between banking and securities into an emaciated and ineffectual symbol, American banks will be experts in the art of creating and marketing securities instruments.

Not only has technology given birth to new markets and market instruments; it has also enabled existing markets to grow to extraordinary size. Transactions on the foreign exchange markets, for instance, ordinarily surpass $200 billion per day. By 1987, international capital flows expanded in volume to more than 50 times world trade.

Some technical innovations were particularly successful. For example, the development of collateralized mortgage obligations (CMOs) by Shearson Lehman created a vast market. (A CMO is simply a floating rate debt security collateralized by a portfolio of mortgages, such as Ginnie Maes, and carrying lower rates than those carried by long-term fixed rate securities.) The U.S. market in these and other mortgage-backed securities exceeded $300 billion in 1985, while secondary market trading reached $1.6 trillion. (In 1987, a single investment bank, Merrill Lynch, lost more than $300 million in the mortgage-backed securities market.) Such trading volumes would have been impossible without modern developments in computer hardware and software. Thus, as new technological developments occur in the future, new financial instruments are likely to follow.

In late 1987, U.S. bond rating agencies, led by Moody's Investors Service, Inc., decided to give triple-A ratings to securities backed by junk bonds. The $150 billion U.S. junk bond market consists of bonds with ratings of double-B-plus (S&P) or Ba1 (Moody's) or lower. Offering yields from 2 percent to 5 percent above those on triple-A securities, junk bonds will provide a basis for a vast pool of new collateralized securities.

SILENT COMPUTERS IN THE OFFICE REPLACE
THE OUTCRY IN THE PITS

It has long been known that "pit trading" with the "open outcry" produces the most efficient and liquid markets. It is this knowledge that underlies the method of floor trading found in the world's stock markets and futures exchanges. Despite its benefits, however, the open outcry may be slowly replaced by automation.

Automation has not been readily accepted in the world's stock and futures exchanges. The first fully automated financial futures market was Bermuda's International Financial Futures Exchange (Intex). Although the automated system enables trades to be executed accurately in less than three seconds from anywhere in the world, Intex has been struggling to survive since it opened in October 1984. Citicorp and McGraw-Hill were forced to abandon an electronic oil and petrochemical trading venture after only six months of operation because of insufficient trading volume. However, the largely automated Tokyo Stock Exchange's bond futures market, which has no trading floor, has been thriving.

Most of the world's futures exchanges have recognized the need for globalization and at the same time are reluctant to encourage automation. Instead, futures exchanges in the United States, Europe, and Asia have been establishing linkages that permit identical contracts to be traded on exchanges on different continents.

The American Stock Exchange established linked trading in stock index options with the European Options Exchange in Amsterdam. In a modestly successful venture, the Chicago Mercantile Exchange (the Merc) has tied up with the Singapore Monetary Exchange for linked Eurodollar futures trading. The Sydney Futures Exchange has attempted tie-ups with the London International Financial Futures Exchange (Liffe) and the New York Commodity Exchange (Comex) for linked trading in U.S. Treasury bond futures and gold futures, respectively. The tie-up has been a dismal failure with negligible trading. The problem with these, and nearly all, exchange linkages is that major and minor exchanges are tied together. Invariably, the smaller exchange does not have sufficient liquidity to draw the major traders of the big exchange.

A number of futures exchanges have established night trading hours. The Chicago Board of Trade introduced a three-hour weekday evening trading session in April 1987, and later in the year it inaugurated a Sunday night session to coincide with the opening of Monday morning business in Tokyo. The Philadelphia Stock Exchange added a four-hour session to its regular trading hours for foreign currency options. However, these attempts to establish around-the-clock trading opportunities in particular contracts will inevitably be outmoded by total automation, which will render trading floors functionally superfluous.

In the United States, the National Association of Securities Dealers Automated Quotations (NASDAQ), in which stocks are traded on video screens, has become the world's third largest equity market. Among U.S. stock exchanges, only the New York Stock Exchange requires that members transact all business on the floor. In 1987, California-based Security Pacific National Bank received authorization from the Federal Reserve Board to create an automated marketplace for domestic government security options.

In Canada, the Toronto Stock Exchange (through its Computer Assisted Trading System) provides fully automated trading and execution of orders. In 1985, Toronto became the first of the world's stock exchanges to establish a trading link with a foreign stock exchange (Amex—the American Stock Exchange).

The Paris Bourse abandoned its traditional trading system (involving 45 licensed stockbrokers) and adopted an automated system developed and operated by the Toronto Stock Exchange. Similarly, the seven Swiss stock exchanges used NASDAQ as a consultant in order to develop an adaptation of the NASDAQ system.

The first section of the Tokyo Stock Exchange has been computerized since 1986 and provides on-line connections to computer terminals at all of the securities companies. Through the Computer Assisted Orders Routing and Execution System (based on the Toronto system), trading of shares is fully automated (with the exception of 250 heavily traded issues that are still traded on the floor). Thus, orders can be immediately executed during trading hours by using this system at any securities company office.

Instinet, a Canadian subsidiary of Reuters (the United Kingdom–based information group), offers an equity trading system that automatically matches buy and sell orders. Used extensively by block traders in the United States, Instinet handles billions of dollars of trading business each month. Although currently opposed by British regulatory authorities, Instinet will eventually be used in the United Kingdom. Within five years, such a system will be used for the execution of small orders.

An event that shocked futures traders in September 1987 foreshadowed the eventual demise of open outcry trading. Reuters successfully concluded negotiations with the Chicago Mercantile Exchange. Under a new agreement that will take effect in 1989, Reuters' 130,000 screens will be used for the automated trading of financial futures and options contracts when the Chicago market is closed. During off-trading hours, the Reuters Dealer Trading System will instantly execute trades, including preprogrammed instructions.

To compete with the Merc, other exchanges will institute similar arrangements. The Matif financial futures exchange in Paris (which made its debut in 1986) is planning electronic trading before and after its regular session. The New York Mercantile Exchange has discussed the electronic trading of oil futures through a tie-up with Reuters. If these developments materialize and flourish, they will signify a big leap in the direction of 24-hour dealing in financial instruments *and* a major weakening of the importance of the open outcry method.

Automation is now rendering the world's stock exchanges accessible to every trader in the free world, regardless of nationality or location. Consequently, competition will become ever more intense and will result in cheaper prices and greater product uniformity.

A small number of securities will always be traded on the floors of the world's major stock and futures exchanges. However, the day is not far distant when trading in the pits by open outcry will be a quaint survival, like the Dixie Land Jazz of New Orleans.

GNOMES NEVER SLEEP

Currencies are uniform and can be traded in vast volumes. Thus, it is scarcely surprising that foreign exchange trading led to the development of the first truly global 24-hour financial market. As early as the 1960s, major international banks used their excess liquidity to exploit significant arbitrage opportunities in the foreign exchange markets. When President Nixon effectively demolished the Bretton Woods Agreement in 1971, he pointed to international bankers, exemplified by the "gnomes of Zurich," as culprits scheming to undermine the U.S. monetary system.

Today, the automated trading of major currencies occurs around the clock in the world's commercial banks, investment banks, and merchant banks. In Tokyo, for example, trading houses (sogo shosha) have established their own foreign exchange trading rooms, while the international offices of Japan's city banks "pass the book" from Tokyo to London to New York to Los Angeles. Foreign exchange trading follows the sun.

The second global financial market, which is now emerging, is trading in government bonds. Government bonds resemble currencies: like money, they are backed by the government that issues them and they can be traded in large amounts.

Government bond yields have been adjusting with increasing rapidity to underlying currency pressures. As a result, attempts by the central banks of the industrial nations to stabilize currency exchange rates and interest rates have begun to adopt the appearance of a zero-sum game. Thus, if foreign exchange rates stabilize, interest rates become increasingly volatile. This may be inevitable, because foreign exchange and interest rates are the expressions of changing economic forces in the world of nations. Like drainage canals alleviating pressure in a riverine system, exchange and interest rates provide the outlet for forces underlying changing global economic factors.

Offshore bond trading (that is, the trading of yen bonds in London or dollar bonds in Tokyo) has grown steadily during the 1980s and will continue to expand as the world's securities markets are deregulated. The development of markets in bond futures in Chicago, New York, London, Singapore, and Sydney has provided investors with a vital means to hedge their positions.

A key event in the development of a 24-hour bond market has been the dramatic increase in the net purchases of American Treasury issues by Japanese investors. In 1985, Japanese purchases of Treasuries totaled $19.2 billion, a threefold increase over the preceding year. This figure, in turn, nearly tripled again in 1986 (reaching about $50 billion). The enormous net investment in U.S. bonds encouraged the trading of Treasuries in Tokyo while New York slept.

In London, the biggest market in the world for the trading of foreign exchange and Eurobonds, global 24-hour trading in Eurobonds has become routine. Eventually, deregulation of the Japan Offshore Banking Market will lead to the relocation of the Euroyen bond market to Tokyo.

If Tokyo, London, and New York are regarded as three corners of a market triangle, then the structure for a unified (and unlinked) global stock market already exists—thanks to the time differences of these cities. A company listed on all three markets can be traded 17.5 hours per day. Any hearty trader determined to doggedly follow the three markets need only adhere to the schedule in Table 4–1.

At the end of each trading day in New York, major American and Japanese brokers pass on unexecuted orders to Tokyo. Similarly, after trading in Tokyo closes, brokers send new or unexecuted orders to London.

In addition to these three major markets, the Amsterdam Stock Exchange (which lists more foreign than local issues) offers 24-hour trading in a selected number of stocks listed on the New York and Tokyo stock exchanges. Not surprisingly, the big Japanese securities companies (except Nikko) are members of the exchange. The Zurich Stock Exchange also offers trading in some major foreign shares.

The 49 market makers on the London Stock Exchange provide prices for more than 200 international stocks. More than half of the dealing in these foreign issues involves investors based outside Britain.

TABLE 4–1
One Day in the Life of a Tripartite Stock Market

	New York	London	Tokyo
New York Stock Exchange opens	09:30	14:30	23:30
London Stock Exchange closes	10:30	15:30	00:30
New York Stock Exchange closes (sleep 4 hours)	16:00	21:00	06:00
Tokyo Stock Exchange opens	20:00	01:00	10:00
Tokyo Stock Exchange closes (sleep 2½ hours)	01:30	06:30	15:30
London Stock Exchange opens	04:00	09:00	18:00

Before long, options on some foreign stocks will also be traded on the London Stock Exchange.

Today, New York and London stand alone as the world's two truly international financial markets. Tokyo is gradually developing the market depth and diversity necessary to compete in 24-hour global trading. During the course of the next five years, Tokyo will join London and New York as an international financial market, providing the same opportunities to international investors.

Eventually, the New York, Tokyo, and London stock markets will be connected by a single computer system so that orders unfilled in one of these markets would automatically be transmitted to the next. Gradually, fixed trading hours will become superfluous and will be abandoned in favor of perpetual computer-executed trading.

GLOBALIZATION OF THE WORLD'S STOCK MARKETS

A market can be simply defined as the area in which buyers and sellers of a product are in communication with one another. More than that, however, it is the area that brings into focus all of the forces that determine prices. In the strict sense of the term, world markets for most commodities have existed for a long time.

The gold prospector in the remote Brazilian jungle sells his nuggets at the trading post in accordance with prices determined in London and Chicago. Similarly, a particular U.S. Treasury bond costs the same in New York or Brasília. If it were possible to buy U.S. Treasury bonds for less gold in Brasília than in New York, New Yorkers would fill their suitcases with gold and take a Brazilian holiday. Market prices would swiftly adjust.

Of course, there will always be arbitrage opportunities between bonds or bills of exchange with different maturity dates when the interest rates diverge. Foreign exchange trading will always flourish. But overall, so long as free competition is unconstrained, efficiency will guide market prices. Keep your eye on the invisible hand.

Today, bonds are traded in dollars, yen, or deutsche marks, and the links among the yields on these securities and currency movements create a chain that encircles the globe. The world's stock markets will eventually follow the bond markets.

Unlike the bond markets, however, most of the world's stock markets are still domestic markets of stocks where locals peruse the inventory and buy in accordance with expectations and fashions. Nowhere is this more pronounced than in Japan. Japanese investors buy stocks as short-term speculative investments on the basis of trends, fads, and rumors.

If an obscure Tokyo stock sheet hints that a certain pharmaceutical company may have discovered a cancer-curing drug, the prices of *all* pharmaceutical stocks in Japan may suddenly rise. During the great bull market of 1986–87, Japan's stock prices rose so high that the average ratio of price to earnings soared to quadruple the comparable multiple prevalent in the United States or Britain.

In the United States and the United Kingdom, where institutional investors are guided by modern portfolio theory and securities analysis is a high-tech art, corporate earnings have acquired cabalistic significance. If a famous stock analyst forecasts that the earnings of a particular corporation will be poorer than expected, institutions will sell their positions and the stock price will decline well in advance of official earnings announcements.

The forces that contribute to the determination of stock prices in different national markets are influenced by market regulations, by the taxation of income from equities and capital gains, by accounting practices, and by a host of sociocultural factors that underlie investors' psychology.

A market's liquidity and the speed with which an investor can sell local equity vary enormously among the world's stock markets. Although these factors will never disappear, their significance as forces in price determination will slowly fade as global stock trading grows. Financial regulators in Japan, France, and Australia have already eased restrictions on equity purchases by foreigners at home and by locals abroad.

In 1986, British net purchases of U.S. stocks exceeded $4.7 billion, a rise of 275 percent over the preceding year. Japanese purchases of U.S. stocks were roughly eight times higher in 1986 than in 1985 and soared again in 1987. Meanwhile, traders and brokers in the United States buy and sell shares listed on all of the world's major stock markets.

Dealers in Britain are now trading American Depository Receipts (ADRs), which represent stock, priced in dollars, of foreign companies whose shares are held abroad. Every business day, London ADR traders scrutinize their screens, searching for arbitrage opportunities among currencies and between the price of the ADR and the price of the under-lying stock.

A demand that exceeded supply caused certain Japanese ADRs to be converted back into common shares and sold to investors in Tokyo. As a result, since 1985 the supply of ADRs in such popular issues as Sony, Matsushita, and NEC has contracted severely. Declining liquidity in the market for Japanese ADRs will send investors directly to the Tokyo Stock Exchange to buy common shares.

Led by the world's multinational corporations, the number of foreign stocks listed on the London and Tokyo stock exchanges has been growing steadily. Swedish companies are listing their shares on the Helsinki Stock Exchange, and in 1987 Nixdorf Computer became the first foreign company to obtain a listing on the Madrid Stock Exchange.

As increasing numbers of multinational corporations regard the world as a single marketplace, a coherent global equity marketplace will gradually emerge. The development of such a marketplace will in turn lead to the routine trading of securities around the clock in the world's major markets. This will lead to price convergence. The day of the global equity market is not far off. The world of international finance is a small world indeed.

CHAPTER 5

JAPAN VERSUS WORLD FINANCE

SUMO

"Japan," my Japanese friend once said to me, "is an island." We were sitting in a coffee shop at midday, and I was busy reading a newspaper article on *sumo* wrestling.

The comment seemed rather obvious, and I grunted noncommittally.

"Actually, Japan is many islands," he continued, apparently intent on gaining my attention.

"Yes, many islands," I agreed without diverting my eyes from the article.

"But for us the Japanese," he continued relentlessly, "Japan is just one island like the circle that surrounds the sumo wrestlers."

At the mention of sumo, I looked up from my newspaper.

"Sumo," he continued, "expresses the essence of Japan. It is unique. It *is* Japan."

"Are you suggesting that Japan is a wrestling match?" I asked.

"Sumo is more than a thousand years old," he continued, ignoring my question. "As with other Japanese rituals and arts, *form, ceremony*, and *appearance* are as important as the activity itself.

"Before a match, each sumo wrestler carefully stamps his feet, claps his hands, throws salt, and, finally, stares with intensity at his opponent. Only the soles of the wrestlers' feet can be in contact within the area enclosed by the circle. Finally, only one wrestler can remain within the circle. The typical match lasts less than half a minute.

"The match represents the collision of power. When the match is over, one sumo wrestler stands within the circle as the solitary victor.

Through a uniquely Japanese combination of *size, skill,* and *harmony,* he occupies the inner circle and in a sense becomes the circle."

"Is that how Japan views competition in business?" I asked. "Does one manufacturer or one bank use its size and skill to dominate the inner circle?"

"No," my friend replied. "There are always at least four to six leaders. If there were only one sumo wrestler, there would be no match; if there were only two, competition would be too limited.

"But, remember, while all of the sumo champion's skills and qualities are indispensable to his victory, size is vital. A sumo wrestler weighing a mere 250 pounds doesn't stand a chance."

CAPITALIZATION

Compared with Japanese financial institutions, U.S. financial institu tions are undercapitalized. In 1986, for example, only two American commercial banks were among the world's top 25 in terms of capitalization (Morgan Guaranty and Citicorp ranked 19th and 21st, respectively). The largest 12 of the world's top 25 banks were Japanese followed by the great universal banks of Switzerland and Germany. The biggest Japanese bank in terms of capitalization (Sumitomo) today has roughly eight times the capitalization of America's best-capitalized bank (Morgan).

Much the same situation holds true for nonbank financial institutions. The best-capitalized American firm, American Express Company, for example, has only about 20 percent of the capitalization of Japan's Nomura Securities Company. In terms of capitalization, the Big Four securities companies are among the biggest brokers in the world.

Capital is as vital to financial industries as food is to the sumo wrestler. Without enough of it, investment banks and commercial banks become too thin to compete. A big capital deficiency can cause a financial institution to wither and die. In the investment banking world, big capitalization means big profits.

Thus, it was the need for increased capital in the early 1980s that forced privately held firms (such as E. F. Hutton and PaineWebber) to go public or to merge with large diversified conglomerates (e.g., Salomon Brothers with the commodities group Philbro and Lehman Brothers with American Express). In 1986, privately held Goldman Sachs (the fourth largest firm on Wall Street) traded a 12.5 percent share of its profits for a $500 million cash infusion provided by Sumitomo Bank, and not long afterward Shearson Lehman Brothers Holdings, Inc. did much the same.

In Japan, all major securities companies, like banks, have been publicly traded for decades. Until recently, however, bank shares and other financial stocks were only thinly traded and maintained stable prices.

Beginning in 1983, bank shares began to rise rapidly. Today, shares in Japan's major banking institutions are trading at 6–10 times the prices that existed five years ago. Price-earnings multiples in the banking sector now range from 60 to more than 150 times.

The share prices of leading securities companies have also rocketed. Nomura Securities Company, for example, which traded at ¥250 per share in 1983, was valued by the market at ¥4550 five years later. This 18-fold increase gave it a price-earnings ratio of 55 (compared to 9 for Merrill Lynch).

By mid-1987, Japan's financial sector had come to represent about 40 percent of the total value of all issues listed on the first section of the Tokyo Stock Exchange. This rise in the total stock market capitalization of Japan's financial institutions has ramifications that extend far beyond Japan's national borders.

Suddenly, Japanese financial institutions have acquired the financial clout to move from their domestic habitat to faraway places with strange-sounding names—such as New York and London. Eventually, the biggest Japanese financial institutions will set up semiautonomous headquarters in these cities and will fiercely compete with local firms for local business.

In just a few years (from, say, 1982 to 1992), Japanese banks and securities firms are being transformed from highly regulated domestic institutions into multinational organizations with extraordinary flexibility and incomparable assets.

THE GIANTS' ETERNAL OBSESSION: MARKET SHARE

Although rice is Japan's traditional staple food, bakeries have been thriving in Japan. According to market research undertaken by Matsushita Electric Industrial Company (the world's largest consumer electric appliance maker), 46 percent of Japanese families eat bread for breakfast rather than rice. Identifying a potential new market, Matsushita invented a new home electrical appliance.

Priced at ¥36,000 ($250), the new machine makes dough, controls fermentation, and bakes a loaf of bread. The housewife (Japanese men seldom cook) need only pour a mix of flour, salt, butter, and dry yeast into the machine; add water; and set a timer. In the morning, fresh-baked bread will be waiting for the family.

The automatic baking machine was introduced by Matsushita in February 1987. Certain of success, Matsushita set initial monthly production at 50,000 units. In less than four months, Toshiba, Hitachi, Sanyo, and Funai Electric were selling virtually identical machines at prices ranging from ¥33,000 to ¥40,000.

Matsushita's optimism was justified, and in 1987 total sales of automatic baking machines in Japan were estimated to be about 1 million units. However, Matsushita will be obliged to share the market with its competitors.

All five producers of automatic baking machines increased production capacity and began competing intensely by establishing differences in design and price. Although Matsushita invented the automatic baking machine, it probably did not resent the sudden surge of competition. In Japan, interindustry competition is viewed as a means of increasing product variety and of improving public recognition.

Not all the producers of the baking machines will necessarily profit immediately from the new product line. But *all* will struggle to secure and hold a particular segment of market share; and all will continue to increase production in accordance with their long-term sales projections.

* * *

In Japan, market share is pursued regardless of immediate costs and short-term losses. Long-term strategy invariably takes precedence over concerns regarding return on investment. In both the manufacturing sector and the service sector, market share is the ultimate measure of performance.

Once market share has been secured, profits will eventually follow. Synonymous with corporate success, market share is the laurel of victory.

The six massive keiretsu (mentioned in Chapter 2) represent a hefty segment of Japan's industrial and financial sectors. These six groupings compete in virtually every area, and member firms in each of them usually produce similar products

Each of the six banks that constitute the core of one of the major keiretsu belongs to an exclusive club (the Six Bank Club). Representatives from each bank (Dai-Ichi Kangyo, Sumitomo, Fuji, Mitsubishi, Sanwa, and Mitsui) meet regularly and discuss collective strategies.

If one company creates a new product, the appropriate company in each keiretsu rushes to produce an identical product in order to lock up a portion of the domestic market. This strategy is pursued to realize long-term objectives rather than to meet short-term sale or profit targets.

Because six or more companies are usually deploying identical techniques to produce almost identical products, competition in Japan is fierce. This encourages a perpetual drive to refine and improve products (while reducing cost) in order to hold market share. It is this dynamic that is responsible for the widespread use and success of quality circles and other devices for which Japanese management has become well known.

In many areas, capital investment is expected to precede profits by a decade or more. Competition with other producers and an expanding market often require expansion of production facilities, which in turn postpones the return on investment.

To keep pace with expanding markets, producers must expand production in advance of demand. This nearly always results in excess capacity. Among manufacturing industries, the creation of excess capacity invariably leads to excess production.

Meanwhile, the excess capacity that results in excess production forces producers to seek new markets for their surpluses. Surplus production, which must be disposed of, can be sold in markets throughout Asia, North America, and Europe at less than production costs.

By offering cut-rate prices combined with outstanding quality, Japanese products can successfully compete with local equivalents. As a result, a domestic problem (*unavoidable surplus production*) is resolved by means of an international solution (*the procurement of overseas market share through predatory pricing*) that leads back to the source of the problem: overcapacity. As foreign demand increases, domestic capacity increases further and a corporation's concern with market share (a domestic issue) is transformed into the relentless drive for world share (a global issue).

Concern with market share is not limited to the manufacture of specific products. When a major Japanese company establishes a new subsidiary in order to provide a new type of service, all of its competitors soon set up identical subsidiaries. Thus, for example, in the mid-1980s all of the major city banks, trading companies, and some corporations set up finance subsidiaries in Luxembourg and London. A primary function of the subsidiaries was to engage in *zaitek*.

ZAITEK

Free Love

Zaitek is to Japan's corporate accountants what free love was to the hippies of the 1960s: it eliminates the need for competition while providing momentary fulfillment. In its most fundamental sense, zaitek is financial arbitrage. It involves the use of moderately sophisticated financing techniques to derive short-term profits from the securities and foreign exchange markets. For zaitekeurs, the world is a playground and the object of the game is to increase annual corporate pretax profits.

Like so many things in Japan, the word *zaitek* is an amalgam of Japanese and foreign elements. *Zai*, which means money, is the root of the Japanese term for finance, *zaimu; tech* is derived from the English word *technology*. The term gives expression to a special Japanese activity that has been growing since the spring of 1984 (when the Ministry of Finance allowed nonfinancial institutions to participate in many financial activities in overseas markets).

Easy

In 1986 and 1987, while the Tokyo stock market was booming, Japanese corporations raised money in the Euromarkets. They floated straight Eurodollar bonds, convertibles, and bonds with warrants attached. In 1987, the coupon prices (the interest rates paid on bonds) on Japanese warrant bonds dropped as low as 1-2 percent. When the proceeds were swapped from Eurodollars into yen, the issuing corporations achieved negative interest rates. That is to say, some Japanese corporations succeeded in being paid to raise money in the Euromarket.

Funds raised in this way were then invested in the Tokyo stock market, in the domestic and international bond markets, and in the volatile domestic bond futures market. Successful corporate investors made big profits; the losers remained mum.

Like Magic

It quickly became common practice for manufacturing companies to derive a hefty segment of pretax profits from financial activities. According to a *Nihon Keizai Shimbun* survey, roughly one third of all publicly listed firms, which are *not* in the financial services industry, profited from zaitek in 1986.[1] The biggest winners were Toyota Motor Corporation, with a cash surplus of ¥123.6 billion (about $850 million), followed by Hitachi, Ltd (¥39.6 billion).

During the period 1985–87, when the yen appreciated against the dollar by 100 percent, most of Japan's manufacturing industries suffered. Zaitek, however, enabled some companies to accomplish the impossible: while their operating profits declined drastically, their total profits remained roughly constant or grew. In 1986 and 1987, many Japanese companies thrived and their corporate surpluses ballooned.

Take the case of Renown, Inc., Japan's largest wholesaler of secondary textile products. In 1986, business was not good and Renown's operating profits declined by 60 percent. However, its zaitek activities saved the year. Zaitek adventures, including $130 million in warrant bonds, gave it a cash surplus that neutralized most of its decline in profits. As a result, 56 percent of Renown's pretax recurring profits for the year ending December 1986 were derived from zaitek.[2]

Not all Japanese companies have been as consistently successful as Renown. In September 1987, Tateho Chemical Industries Company (Tateho Kagaku Kogyo) suffered losses in the Tokyo bond futures market which exceeded its net worth.

Tateho, established in 1966, is a small rural firm (about 300 employees) with a virtual domestic monopoly on the production of electro-fused magnesia (used in the steel refining industry). To counterbalance severely declining profits resulting from poor sales (the decaying Japanese steel industry and the strong yen were the culprits), Tateho's accountant invested heavily in Japanese government bonds.

As with Renown, although Tateho's operating profits were in a tailspin, the company's balance sheets looked wonderful. For the year ending March 1987, its operating profits were more than 63 percent

---

[1] *Japan Economic Journal*, September 5, 1987.

[2] Statistics regarding Renown, Inc. were obtained from the *Japan Economic Journal*, September 5, 1987. Other major companies which suffered annual operating losses in fiscal 1987 while earning zaitek profits included Nissan, Sony, Victor Co. of Japan, and Sanyo.

lower than those of the preceding year, but its ordinary profits were 47 percent higher. Zaitek, take a bow.

In late May 1987, however, when the bond market proved to be a bad bet, Tateho's 40-year-old accountant attempted to counterbalance trading losses by buying contracts on the bond futures market. With an investment position of about ¥400 billion (or about 23 times the company's net worth!), Tateho incurred officially announced losses of ¥28 billion against net assets of ¥16.9 billion. Thus, zaitek produced its first disaster. Or, more accurately, a small corporation devoid of financial savvy failed to establish controls on its corporate investments.

World markets quivered for a moment. Traders and portfolio managers imagined other Japanese companies on the brink of similar calamities. What monsters could be lurking in the deep, opaque waters of Japanese corporate accounting and cash management? Nevertheless, like all nightmares, this one was soon forgotten.

The Rise of Corporate Finance in Japan?

Japanese corporations do not have finance departments. Instead, corporate finance is subsumed by the accounting division, which has not traditionally had a major role in corporate management. In Japan, accountants never become company presidents and rarely rise to the level of director.

The purpose of finance in the majority of Japanese firms is to maintain banking relationships and to assure the smooth transmission of capital to each segment of corporate operations. The finance section of a corporation may on rare occasions voice disapproval of a management decision but can never countermand it.

Zaitek could alter this traditional arrangement. Gradually, the personnel structure of Japanese corporations may change as corporate finance becomes a vital part of corporate profits. If zaitek continues to stuff company coffers, financial decision making will play an ever greater role in management.

Or Is Zaitek Building a Sand Castle?

Just as starving drug addicts use heroin highs as a substitute for food, Japanese companies have been compensating for declining export earnings by shooting cash into the domestic capital markets. Often speculating with borrowed money, Japanese businesses have been attempting to counterbalance eroding profit figures by speculating on the stock and futures markets. Partly as a result, the broadly defined money supply (in mid-1987) has been increasing by 9–11 percent, while inflation has been almost flat.

Windfall profits from the stock market and real estate markets have been keeping troubled companies solvent. However, just as heroin cannot be a permanent substitute for protein, zaitek cannot be a permanent substitute for production.

There can be little doubt that a serious market correction could lead to a plethora of Tateho-style incidents. However, Japanese industry's carefully constructed sand castle will not be washed away by the waves of a financial crisis. The Big Four securities companies, with their vast retail sales networks, enormous capital, and considerable funds under management, will support the domestic markets because it is in *their* best interest to avert publicized crises. Thus, zaitek may be a bridge that is enabling Japanese industry to walk across a temporary gulf in profitability created by the strong yen.

THE FUTURE OF FUTURES

In October 1985, a single bond futures contract was introduced on the Tokyo Stock Exchange. Based on price indexes for fictitious issues of 10-year government bonds, it was the first financial futures contract traded in Japan during the postwar period. Thus, for the first time in 40 years, investors were given a means to hedge positions or sell short.

After an initial setback, the market thrived. Domestic firms ranging from Toyota Motors to Tateho Chemical participated in the market. In less than one year, the new futures instrument became the most actively traded coupon futures contract in the world. Today, only the Eurodollar futures market is bigger.

On July 13, 1987, trading in the contract began on the London International Financial Futures Exchange (Liffe). For Japan's zaitekeurs, however, the London contract was a superfluous invention. Trading during business hours in Tokyo has been more than enough to keep corporate accountants happily busy.

In June 1987, trading in a stock average futures contract (consisting of a package of 50 stocks) began on the Osaka Stock Exchange. As with the bond futures contract in London, participation in the Osaka stock average futures was middling. Trading in stock index futures (based on the Nikkei Stock Average of 225 issues or the Tokyo Stock Exchange Average of all issues listed on the first section) is likely to begin on the Tokyo and Osaka stock exchanges in 1988.

It is also likely that the Ministry of Finance will authorize the establishment of an integrated market that includes trading in additional financial futures as well as interest rates and currency. This development will add a new dimension to zaitek speculation.

Stock index futures based on Japan's Nikkei 225 were first traded on the Singapore International Monetary Exchange (Simex) in late 1986. Trading was thin, largely because Japanese law prohibited Japanese investors from trading in the instrument.

The May 1987 decision by the Japanese Ministry of Finance to allow domestic institutions to participate in foreign futures and options markets has enhanced the prospects for Simex's Nikkei contract as well as for futures trading throughout the world's exchanges. Soon after the decision, 307 domestic financial institutions quickly became active players in the world's major futures exchanges. Gradually, limits placed on overseas futures trading by Japanese financial institutions will be raised or eliminated.

Japanese financial institutions, which are among the world's biggest investors in securities markets, have the potential to become major players in financial futures and options markets throughout the world. In 1987, the Big Four securities companies bought seats on the Chicago Mercantile Exchange (the Merc) and the Chicago Board of Trade (CBT). In 1987, Japanese trading interest focused on the CBT's Treasury bond contracts and the Merc's S&P 500 stock index contract.

As Japanese investments in overseas securities grow ever larger, Japan's investors will turn to the diversity of the world's futures markets as a means of hedging their investments. Futures contracts will be used as a technique for allocating assets among the world's major markets.

Before long, Japanese institutional investors will swiftly move in and out of market sectors by trading enormous volumes of futures contracts. In far less than a decade, Japanese investors are likely to account for at least half of all global futures trading. This fact— conjoined with the size of Japan's domestic stock and bond markets— has encouraged the world's futures exchanges to try to arrange tie-ups with Japan's stock exchanges.

Japanese authorities, however, have been largely uninterested in arranging such tie-ups. They perceive automated trading as the way of the future. The Tokyo Stock Exchange, for example, is developing technology that would fully automate futures trading. Thus, the International Financial Futures Exchange (Intex), Bermuda's tiny futures exchange (mentioned in Chapter 4), will someday be the model for futures and options trading in Japan.

MIXED BLOOD

According to the Aspirin Count Theory, a leading U.S. stock market indicator, the market will slump approximately one year after American aspirin production increases and will rise about one year after it decreases. There are other, similar, indicators that establish market correlations with ice cream sales, the performance of particular football leagues, and the length of women's skirts. Equally frivolous, but more concrete, is the relationship that currently obtains between migration policies and financial market regulation.

In countries that exercise an absolute ban on the emigration of residents (e.g., the Soviet-bloc nations), there are virtually no financial markets. Countries that severely curtail the emigration of residents (e.g., China or Taiwan) have only marginally developed capital market structures. In countries that permit free emigration, the degree to which immigrants are admitted and rendered eligible for citizenship correlates with the degree of capital market regulation.

Thus, at one end of the continuum are Britain and the United States, with highly developed securities industries and a willingness to admit immigrants and grant them citizenship in accordance with long-standing regulations. At the other end of the continuum is Japan.

It is difficult, almost to the point of impossibility, for an immigrant to become a Japanese citizen. Furthermore, Japan is one of the few countries in the world in which birthplace entails no rights to citizenship. Citizenship in Japan has been traditionally determined on the basis of the newborn's patrilineage. The *koseki*, a document detailing the patrilineal descent (and affinal links) of each Japanese has been the only determinant of citizenship. Thus, children born in Japan of Japanese mothers and nonresident fathers have not been Japanese nationals. No other country has insisted upon such strict requirements for citizenship. And no other country in the free world has maintained such highly regulated and restricted financial markets.

It is unwise to draw conclusions from whimsical indicators. Nonetheless, Japan has a long history of maintaining harsh rules determining in-groups and out-groups. Indeed, throughout most of the Tokugawa era (1603–1886), Japanese who ventured outside the archipelago were executed if they dared to return. The regulations that have dictated who is Japanese are the product of the same sociopolitical traditions that have given rise to financial market regulations.

In 1985, the government liberalized citizenship requirements, allowing children born in Japan of Japanese mothers and foreign fathers to be made citizens—following the completion of necessary paperwork at the local-level government ("ward") office. The government firmly gave its directives to the local bureaucrats who were expected to implement them.

Few were surprised, however, when the local bureaucrats hesitated to administer the government directives. There were no refusals, nor were public objections voiced. Instead, the bureaucrats simply demanded successive and extensive documentation from all applicants. Those applying for citizenship on their children's behalf were required to provide materials determined by the bureaucrats. Local offices requested letters from the employer of the child's father. Others insisted upon scrutinizing the birth certificates of the child's paternal grandparents. The requests for supporting materials were varied and irrelevant, and the delays were innumerable.

Some applicants, weary of the process and hoping for an easier time in the future, abandoned their applications. Others complied with all requests, persisted relentlessly, and eventually procured Japanese citizenship for their Japanese-born children. Meanwhile, the application procedure has gradually become more standardized and the number of approved applications has been increasing.

Japan's financial markets resemble its half-native children. Sired by foreign forces, yet born in 19th- or early 20th-century Japan, the capital markets and money markets were nearly all based on U.S. and European models. Just as the half natives combined foreign and Japanese facial features while speaking Japanese with native fluency, so too the financial markets bore the imprints of foreign structures *and* indigenous practices while operating exclusively in a Japanese mode.

Inspired by Western capital structures, Japanese financial markets had no room for foreign participants. Although the Japanese monetary system was influenced by—indeed, was a component of—the international financial nexus, Japan denied its capital markets a role in global finance. Prior to the 1970s, foreign securities firms were excluded from the brokerage industry. Prior to 1986, foreigners could neither join the Tokyo Stock Exchange nor participate in pension fund management. Today, although several Japanese securities firms have become primary dealers in the U.S. Treasury market, foreign institutions are precluded from full underwriting participation in the bellwether 10-year Japanese government bonds.

The opening of Japan's financial markets has proceeded in much the same way as the naturalization of half-native children. Once completely closed to all foreign institutions, Japanese financial markets initiated the process of compromise with foreign elements during the 1960s. At first, some developments allowed by law were not implemented in practice. Thus, the law regulating foreign securities companies positively sanctioned the opening of securities branches that were 50 percent owned by banks. Until recently, however, regulators ignored the provisions and denied access. In the 1980s, under the orchestration of the Ministry of Finance, the Japanese financial markets began to open with increased rapidity, and they will continue to do so.[3]

More foreign securities firms will soon join the Japanese stock exchanges. Stock index futures will be traded in Tokyo. Shelf registration, floating rate notes, domestic commercial paper, and other new instruments and procedures will be introduced while this book is in press.

Meanwhile, Japan's domestic institutions are being granted un-

---

[3]The Ministry of Finance regulates all financial institutions in Japan, as well as the budgets of all government ministries. It also establishes and administers the national tax structure. This comprehensive authority has made it the most powerful and prestigious arm of the Japanese government. The minister of finance is appointed by the prime minister and is a possible future candidate for the nation's top political position.

The Ministry of Finance contains seven distinct bureaus, which oversee the areas of their precisely defined responsibilities: Finance, International Finance, Banking, Securities, Budget, Tax, Customs, and Tariff. The bureaus are in turn segmented into from 6 to 13 divisions, each of which consists of a number of sections.

Collectively, the seven bureaus control the Japanese economy. Fiscal policies are implemented by the various bureaus through taxation, debt expenditures, loans, and investments. The ministry's policies, determined through consultation with the prime minister, are communicated overtly through legislation (introduced by the ministry and approved by the Diet) and more discreetly through "administrative guidance." Administrative guidance is usually communicated verbally by the appropriate bureau to the institutions that it regulates. Although such guidance is not supported or enforced by the rule of law, delayed negative sanctions are imposed on institutions that flout it.

expected (and sometimes unwanted) freedoms. Interest rates on large bank deposits, money market instruments, and a broad range of financial transactions have been deregulated. By 1990, interest rates on small deposits will be determined by market forces. Previously prohibited financial instruments (certificates of deposit, repurchase arrangements, banker's acceptances, treasury bills, stock futures) have made their official appearances. Foreign currency swaps and Euroyen borrowing are now routine.

Beginning in 1988, Japanese corporations will be authorized for the first time since 1933 to issue straight bonds on the domestic market with only a bank guarantee. As a result, small expanding companies will be able to issue unsecured bonds. This move may revive the desultory domestic bond market, which was forced into obsolescence by the more modern Eurobond market.

Today, Japanese banks are permitted to deal in government bonds, while securities companies are gaining freedom to deal in money market instruments. Indeed, during the mid-1980s Japan's "open market," once a tiny portion of the money market, far outgrew the interbank market.

Japan's financial deregulation can be viewed as one instance of the global deregulatory trend mentioned in Chapter 4. It is more than that, however. Not only are Japan's half-native children becoming citizens, but their foreign past has become irrelevant. They have been naturalized and are now as native as automobiles.

Japan's domestic financial deregulation will facilitate the growth and internationalization of the biggest Japanese banks and securities companies. A handful of these institutions are now taking their places among the world's most successful bankers and brokers. In addition, as mentioned in Chapter 4, Japan's insurance companies and trading companies have been setting up financial subsidiaries in Europe to participate in the Euromarkets and generate profits from zaitek.

THE BIGGEST OVERSEAS ASSETS IN THE WORLD

Several centuries ago, a tiny European country famous for its tulips seized control (through the organizational skills of its official agent) of the largest archipelago in the world. The Dutch East Indies, which was 46 times the size of Holland, gave the Dutch a global monopoly on the production and sale of a number of rare spices. Throughout history, nation-states have dramatically expanded their overseas assets and in the process have often multiplied their national wealth and global political power.

Although (sadly) the annexation of sovereign territory is not an obsolete practice, it is not conventionally viewed as a component of macroeconomics. At least among the world's "civilized" industrial nations (those who belong to that respectable club, the Organization for Economic Cooperation and Development—OECD), overseas assets consist of foreign securities, bank deposits, real estate, and plant and equipment that a nation's government, corporations, banks, and individuals purchase in accordance with the law of the land.

In 1986, Japan engaged in an overseas buying spree. That year saw a major expansion in the net size of its overseas assets. According to a May 1987 report submitted by the Minister of Finance to Japan's cabinet, overseas assets held by the Japanese government, corporations, and individuals totaled $727.31 billion at the end of 1986. After subtracting debts, this gave Japan net overseas assets of $180.35 billion, the largest in the world.

Japan's overseas assets in 1986 soared 39 percent over the level of the preceding year. Investments in foreign bonds, representing 35 percent of the country's total overseas assets, were responsible for a large part of the increase. In 1986, Japan's investments in foreign securities rose 129 percent over the 1985 level. Nearly one half of the $257.93 billion in foreign securities consisted of U.S. Treasuries. Investments in foreign stock, foreign real estate, and corporate acquisitions, though not of staggering proportions, were also substantial.

* * *

Japan cannot afford to buy the world. Perhaps if it could, it would. Nevertheless, Japan's overseas investments will continue to grow at a rapid rate. However, the proportional values of the major sectors of those overseas investments will change.

Direct investment will grow rapidly during the course of the next five years, as Japanese manufacturers attempt to rationalize their industries by moving production to countries with low labor costs. Furthermore, foreign investment, by enabling certain Japanese industries to avoid domestic restrictions on expansion within Japan, will sometimes increase independently of labor costs in particular sectors. Because of constraints in the domestic market, many smaller Japanese firms are forced by the severity of competition at home to expand into overseas markets. Even the largest Japanese companies have found that their growth (and their ability to achieve economies of scale) depends on overseas expansion.

During the next several years, efforts will be made to reduce trade friction by increasing the role of foreign-produced goods in foreign trade. Concurrently, investment in foreign services will mushroom. Soon, Japan's aggregate investments in services and real estate will surpass its direct investments.

While Japan's purchases of foreign bonds will rise to a net level of about $200 billion per year (double the current level) before reaching a plateau, investment in foreign stocks will expand exponentially for some time to come. As a result, Japanese investors will become increasingly vital market movers in New York and eventually in London.

An inevitable further strengthening of the yen against the dollar will result in an increase of Japanese purchases of real estate in the United States and Hong Kong (the Hong Kong dollar is tied to the U.S. dollar)—a bargain that few Japanese investors will be able to neglect. In the United States, Japanese buyers will soon begin to look beyond the familiar cities (Honolulu, Los Angeles, New York, Boston) to other promising real estate opportunities. Concurrently, they will buy and build more factories in order to lower production costs and lessen trade friction.

* * *

The following sections will briefly discuss eight instances of Japanese overseas investment:

1. Competitive collaboration.
2. Venture capital.
3. Direct investment in overseas production facilities.
4. Mergers and acquisitions.
5. Investment in U.S. real estate.
6. Investment in foreign securities.
7. The Big Four securities companies.
8. The city banks.

By no means exhaustive, these discussions are intended to provide an indication rather than a demonstration of Japan's expanding role in overseas markets.

COMPETITIVE COLLABORATION

Collaboration among competitors in Japan is at least as old as the zaibatsu holding companies. Top executive officers from competing companies traditionally meet on a regular basis to discuss industry-wide developments and political strategies. Umbrella organizations (such as Keidanren, the Federation of Economic Organizations) and industry-wide organizations (such as the Japan Industrial Technology Organization, or Zenshinren, and the National Federation of Credit Associations) are popular in Japan and have acquired considerable political clout.

In Japan, "cooperative competition" often takes the form of "research associations" created by members of particular associations or a smaller number of competing industries. Intended to pool funding and personnel in an effort to pioneer a new sector or solve a vital problem, such joint undertakings accelerate research and development (R&D).

Discoveries or new products resulting from joint research ventures are, of course, shared among the participating companies. Often, these cooperative ventures have been fallaciously construed by Japan's trading partners as unequivocal evidence of "Japan, Inc."

Although the discoveries of a research association are shared, fiercely intense competition exists among its members. Moreover, individual companies conduct their own in-house R&D in addition to engaging in collaborative ventures. Joint research ventures have become increasingly common among members of the European Economic Community (EEC), and some have been instituted in the United States (see, for example, the discussion of Sematech in Chapter 1).

During the 1960s, many individual Japanese companies sought opportunities to enter into joint marketing or production ventures with foreign partners. These ventures were pragmatically perceived as a tactic to learn about new practices, procedures, and products. Once a Japanese firm learned everything about its partner's business, the venture was usually terminated. As a result of the proliferation of such joint production ventures in North America and Europe, the term *competitive collaboration* acquired a definition in the West that diverged from its meaning in Japan.

In the West, this term was used to signify an unbalanced situation in which a Japanese corporation, with a "hidden agenda," would pursue interests capable of damaging its foreign partner. Thus, for instance, Japanese companies have been accused of using business connections resulting from collaborative arrangements as a means of ferreting out information from the customers of partners or of conducting more general market research that they will use as a tool for competing against their partners in the future.

Despite its negative connotations, competitive collaboration between Japanese and foreign companies has become increasingly common. Many European and American companies welcome the opportunity to develop a new product that can utilize leading edge Japanese technology.

Joint ventures between Japanese and foreign companies have become particularly popular in the auto industry. Thus, for instance, General Motors has collaborated with Toyota Motors and Suzuki Motors to produce vehicles in North American factories and has become a junior partner in a joint venture with Isuzu to produce vans in Bedford, England. Similarly, Volkswagen A.G. and Toyota Motors will jointly produce pickup trucks (designed by Toyota) in West Germany beginning in 1989. In 1987, Daimler-Benz A.G., one of the largest manufacturers of vehicles in Europe, entered into a joint venture with Mitsubishi Motors. Daimler and Mitsubishi will jointly develop and produce vans in Europe. Both sides should benefit. Daimler will gain access to distribution channels in Japan, while Mitsubishi will gain similar access to distribution networks in Europe.

Joint ventures between Japanese and foreign competitors have not been limited to the manufacturing sector. In the capital management industry, for example, many Japanese banks and capital management firms have entered into joint ventures with British and American counterparts. In some instances, the Japanese partner has managed funds that are marketed by its Western partner; in other instances, a new foreign based company has been created (e.g., Yamaichi-Murray Johnstone in Glasgow).

Despite hostility in the United States and the European Community, competitive collaboration is likely to gain in importance during the course of the next decade. The technological know-how and significant capital of Japan's corporations will offer North American and European companies appealing opportunities to gain new knowledge, new products, vital funding, and access to Japanese contacts.

VENTURE CAPITAL

Declining Japanese industries (from steel to trading companies) have found it vitally necessary to diversify into new growth sectors. This is particularly difficult to achieve in Japan, where opportunities for mergers and acquisitions are severely constrained (see the discussion below).

Members of a single keiretsu often band together to share the cost and risk of creating a new undertaking. For example, to move into the communications sector, five Mitsubishi group chemical companies created a jointly owned telecommunications firm (Newcom Five, Ltd.) in 1987. The new firm will provide a network of high-speed digital telecommunications lines linking major Japanese cities. Also in 1987, another Mitsubishi group member (Mitsubishi Corporation—the largest trading company in Japan) established an advertising firm (Media Five).

An alternative to the creation of new companies or the strategic collaboration of a joint venture is the venture capital enterprise. Venture capital enterprises involve investment in new, unproven undertakings. By participating in the risk of new ventures (the total sum of an investment is usually unsecured—hence the term *risk capital*), investors receive a significant portion of the equity in the business. Thus, if a venture succeeds, investors can reap substantial gains.

In the United States, for example, specialized venture capital firms—which perpetually search for a diversity of new companies in which to invest—have developed into a $25 billion industry. In addition, many old-line corporations have also sought one or two venture capital opportunities in order to expand into a new field or to derive beneficial information and new products.

Similarly, in Japan during the 1980s the Big Four securities firms set up venture capital subsidiaries (such as Yamaichi's Uni Ven Company, Ltd.) that were intended to derive long-term capital gains from venture capital investments. Although the primary focus of these subsidiaries has been domestic venture businesses, they have engaged increasingly in overseas investments.

In addition to establishing specialized venture capital companies, many Japanese companies have actively pursued opportunities to invest in "start-up" overseas enterprises, particularly in the United States. Thus, for instance, Mitsui U.S.A., the American subsidiary of Mitsui Bussan (Japan's second largest trading company), poured ¥1.5 billion into nine new U.S. companies between 1984 and 1987. Mitsui's investment represents about 2 percent of the Japanese funds that have been directed into U.S. venture capital investments since 1984.

Venture capital investments enable Japan's mature industries to enter new businesses and offer high-technology companies a means of procuring new products at a fraction of in-house development costs. Discoveries in foreign high-technology areas can be purchased in advance by channeling funds into a promising overseas start-up. In this way, Japanese companies can gain access to the newest American or European technology.

Foreign firms benefit significantly from the presence of Japanese partners. Cash investments from Japan assure adequate funding for research. Furthermore, Japanese investors, because of their long-term view, tend to be more willing than Western investors to engage in undertakings with considerable start-up time. Sometimes a Japanese investor will provide the venture company with engineering assistance. Following the development of a product line, a Japanese partner can provide a manufacturing plant or a bridge to Japanese distribution.

Start-up companies in a variety of high-technology fields will proliferate throughout the industrial world during the next several years. Japanese investors, motivated as much by the opportunity to procure new technology as by windfall profits from equity appreciation, will quickly emerge as a vital source of funding. This, in turn, will give Japanese corporations increasing access to their trading partners' leading edge research and development.

DIRECT INVESTMENT IN OVERSEAS PRODUCTION FACILITIES

Overseas direct investment offers Japan's manufacturers a number of benefits that justify the often unpleasant task of sending managers and middle managers abroad and hiring large numbers of foreign employees. Improved market access, lower labor costs, access to superior market information, and opportunity to reduce Japan's surpluses (and thus trade friction) are the most obvious reasons for shifting production abroad.

In addition, overseas production units enable corporations to establish foreign currency microcosms in which all of a firm's subsidiaries in a particular country can form a self-contained economy. Thus, production costs can be paid, revenue earned, and profits invested—all in one foreign currency.

During the past several years, there have been repeated complaints, particularly by the European Community, that Japanese overseas factories are "screwdriver operations," devoted primarily to the assembly of imported components. European trade representatives allege that Japan has deliberately planned its overseas production to maximize the use of unskilled workers and minimize the integration of its production into local economies. Japanese trade representatives have dismissed these allegations as "Japan bashing" and maintain that screwdriver operations are the necessary precursors to full production facilities. Both the European and the Japanese contentions are well founded.

On the one hand, Japanese manufacturers, particularly the Japanese auto makers, *are* developing their overseas factories into mirrors of their domestic plant and equipment. On the other hand, however, Japanese companies prefer to avoid training foreign personnel. From the Japanese perspective, "job hopping" is a Western trait and money spent on training foreign staff is money eventually lost. Furthermore, the structural approach of Japanese manufacturers differs from that of Western manufacturers. A focus on product in preference to national integration is a vital component of Japan's international operations. This point will be discussed further in Chapter 6.

* * *

Japanese overseas direct investment in 1986 climbed $14.01 billion, an increase of more than 30 percent over the level of the preceding year. In the United States, for example, Japanese direct investment rose from $16 billion in 1984 to $24.4 billion in 1986 (representing about 11.5 percent of total foreign direct investment in the United States).

Japanese corporations have been enthusiastically building and buying factories in the United States and the European Economic Community. The industries that have triggered the most trade friction (such as the automobile and electrical machinery industries) are likely to increase overseas direct investments the most quickly.

The bulk of Japan's direct investment in manufacturing facilities has been channeled toward new factories rather than toward the purchase of existing plants (or of entire companies owning needed factories). In the United States, for example, Japanese manufacturers often build their own plants and subsequently hire nonunion employees who are receptive to the practices of traditional Japanese management. It is estimated that more than 200,000 Americans are currently employed by such plants. However, as mentioned above, Japanese acquisitions of American and other foreign companies will become increasingly common during the next decade.

The Japanese auto industry (which accounted for roughly half of Japan's trade surplus with the United States in 1986) has spent or plans to spend a total of about $4.5 billion on U.S.-based plant and equipment during the 1980s. By 1990, Japanese factories in the United States will have the capacity to produce about 2 million cars per year (more than Japan's total auto exports in 1986)—about 25 percent of total American production.

Japanese auto production facilities have been among the most visible direct investments throughout the world. In the United States alone, more than 350 Japanese companies that manufacture auto parts have established factories in order to supply Japanese *and* American manufacturers.

Honda Motor Company, Japan's fourth largest automaker, expects to export 70,000 cars annually from the United States (of which 50,000 will go to Japan) when its new car assembly plant in central Ohio is operational, in 1989. Similarly, in the United Kingdom, Nissan, for example, plans to produce 100,000 cars annually by 1991, of which one third will be exported to members of the European Community. In Mexico, Honda Motor is investing $41 million in a motorcycle factory, while Nissan Motor has plans to export 90,000 engines annually from Mexico to its factory in Tennessee.

In 1986, West Germany had a trade deficit with Japan of 15 billion deutsche marks ($8.15 billion), about one third of the total European Community deficit with Japan. Roughly 10,000 Germans are employed by 650 subsidiaries of Japanese companies. Although Japan's direct investments in West Germany have been only a small fraction of its investments in the United States and Britain, they have been expanding dramatically, reaching 1.3 billion deutsche marks ($706 million) in 1986 (five times the 1983 level).

In Hong Kong, Japan is the second largest foreign investor (after the United States). Nine Japanese department store chains account for nearly one third of Hong Kong's department store sales. In 1986, Japan spent $502 million in Hong Kong, $493 million in Singapore, and $436 million in South Korea. Japan's direct investments in all of the newly

TABLE 5–1
Japanese Auto Factories Sprout in the U.S.

Company	Investment Cost ($ millions)	Annual Capacity (units)	First Year of Production
Honda Motor	530	360,000	1982
Nissan Motor	745	240,000	1983
Toyota Motor (with General Motors)	400–500	250,000	1984
Mazda Motor	450	300,000	1987
Toyota Motor	800	200,000	1988
Mitsubishi Motor (with Chrysler)	600	240,000	1988
Fuji Heavy (with Isuzu Motor	500	240,000	1989
Honda Motor	380	150,000	1989

Source: "Special Survey, Japanese Management," *Japan Economic Journal* September 5, 1987, p. 8.

industrialized nations will increase considerably during the next five years, as a variety of Japanese businesses open subsidiaries to exploit cheap labor and large market bases.

Japanese companies are discovering that zaitek is not the only way to convert losses to profits. In 1986, Aiwa Company (an audio equipment producer and exporter that is 54.7 percent owned by Sony Corporation) suffered a 25 percent decline in sales, resulting in an after-tax loss of ¥5.7 billion (about $38 million). The appreciation of the yen had rendered Aiwa's products noncompetitive in world markets.

Based on the expectation of continuing sales declines, Aiwa decided to immediately move a large portion of its total domestic production to Singapore, where the cost of labor was far lower than that of Tokyo. Within eight months of the decision, 1,200 jobs at Aiwa's Tokyo facility were terminated (primarily through early retirement and offers of unusually large severance payments). By the end of 1987, Singapore production will constitute an estimated half of Aiwa's total output.

The Aiwa strategy is likely to be mirrored increasingly by those

Japanese industries that are squeezed by the strong yen. In 1987, such leading Japanese electronic firms as Sony, NEC, and Matsushita Electric Industrial announced plans to invest in Singapore.

As more and more Japanese firms, for a variety of reasons, expand overseas production, growing numbers of local nationals will become dependent on them. The more jobs Japanese employers control in particular countries, the greater the influence of Japanese companies will be on local economies. When Toshiba Corporation was faced with trade sanctions in 1987, Toshiba immediately pointed to the 4,500 Americans that it employed.

MERGERS AND ACQUISITIONS

White Elephants

In Japan, mergers are not unusual. According to the Japan Fair Trade Commission, during the decade from 1976 to 1985, mergers averaged about 1,000 per year. This compares with a comparable figure of nearly 3,000 in the United States.

Mergers most commonly occur when, under the guidance of MITI or the Ministry of Finance, companies facing immediate or likely bankruptcy are merged with firms in the same industry. In 1986, for example, Heiwa Sogo, Japan's sixth largest mutual savings bank, was faced with insolvency and merged with Sumitomo Bank.

Most mergers or acquisitions in Japan during the postwar period have involved businesses within the same industry. Mergers are usually initiated by an appropriate ministry or by the selling firm. The majority have entailed acquisitions of subsidiaries by parent companies or mergers among subsidiaries at the parent's initiative. In some cases, the acquisition of a small distributor by a major corporation is accomplished through the discreet transfer of a block of shares. Companies needing land sometimes buy real estate companies to acquire their holdings.

While acquisitions in Japan are far more unusual than mergers, hostile takeovers are as rare as white elephants. Frowned upon by industrialists and the bureaucracy, they have been firmly opposed by the government. Thus, for instance, MITI overtly prevented Sanko Steamship from taking over Japan Line in 1973. Minebea Company's hostile bid for Sankyo Seiki Manufacturing Company in 1985 (still under negotiation in late 1987) is an example of this underhanded and immoral approach.

A *hostile* takeover of a Japanese company by a foreign company has not yet occurred. Foreign acquisitions of Japanese companies are feasible and occur infrequently. Between 1978 and 1984, only 20 Japanese companies were acquired by foreign organizations, all after prolonged and friendly negotiations.

Between 1984 and 1987, a handful of foreign (primarily U.S.) firms purchased small, beleaguered Japanese companies. Kodak Japan, for example, bought three units of Kusuda Business Machines Company as well as a small share of a local camera producer (Chinon Industries, Inc.). With few exceptions, the Japanese companies acquired by foreign interests have been small and financially troubled. Thus, foreign buyers are perceived as occasionally acceptable agents in minor domestic mergers.

One of the many comparative strengths of Japanese corporate structure has been the system's hostility toward hostile takeovers. Japanese corporations can conduct business without building defenses that could preclude the accumulation of valuable assets or inhibit long-term research and development strategies. Because the Japanese shareholder is *not* a shareholder in the American sense (that is, the minority shareholder is not truly an owner but rather a corporate supporter, an agent expressing goodwill), the shareholder's interests are irrelevant to corporate strategy.

Mergers and Acquisitions in Japan

A Japanese corporation is viewed as an organic whole that consists of relationships—among employees, between employees and suppliers, and between customers and employees. Traditionally, employees stay with a single company throughout their working lives. Job-hopping is still rare among blue-chip corporations, and people who are not hired directly out of a university (latecomers) can seldom hope to advance to the highest levels of management. The corporation's relationships with its customers are carefully nurtured, and, depending on the business, corporate employees often cultivate business friendships with their customers.

In Japan, ideally, long-term relationships transcend immediate financial constraints. This means that the established networks among companies and between a company and its employees are believed to be more durable and important than the short-term problems that may threaten to interrupt them. The relationships that link people within a company are believed to be as vital and inviolable as Japanese culture itself. Thus, declining industries make every possible effort to retrain unneeded employees rather than dismiss them. In the banking and securities industry, employees are fired only for a major act of wrongdoing.

The primary reason for a corporation's existence is to enable people to work and prosper. In this sense, a corporation belongs to its employees rather than to its shareholders. The letter of the law is thus incidental to the pragmatic fact that management and staff, by running and maintaining a corporation, are more than its heart and blood. They are its soul.

Because corporate vitality and identity are inseparably linked with employees, a Japanese corporation's personnel department embodies a significance and wields a degree of power not found in non-Japanese corporations. By simply refusing to amalgamate, the personnel departments of two corporations considering a merger can subvert merger plans.

Of course, this ideal model is not always realized. However, the myth that relationships are never severed and that the corporation *is* a tightly knit family is paramount. Thus, the sale of a company is tantamount to the sale of family members and has "implications of immorality and social irresponsibility."[4] The word *nottori*, a term applied to airline hijackers, is sometimes used with reference to corporate takeovers.

To prevent a reemergence of the dismantled zaibatsu, the Occupation authorities revised Japan's Commercial Code, making holding companies illegal and allotting considerable power to a shareholder with as little as one-third ownership. In the absence of a holding company, expansion through the acquisition of companies in nonrelated businesses is difficult. The vital power associated with one-third ownership makes it virtually impossible to gain control of a company through a tender

---

[4]James C. Abegglen and George Stalk, Jr., *Kaisha: The Japanese Corporation* (New York: Basic Books, 1985), p. 202

offer for shares. Since World War II, there have been only two tender offers in Japan (both friendly).

It is sometimes possible for a block of investors (termed a *kaishime*, or "corner group") to buy one third or even one half of a corporation's shares, thus gaining a major voice in the corporation. Because of beneficial cross-shareholding, however, there are few, if any, publicly listed companies in Japan with a float equivalent to more than two thirds of outstanding shares.

Finally, the Commercial Code prohibits corporate mergers without the *unanimous* consent of the directors of the corporations to be merged. However, even after such consent has been achieved (usually following years of negotiations), redundancy is not easily eliminated. Workers are not ordinarily fired in Japan's "lifetime employment system," while new positions can be difficult to create. Employees identify primarily with the entity for which they worked prior to the merger. As a result, factions based on premerger corporate definitions become firmly established.

In 1971, for example, the Kangyo Bank merged with the Dai-Ichi Bank to form a sprawling entity, the Dai-Ichi Kangyo Bank. The new bank ranked first among Japanese commercial banks in the number of its branches and employees and in the size of its asset base. In Japan, where bigger is always better, the bank thrived. But there were problems.

For more than a decade following the merger, employees considered themselves as "Dai-Ichi men" or "Kangyo men." Frequently, the Dai-Ichi group looked down on the Kangyo group. Only employees hired after the merger were indifferent to the distinction. Although all the directors of both banks had approved the merger, some former directors of the two banks inhibited the smooth merging of the separate work forces. The result was inefficiency. Fifteen years after the merger, the Dai-ichi Kangyo bank, plagued by redundancies, ranked below many other city banks in profitability (return on assets).

M&A Could Help Restructure Japanese Industry

Because of the problems and barriers involved in mergers or acquisitions, Japanese corporations have traditionally diversified through the introduction of new product lines. When necessary, new subsidiaries are established to develop, to manufacture, and to market leading edge products.

The maturing of many Japanese industries, the gradual internationalization of Japan's corporate sector, and the need to rapidly establish new products are leading to a recognition of the need for diversification through acquisition. Invariably, Japanese domestic acquisitions entail the purchase of a small company by a large company.

In 1986, for example, Tokyo-based Orient Leasing Company (in terms of capital, the fourth largest financial services company in the world) acquired Akane Securities (a third-tier securities company). At about the same time, Kanematsu Semiconductor Corporation acquired Pacific Electronic Trade Corporation. Megamergers, such as Chevron's $13.2 billion acquisition of Gulf Oil or General Motors' $5 billion acquisition of Hughes Aircraft, have not yet occurred in Japan. Leveraged buyouts on the scale of the Kohlberg Kravis acquisition of Beatrice Foods are currently inconceivable in Japan. Indeed, no Japanese-owned company has ever been acquired in a leveraged buyout.

Takami Takahashi, the president of Minebea Company, one of the world's leading manufacturers of miniature ball bearings, is one of Japan's few corporate raiders.[5] In addition to making 15 domestic acquisitions, Minebea paid $139.2 million in 1985 to acquire the U.S. firm New Hampshire Ball Bearings, a supplier to the Pentagon. At that time, U.S. sentiment did not weigh strongly against Japanese acquisitions of strategically important U.S. firms. Minebea's purchase of New Hampshire Ball Bearings stands in sharp contrast to Fujitsu's failed attempt to acquire Fairchild (discussed in Chapter 1).

Today, most Japanese industrialists openly condemn "the trend of trading Japanese corporations as if they were merchandise."[6] Privately, however, some Japanese bankers and industrialists admit that profit margins can be increased by buying existing businesses rather than developing new sectors from scratch.

In the retailing industry, it is often more profitable to buy an existing chain of stores with established market share than to open new stores. Where Japanese legislation restricts the opening of supermarkets,

---

[5]See the discussion of Minebea in Aron Viner, *Inside Japanese Financial Markets* (Homewood, Ill.: Dow Jones-Irwin, 1987), pp. 89–90.

[6]See "Mergers & Acquisitions, Cash-Rich Companies Go on Overseas Shopping Spree," *Japan Economic Journal*, November 29, 1986.

for example, the acquisition of new outlets may be the only means of domestic expansion. As Japanese companies become accustomed to buying foreign businesses, domestic acquisitions are also likely to become more frequent.

Targeting the United States: M&A Departments in Japanese Financial Institutions

Cash-rich Japanese companies have begun to actively seek acquisition targets in the United States. The strong yen has made many U.S. companies seem cheap by comparison with their Japanese counterparts. According to the Sanwa Bank, publicly disclosed Japanese takeovers (including joint venture investments) of foreign companies increased from 31 in 1985 to 78 in 1986, with more than half of these (25 and 47, respectively) in the United States. The majority of the deals, however, were small acquisitions, ranging from $1 million to $20 million.

Although hostile takeovers are a customary avenue for acquisitions in the United States, Japanese buyers have rarely chosen this method (the outstanding exception of Dainippon Ink is discussed later). Most Japanese companies move into foreign markets slowly and negotiate to buy companies in related industries. Their aim is to reduce production costs (and protectionist pressure) by manufacturing in the United States. In some instances, a foreign acquisition offers the opportunity to diversify away from old-line and unprofitable businesses. In other instances, foreign acquisitions permit declining industries to reduce their production costs. In the American steel industry, for example, the biggest steel companies have sold part of their equity to Japanese firms.

Japanese corporations that seek targets for purchase often turn to the domestic banks with which they have had long-term relationships. Traditionally, Japanese banks functioned as main banks or shareholders when they worked behind the scenes as intermediaries in mergers and acquisitions. Before the 1980s, most Japanese banks were only rarely involved in mergers and acquisitions (M&A) and none of them had established an M&A department. Osaka-based Sanwa Bank was the first Japanese bank to establish an M&A team (in 1983), and it has been Japan's leader in the M&A field, completing 20 deals between 1983 and 1986.

Unlike other banks in Japan, which have ordinarily provided M&A advice and information as a service to clients, Sanwa has charged its clients a fee for its M&A services and has aggressively cultivated a role as intermediary in or initiator of mergers and acquisitions. As a result, the bank earned ¥100 million in M&A commission fees in the first half of 1986.

In 1985, for example, Sanwa arranged (in collaboration with Morgan Stanley) for Fujisawa Pharmaceutical to buy 22.5 percent of Lyphomed, Inc. of Chicago. In November 1986, Sanwa advised Hitachi Zosen Corporation in the $70 million purchase of Clearing, Inc. (a maker of metal-forming presses) from U.S. Industries, Inc. (a subsidiary of Hanson Trust PLC). Similarly, in January 1987 Sanwa (in collaboration with Sonnenblick-Goldman, a mortgage brokerage firm) encouraged its client Kokusai Motorcars Company (Japan's biggest taxicab and livery service) in a $319 million acquisition of the Hyatt Regency Maui from VMS Realty.

As Japanese corporations seek overseas acquisitions, their traditional banking partners have been steadily drawn into the field. The Long-Term Credit Bank of Japan, for instance, participated in two U.S. acquisitions in December 1986. It advised Sumitomo Rubber Industries, Ltd. when it acquired 80 percent of Dunlop Tire Corporation in a $240 million deal, and it arranged for a unit of Mitsui & Co. to buy the American Acceptance Corporation from Fidelity Bank.

Although the Big Four Japanese securities firms have M&A departments in Japan, they have only recently begun to develop similar capability in their overseas subsidiaries. Usually, when Japanese corporations seek a U.S. acquisition, they utilize a major American investment bank with proven expertise rather than a domestic securities firm. During the past several years, for example, Morgan Stanley & Co. (which has M&A departments in Tokyo as well as New York) has advised the Industrial Bank of Japan, Nippon Kokan, Sanwa Bank, and Fuji Bank on transactions worth an estimated $1.8 billion.[7]

Japanese Financial Institutions Go Shopping in New York, Chicago, and Los Angeles

While Japan's banks and securities companies expanded their M&A departments and went scouting for their clients, some of them made acquisitions on their own account. In 1985, for example, Nomura

---

[7]See Michael R. Seist, "Japanese Seek Role as Takeover Advisers," *The Wall Street Journal*, May 4, 1987, p. 6.

TABLE 5–2
A Sampling of Major Corporate Acquisitions in the United States by Japanese Firms, 1984–1987

U.S. Firm Acquired	Japanese Buyer	Equity (percent)	Price (millions)	Year
National Steel	Nippon Kokan	100	425	1984
Bank of California	Mitsubishi Bank	50	292	1984
Continental Illinois Leasing	Sanwa Bank	100	64.5	1984
Martin Marietta	Nippon Kokan	40	45	1984
Thin Sheet Metals	Nishan Steel	100	25.8	1985
New Hampshire Ball Bearings	Minebea	100	132.9	1985
TREA Industry	Toray Industries	100	10.3	1985
Sun Chemicals (Graphic Arts Materials Group)	Dainippon Ink	100	550	1986
Bell and Howell (Visual Communications Division)	Eiki Industrial	100	25.8	1986
Clearing Inc.	Hitachi Zosen	100	70	1986
Dunlop Tires	Sumitomo Rubber	80	240	1986
CBS Records	Sony Corp.	100	2,000	1987
Westin Hotels & Resorts	Aoki Corp (& Bass Group)	100	1,530	1987
Reichhold Chemicals	Dainippon Ink and Chemicals	100	540	1987

Sources: *Nihon Keizai Shimbun, Financial Times,* and *The Wall Street Journal.*

acquired 50 percent of Babcock & Brown, a New York–based real estate leasing firm. In December 1986, Nomura Babcock & Brown Real Estate, Inc. paid $50 million to acquire a 50 percent stake in New York's Eastdil Realty, Inc., a real estate investment banking firm owned and founded by Benjamin V. Lambert with an extensive Japanese clientele. Indeed, no sooner was the deal closed than Eastdil concluded the arrangements for Shuwa Investment Corporation (see below) to buy the Arco Plaza in Los Angeles. Eastdil now functions as the real estate investment banking arm of Nomura's U.S. operations. Under Lambert's guidance, Nomura will engineer complex U.S. real estate investment opportunities for Japanese investors.

In 1985, the Industrial Bank of Japan (IBJ) bought 75 percent of J. Henry Schroder Bank & Trust Company from Schroders (a U.K. banking group). A year later, while Nomura concluded its purchase of Eastdil, J. Henry Schroder Bank & Trust arranged to pay $234 million to acquire Aubrey G. Lanston & Co., one of the few remaining independent primary bond dealers. Before the ink was dry on the legal documents, the IBJ increased its stake in Schroder to 95 percent and changed the name of the institution to IBJ Schroder Bank & Trust Company.

A big spender in the American financial market has been Fuji Bank (Japan's most profitable bank in fiscal 1987), which in 1984 paid $425 million for two finance subsidiaries of Walter E. Heller International. By means of this acquisition, Fuji hoped to provide a majority of Japanese corporations in the United States with leasing and factoring services. At the time of the purchase, the two units had aggregate nonperforming debts of $400 million. In 1986, Fuji Bank added $300 million in equity to Heller International Corporation, bringing its total commitment to $1.15 billion, the largest single investment in the United States by a Japanese financial institution. Under Fuji management, Heller International has become a major lender in American leveraged buyouts (financing more than $1 billion in 1987) and after four tough years will finally move from the red to the black in 1988.

In 1985, Sanwa Bank paid $50 million for Continental Illinois's leasing subsidiary (the 13th largest leasing unit in the United States), which is now the major component of Sanwa Business Credit Corporation. This was the first Japanese purchase of a U.S. leasing operation. In the expectation that all U.S. interstate banking regulations will disappear, Sanwa Bank has plans to convert the leasing offices into part of a broad network of national banks.

In 1986, Sanwa bought Lloyds Bank California (a unit of London-based Lloyds Bank PLC) for $263 million. The acquisition was merged with Sanwa's Golden State Sanwa Bank, making it the sixth largest bank in California. Continuing its acquisition strategy in 1987, Sanwa agreed in principle to buy a primary bond dealer, Brophy, Gestal, Knight & Co. L.P. (formerly Refco Partners) for about $75 million.

Although the deal will not be concluded until the political climate is favorable, it is likely that Sanwa will soon join the Industrial Bank of Japan as owner of a primary dealer subsidiary.

Rumors that one of the Big Four was contemplating acquisition of a U.S. broker with an extensive retail network wafted through the streets of New York's financial district throughout 1986 and 1987. There can be little doubt that such an acquisition will be made when the political climate is favorable.

Meanwhile, Nippon Life, Sumitomo Bank, and Yasuda Mutual Life have each paid tidy sums ($538 million, $500 million, and $300 million respectively) for pieces (13 percent, 12.5 percent, and 18–25 percent) of premier Wall Street investment banks. In a more conservative fashion, Sumitomo Life bought 2 million shares (1.5 percent) of the British Merchant bankholding company, Kleinwort Benson Lonsdale PLC.

Like Japan's industrial corporations, Japan's financial institutions realize that it is usually more economical to buy a foreign unit (with customers and foreign staff in place) than to create a foreign subsidiary from scratch. Because of their massive equity capital, Japan's securities companies, banks, and insurance companies are well positioned to buy anything they want from the Atlantic to the Pacific.

TABLE 5–3
Japanese Financial Institutions Buy Pieces of Wall Street

U.S. Investment	Japanese Buyer	Equity (percent)	Price (millions)	Year
Babcock & Brown	Nomura Securities	50	—	1985
Henry Schroder Bank and Trust	Industrial Bank of Japan	95	—	1985
Eastdil Realty	Nomura Securities	50	50	1986
Aubrey G. Lanston	Industrial Bank of Japan	100	234	1986
Goldman Sachs	Sumitomo Bank	12.5	500	1986
Shearson Lehman	Nippon Life Insurance	13	538	1986
PaineWebber	Yasuda Mutual Life Insurance	18–25	300	1987

The First Leveraged Buyout in Japan

A leveraged buyout involves the purchase of a controlling interest in a company through the use of borrowed funds. Because the funds are borrowed against the assets of the acquisition, the lender usually gets an equity share in the acquired company. Ordinarily, the loans are repaid by selling a portion of the acquired company's assets and by using its cash flow. The technique of financing corporate takeovers through leveraged buyouts gave birth to the junk bond market in the United States.

In June 1987, Prudential Asia Investment of Hong Kong (a newly created merchant banking subsidiary of Prudential Insurance of America) concluded a leveraged buyout of Simmons Japan (a U.S.-affiliated bed manufacturer with a 70 percent share of Japan's Western bedding market). Arranged by the Industrial Bank of Japan, the ¥4 billion ($26.7 million) acquisition was the first leveraged buyout to occur in Japan and one of the first in East Asian history.

A combination of long-term loans and subordinated debt as well as equity, the deal is noteworthy because it could point the way for Japanese companies to arrange similar deals at home. As a result of the buyout, a U.S. subsidiary company became an independent Japanese company under foreign ownership.

It is highly likely that in the next several years a Japanese market will gradually develop for the unsecured, subordinated paper that is generally used in leveraged buyouts. Thus, medium-sized Japanese corporations may soon undertake leveraged buyouts of Japanese firms. This, in turn, may lead to a new Japanese market in yen-denominated high-yield low-grade securities.

A Japanese Corporate Raider Bares Its Teeth in the United States: The Case of Dainippon Ink

Japan is a patrilineal society in which inheritance of the family name and property passes from father to sons. Sometimes a man with a daughter and no sons will "adopt" his daughter's husband. In such cases, the son-in-law legally takes his wife's surname and becomes his father-in-law's heir.

Shigekuni Kuriyama spent part of his childhood in California and in 1958 graduated from New York University's Graduate School of Business. In 1959, he married the daughter of Katsumi Kawamura, the second-generation owner of Dainippon Ink and Chemicals, Inc. Kawamura had no sons and arranged to have his wife's husband adopt his surname and someday take the reins of the family company. Shigekuni Kuriyama became Shigekuni Kawamura, and in 1978 he assumed the presidency of Dainippon Ink.

Dainippon (which means "great Japan"), the largest printing company in Japan, produces printing inks, synthetic resins, paper, and plastics. In 1976, the firm purchased Kohl & Madden Printing Ink Corporation, a small U.S. maker of printing inks. A smaller but similar Indonesian company was acquired the following year. In addition, joint ventures with domestic and international companies were arranged in order to expand Dainippon's marketing capability and product lines.

Ten years after these acquisitions, in 1986, the firm earned pretax profits of $363.9 million (¥55.32 billion) on $2.7 billion in annual sales. Every year for the past 38 years, Dainippon ink has posted growth in pretax profits. Dainippon's yearly dividend of ¥6 (about four cents) has been very high by Japanese standards.

With the encouragement of his father-in-law, Kawamura has used an increasingly aggressive style of mergers and acquisitions to establish an international network in printing inks and specialty chemicals. In 1979, Dainippon Ink engaged in a bitter bid battle to acquire Polychrome (a U.S. producer of ink and printing plates) from Rhône-Poulenc (a French chemical firm).

In 1986, under Kawamura's direction Dainippon negotiated to buy several companies in the West German Hartmann Group. At the same time, it undertook discussions to buy the profitable graphic arts materials group of the American firm Sun Chemicals Corporation.

When the talks with Sun Chemical failed, Dainippon shocked the American firm's management by making a hostile bid to buy the entire company. Faced with the possibility of a hostile takeover, Sun Chemical quickly capitulated and sold the division for $550 million, a price which analysts considered to be quite high.

In 1987, Dainippon again initiated merger discussions with a U.S. company, this time with New York–based Reichhold Chemicals, a producer of chemicals (adhesives and polymers) used in plastics, photography, and various industrial processes. In June, the discussions broke down because Reichhold wanted $70 per share, while Dainippon offered less than $60.

In a repetition of its strategy with Sun Chemical, Dainippon launched a hostile tender bid. Offering $52.50 per share (about $473 million) for control of the American firm, Dainippon angered Reichhold's management, which rejected the offer out of hand and unsuccessfully sought another buyer. Finally, two months later, Reichhold agreed to a $60 per share offer worth about $540 million.

Decision-making power is far more centralized at Dainippon Ink than at other Japanese companies. Kawamura, as a third-generation corporate president, wields considerable authority and does not need to rely on the consensus of his corporate directors. This makes Dainippon one of the few firms in Japan in which decisions can be rapidly implemented.

The American education and American management philosophy of the company's president are in no small part responsible for Dainippon's distinctly foreign strategy of expansion through acquisition. Thus, Dainippon Ink is in certain respects a Japanese company that acts like an American company.

TABLE 5–4
Major Acquisitions by Dainippon Ink

Date	Company	Amount (millions)
May 1976	Kohl & Madden Printing Ink Corporation	6.00
September 1977	P.T. DIC Indonesia	0.42
March 1979	Polychrome Corporation	6.26
September 1986	Several Hartmann Group firms	3.00*
December 1986	Part of Sun Chemicals, Inc.	550.00
August 1987	Reichhold Chemicals, Inc.	540.00

*5.5 million deutsche marks.

Source: Damon Darlin and Masayoshi Kanabayashi, "Dainippon Ink Takes Another Bold Step", *The Wall Street Journal*, June 29, 1987, p. 18.

Will Some Japanese Companies Begin to Imitate
Dainippon Ink's Aggressive Overseas M&A Strategies?

Many Japanese corporations are studying Dainippon Ink's overseas acquisitions. The smooth integration of a group of foreign companies into a single Dainippon global network will be analyzed not only by Dainippon's domestic competitors but by major corporations throughout Japan. In addition, the M&A departments of Japanese banks and securities houses will assess the success of Dainippon Ink's rapid expansion in the hope that it will provide Japanese companies with an example to emulate.

If Dainippon's corporate profits continue to grow and if no political problems (trade friction) develop from the foreign purchases, then sooner or later another Japanese company will attempt a hostile acquisition in the United States. The outcome of *that* attempt will also be carefully watched. If a pattern of successful Japanese hostile takeovers in the United States gradually emerges, the stage will be set for a flood of Japanese tender offers for major and minor foreign companies.

Because Japanese corporations are patiently watching and waiting, it will be years before Japanese M&A becomes a potent force in the United States and Europe. By the early 1990s, however, Japanese corporations will be active practitioners of the overseas M&A strategy pioneered by Dainippon Ink's Shigekuni Kawamura.

REWRITING THE RECORD BOOKS: THE CASE OF
JAPANESE INVESTMENT IN U.S. REAL ESTATE

Buying America for Fun and Profit

Because of its Pacific location, Hawaii has long held a special appeal for Japanese honeymooners and investors. Hawaii is a familiar place for the Japanese, and Japanese capital investment, not surprisingly, has been flowing steadily from Japan to Oahu (the island dominated by Honolulu) for nearly a quarter century.

In the late 1970s, the Japanese billionaire and power broker Kenji Osano bought the Waikiki Beach Hotel, the Royal Hawaiian, and a number of other similar resort properties in Oahu. A variety of Japanese investors continued to buy Hawaiian hotels during the 1980s, and in 1986 Azabu (a Tokyo retailer) bought three hotels, including the Hyatt Regency Waikiki, for a total of $270 million. As a result, today about 85 percent of the roughly 20 ocean front hotels on Waikiki Beach are owned or controlled by Japanese investors.

In addition to Hawaii's most valuable hotels, Japanese interests have acquired shopping centers, condominiums, and office buildings in Honolulu. Major resort properties on the islands of Kauai and Maui have also been acquired by Japanese investors.

Other portions of Pacific America have attracted Japanese real estate investment for a long time. Los Angeles, home to an estimated 1,000 Japanese companies, is familiar hunting ground. Japanese interests control an estimated 25 percent of downtown Los Angeles.

In 1986, conservative Japanese real estate buyers looked far beyond the Pacific to New York, Boston, and Washington. By the end of December 1986, the Japanese had surpassed the British as the largest foreign investors in the $2.5 trillion American commercial real estate market.

Because Japanese institutional investors have limited domestic opportunities to invest their excess cash, they have been hungry for foreign investment opportunities. The U.S. real estate market offers Japan's institutional and corporate investors an economical meal. There are some sound reasons for this:

1. *Low prices.*
   - The prices of U.S. office buildings have been depressed. By comparison, land prices in central Tokyo increased by 75 percent in 1986. In Japan, the ratio of the cost of land to the value of the building standing on it is usually about 3:1—in the United States, it is usually about 1:3.
   - Because of high land prices, profits from renting a new Tokyo office building do not begin to appear for at least 10 years, while it takes about 30 years for returns on Tokyo real estate investments to match the annual capital gains on Japanese stock investments.
   - Japanese companies can borrow yen at low interest rates in Japan (using their domestic real estate and securities holdings as collateral) and convert the borrowed yen to dol-

lars at a rate that has improved by more than 85 percent since the yen's low against the dollar in mid-1985. Many real estate investors borrow dollars at Japanese interest rates from the American branches of Japanese banks.

2. *Low taxes.*
   • As in the United States, land in Japan is not depreciable for tax purposes. However, a U.S. real estate investment yields a far larger tax deduction than one in Japan because the bulk of the cost of the U.S. investment is in the building rather than the land.
   • Depreciation schedules on commercial property, at 60 years, are far longer in Japan than in the United States.
3. *High yields.*
   • Japanese real estate is far more expensive than comparable U.S. properties and can provide a return of only one third to one fourth of the return available in the United States.
   • With 100 percent financing (from a bank loan), an 8 percent return (from rental income) will enable a Japanese buyer to repay the principal and interest on a loan in 20–25 years. This means that a Japanese buyer can own blue-chip American property *without using its own capital.*
4. *Low political risk.*
   • The United States has the best ratings for political risk in the world.

Japanese investment in U.S. real estate totaled $5.5 billion in 1986, a rise of 366 percent over the level of the preceding year. The figure was expected to double again in 1987. While all of Japan's major financial institutions, real estate firms, and construction companies have been active in the U.S. real estate market, Japan's big insurance and real estate companies accounted for 35 percent and 27 percent, respectively, of all Japanese real estate investments in the United States.

More than half of the Japanese real estate investments have been office buildings in a few U.S. cities (such as Manhattan and Los Angeles). Japanese investments in the best office buildings (fully leased with blue-chip tenants) were so significant in 1986 that, according to some estimates, they boosted prices for prestigious office towers in these cities by 8–15 percent.

Life Insurance Companies Are Learning the Ropes

Japan's leading life insurance companies, which together constitute Japan's biggest institutional investors, have been internationalizing their investment portfolios. While their purchases of foreign bonds grew by 60 percent between the end of 1985 and December 1986, their investments in foreign real estate doubled during the same period.

Although Japan's Ministry of Finance has permitted overseas real estate investments for some time, it has advised (through "administrative guidance") institutional investors to limit their exposure and temper their lack of experience by engaging in joint ventures. The life insurance companies' real estate purchases require special ministry approval, which is granted on a "case by case" basis.

In addition, total real estate investments, as a proportion of investment funds, are limited to 20 percent. However, aggregate industry assets have been growing by 15–20 percent per year. This means that Japan's institutional investors have billions of dollars earmarked for real estate investment. A hefty portion of this money is destined to flow abroad.

Dai-Ichi Life Insurance Company, for example, operates a special division for overseas real estate investments. The division's joint ventures with Japanese and foreign partners have included the AT&T Center in Los Angeles and the Citicorp Centers in San Francisco and New York.

Sumitomo Life Insurance bought an approximately $300 million convertible mortgage on a major New York office building in late 1987. Still under construction, the 650,000-square-foot building (425 Lexington Avenue) was not scheduled to open for nine months. Under the terms of the mortgage, Sumitomo will have the option of converting the mortgage into 49 percent of the equity in the building.

Convertible mortgages offer a special appeal to conservative Japanese investors. After buying such a mortgage, Japanese managers can watch the appreciation in the rental value of the property. If the rental market stagnates, the buyer can decide not to convert the mortgage. This strategic advantage is likely to make convertible mortgages ever more popular among Japanese buyers.

Sumitomo Life and Dai-Ichi Life, like other Japanese life insurance companies, book (record on the balance sheet) foreign real estate investments as stocks. This sleight of hand is achieved by means of the rationalization that the newly purchased buildings are owned by subsidiaries whose stock is wholly owned by the insurance companies. As a result of the accounting convention, the real estate investments become just one component of securities investments. If the real estate investments are successful, they can counter foreign exchange losses in the bond market; if they are unsuccessful, the losses are concealed within the firms' total overseas securities portfolio.

The Highest Bidders

Beginning in 1986 and continuing throughout 1987, Japanese buyers of American property demonstrated their willingness to substantially outbid other investors. The strength of the yen against the dollar, windfall profits from the Tokyo bull stock market, and opportunities to borrow at lower interest rates in Japan than in the United States have encouraged Japan's investors to pay prices that have stunned American real estate brokers. Because Japanese investors analyze U.S. market prices in terms of Tokyo real estate valuation, they willingly make purchases that yield 1–1.5 percent less than those expected by U.S. investors.

The most aggressive Japanese buyer in the United States has been family-owned Shuwa Investment Corporation, which has spent $2 billion on U.S. real estate and plans to spend $1 billion per year on American property. Shuwa (which means "excellent harmony") owns 45 buildings in Tokyo (4.8 million square feet), where it ranks with the major keiretsu real estate companies (Mitsubishi, Mitsui, Sumitomo) as one of the biggest office landlords.

The owner of closely held Shuwa, Shigeru Kobayashi, has commented that he wants to buy a building in every American state. Shuwa has purchased office buildings in New York, Boston, and Washington, D.C., and has become a major landlord in Los Angeles (where it owns about 12 percent of the downtown area) and the San Francisco Bay area (where it owns many condominiums and commercial properties).

The prices paid by Shuwa have set records in the U.S. real estate industry. In a September 1986 cash deal, for example, Shuwa bought Arco Plaza in Los Angeles for $620 million. This was the biggest all-cash real estate transaction in U.S. history. Later that year, Shuwa bought Capital Cities/ABC, Inc.'s New York headquarters for $174.2 million and the PaineWebber building in Boston for $100 million. In a

July 1987 leaseback agreement, Shuwa bought the Washington, D.C., headquarters building of *U.S. News & World Report* magazine for roughly $80 million. At $480 per square foot, this was by far the highest price ever paid per square foot for an office building in the U.S. capital. Three months later, Shuwa acquired a full city block in downtown Los Angeles (paying $76.7 million—a record California land price) that it will develop into a $650 million hotel, office, and retail complex.

Shuwa has not been the only Japanese firm to set records in the U.S. real estate market. In November 1986, Dai-Ichi Real Estate paid $94 million for Manhattan's famous Tiffany Building. This set a record as the highest price ever paid per square foot of retail space in the United States. The following month, Mitsui Real Estate Development Company, Ltd. (Mitsui Fudosan) paid $610 million for the Exxon Building in New York's Rockefeller Center. This was a record payment for a Manhattan office property. During the same month, family-owned Kato Kagaku Company (a major producer of glucose) bought Manhattan's Tower 49 for $303.5 million, a record price per square foot for a U.S. office building.

Sumitomo Realty and Development Company (Sumitomo Fudosan), which has made enormous investments in Tokyo office buildings for leasing, has simply extended its strategy to the United States. In June 1987, for example, the firm bought one of the best-known buildings in Manhattan, 666 Fifth Avenue, for $500 million (about $365 per square foot).

The Sumitomo approach exemplifies the current preference of Japanese investors for landmark buildings, famous hotels, and fully leased rental properties in prime locations. This assures an immediate yield on the investment and obviates the many risks involved in undertaking a new real estate development. Although the majority of Japanese buyers who come to the U.S. market now prefer to buy existing office buildings or hotels, this strategy will gradually change.

Other Strategies

In late 1986, Mitsubishi Estate Company (Mitsubishi Jisho—the largest office building leasing company in Japan) began a $1.4 billion (¥200 billion) joint venture housing and resort development near Palm Springs, California. The five-year project will involve the construction of 2,500 housing units, a convention center, five 18-hole golf courses, and a number of hotels.

Mitsui Real Estate, a pioneer in Japanese real estate development, has also purchased a California site (in San Diego County), where it will build an industrial estate. In Hawaii, similarly, Japanese investors are engaging in joint development ventures with local partners. These developments mark the beginning of a significant trend in Japan's American real estate development.

Japanese investors have begun to look beyond buying famous buildings in famous cities. The strategy of Sumitomo Life Realty is an example. In 1985 Sumitomo Life purchased the Boston headquarters of Wang Laboratories (Burlington Business Center I on Route 128), and in 1987 it put up $145 million for the construction of an office block in central Los Angeles. Shuwa Corporation will soon buy buildings in such American cities as Atlanta, Dallas, Phoenix, and Seattle.

During the next several years, Japanese buyers will diversify their investments from blue-chip properties to higher-return second-tier investments scattered throughout the United States. Japanese construction companies will help build new buildings with money provided by Japanese investors and Japanese banks will become a leading source of real estate financing in the United States.

Although a large portion of Japanese overseas commercial real estate purchases has been in the United States, Japanese buyers have also begun to consider central London, which, after central Tokyo, is the highest-rent district in the world.[8] In June 1987, Ohbayashi Corporation, one of Japan's Big Five civil engineering groups, paid an astounding £3,575 ($5,895) per square foot for Bracken House, the headquarters of the *Financial Times*. This was by far the highest price ever paid for a property in The City. Similarly, across the Channel in Paris, Kowa Real Estate Investment Company invested FFr2.5 billion ($435 million) in a property development project on the left bank near the Montparnasse railway station.

After central Tokyo and central London, the highest rents in the world are paid in Hong Kong. Not surprisingly, Japanese investors

---

[8]In 1986, rents in The City of London were roughly 40 percent of the rents in central Tokyo and twice as high as rents in downtown Manhattan.

know Hong Kong (regarded as the gateway to China) quite well. Japan has been one of Hong Kong's three most active traders (along with the United States and China). Japanese investors, who have spent an estimated $700 million on Hong Kong real estate, own major office blocks in the central business district as well as extensive holdings in Kowloon.

* * *

Not content with joint ventures alone, Shimizu Construction Company (Shimizu Kensetsu—the biggest of Japan's civil engineering contractors) bought a minority stake in California-based Dillingham Construction Corporation. The other big Japanese construction firms are likely to follow the Shimizu initiative and undertake acquisitions of American (or British or Hong Kong) construction firms.

Joint ventures between Japanese and foreign companies are also likely to proliferate. For example, Kumagai Gumi, Japan's sixth largest construction firm, has joined Zeckendorf Company in a number of hotel and residential projects in New York. In Hong Kong, Kumagai Gumi has set up a partnership with a local firm, Cheung Kong, and is developing a vast industrial and residential complex. In addition, the Hong Kong arm of Kumagai Gumi is building the new Bank of China headquarters, the second cross-harbor tunnel, and a building for China International Trust and Investment. In London, Kumagai Gumi is renovating office buildings for the Nomura and Daiwa securities companies.

* * *

Soon, the Ministry of Finance will permit trust banks and life insurance companies to directly invest corporate pension funds in offshore real estate. This will result in further growth of Japan's overseas real estate investments. Japanese buyers will expand their ventures in London, Hong Kong, and other major world cities. Japan's financial institutions will become the number one foreign buyers in the U.S. real estate market—and will hold that position for a long time to come.

They will not be alone. Japanese real estate firms, construction companies, and rich individuals will select their investments with care and will outbid all comers. From mansions in Monterey, California, to shopping malls in Indiana to the most prominent Manhattan towers, the names on the deeds will be Japanese.

THE FLOODGATES SLOWLY OPEN: THE CASE OF JAPANESE INVESTMENT IN FOREIGN SECURITIES

The Ocean of Money

The Japanese like to save money. They save more money than any other nation in the world (about 17.5 percent of disposable income in 1986). The accumulated savings finds its way into bank accounts, securities investments, and insurance policies.

For example, the outstanding value of Japanese life insurance contracts reached $6.4 trillion (¥967.4 trillion) at the end of 1986, which represents an average of $53,000 (¥7.95 million) for every Japanese citizen—the highest in the world. This in turn has made Japan's life insurance companies the biggest and richest investors in history. With total assets of about $430 billion (¥60 trillion), Japan's 23 life insurance companies have more money than a great many sovereign governments.

Nippon Life, the biggest insurance company in the world, holds assets of $105 billion, which include 3 percent of all listed equity in Japan and the nation's second largest private real estate holdings. When Nippon Life casts its gaze abroad, foreign brokers snap to attention and foreign markets respond. The mere rumor that Nippon Life and a few of its pals may stay away from a particular auction of U.S. Treasuries is enough to depress the market. So, in 1986, when the top 10 Japanese life insurance companies increased their foreign investments (mainly U.S. securities) by 35–40 percent, the Dow Jones Averages soared.

This magnitude of financial power, if coordinated, can be awesome. The biggest life insurance companies, prohibited by Article 65 from raising funds through debt issues, are major participants in the foreign exchange markets. It is generally believed that through trading on the Tokyo foreign exchange market, the insurance companies often move and occasionally manipulate the yen-dollar exchange rate.

Collectively, Japan's financial institutions hold a cash pool of vast proportions. At the end of March 1987, Japan's personal savings totaled nearly $4 trillion (¥554 trillion). Corporate surplus funds then exceeded $1.5 trillion (¥200 trillion), while corporate pension funds were worth $140 billion (¥20 trillion) and were growing at the rate of 22 percent per year. In addition, there were the investment trusts (¥35 trillion) and special funds in trust termed *tokkin* (¥27 trillion) For several reasons,

TABLE 5–5
Where Some of the Domestic Money Is

	Percent Share of Funds			
Type of Institution	1965	1975	1980	1986
City and regional banks	40.8	32.5	29.6	29.0
Finance Ministry trust fund	10.0	15.5	19.6	20.4
Mutual and credit unions	14.0	14.2	13.2	12.1
All insurance companies	5.2	5.8	6.3	8.3
Farm banks	7.1	7.3	7.5	7.4
Trust accounts of all banks	7.2	7.3	7.2	7.3
Long-term credit banks	5.4	5.1	4.4	4.4
Postal life insurance fund	2.5	2.4	3.0	3.7
Trust banks	1.8	1.5	1.2	1.2
Other	6.0	8.4	8.0	6.2
Total	100.0	100.0	100.0	100.0
¥ trillion	50.0	276.5	509.3	888.4
$ billion*	357.1	1,971.4	3,637.9	6,345.7

*$1 = ¥140.

Source. The Economist.

only a tiny portion of this ocean of capital has so far found its way into overseas investments.

Buy Japan

Japanese portfolio managers have traditionally been strongly averse to overseas markets. Part of their reluctance to buy foreign securities can be attributed to conservative investment principles that dictate putting funds in the home market where conditions are familiar and foreign exchange risk is absent. Managers of pension and trust funds have sought a modest 8 percent return, which they have secured by investing in domestic loans, stocks, and government bonds.

Furthermore, Japanese portfolio managers—like their American counterparts—have distrusted all things foreign and until recently saw little need to study foreign issues or journey abroad. Thus, they lacked the expertise necessary to follow foreign securities markets.

In addition, the Ministry of Finance maintains strict limits on the proportion of trust and pension funds that can be invested abroad. In March 1986, the limits were raised. Insurance companies and trust banks were authorized to invest as much as 25 percent of their portfolios in foreign securities and real estate. Nevertheless, at the end of 1986 Japan's biggest single group of investors, the 23 domestic life insurance companies, had only 11 percent of their assets (about ¥7.3 trillion, compared to total assets of ¥62.5 trillion) in foreign securities. As this percentage grows, the market-moving power of Japan's financial institutions will increase dramatically.

From Japan to New York and Other Foreign Places

The domestic reservoir is now feeding foreign markets. Net purchases of foreign stocks by Japanese investors in 1986 totaled $7.048 billion. This was 138 times more than the level in 1984. (Roughly 60 percent of these equity investments—$3.3 billion—were in blue-chip issues listed on the New York Stock Exchange. The appreciation of the yen against the dollar and the U.S. bull market made American equities seem cheap and desirable, and the yields were not unappealing.) As a result, the Japanese became the second largest foreign investors in U.S. stocks after the British. Japanese investments in overseas equities were expected to more than triple in 1987, and the proportion directed to U.S. issues were expected to rise to more than 80 percent, or about $20 billion.

Japanese investments in foreign stocks were small, however, compared to Japanese investments in foreign bonds, which in 1987 exceeded $72 billion. About half of this amount was spent on U.S. Treasury issues. Japanese purchases of foreign bonds, like Japanese foreign equity investments, have grown considerably. The case of the insurance companies surveyed in Table 5–6 illustrates this.

At the end of March 1987, roughly 60 percent of Japanese foreign bond holdings were dollar denominated, primarily in the form of U.S. Treasury issues. The big investors in the U.S. Treasury market have been trust banks, life insurance companies (led by the two giants, Nippon and Dai-Ichi), and Norinchukin Bank. Norinchukin, which collects deposits from all of the agricultural cooperatives, is the sixth largest bank in Japan and the largest in terms of domestic deposits. Norinchukin currently holds roughly one sixth of all U.S. Treasuries purchased by Japanese institutions. Foreign securities purchased by the life insurance companies represent about 30 percent of all Japanese

TABLE 5–6
Japanese Life Insurance Companies' Investments in Foreign Securities

Year*	¥ Billions	Percent of Total Portfolio
1975	13	0.1
1980	669	2.5
1985	4,668	8.7
1986	7,307	11.7
1987†	10,340	n.a.

*Fiscal year ending March 31.
†At May 31.

Source: Nippon Life Insurance Company.

foreign holdings and a roughly comparable share is held by the seven trust banks.

As a result of the yen's appreciation against the dollar, unrealized (paper) foreign exchange losses on Japanese institutional holdings of American securities were considerable. For example, the 23 life insurance companies collectively wrote off foreign exchange losses totaling $14.8 billion (¥2.238 trillion) for the year ending March 31, 1987. However, these paper losses have not discouraged Japan's institutional investors from diversifying their portfolio holdings into foreign, particularly U.S., markets. The decline of the dollar has simply reduced the foreign currency expense of buying dollar assets and also the probability of future exchange rate losses that could result from holding them.

From Drizzle, to Downpour, to Flood

During the course of the next five years, there will be a doubling in the percentage of their total assets that the life insurance companies and the trust banks invest in foreign securities. The current level of about 11 percent will begin to approach the ceiling of 25 percent established by the Ministry of Finance. Such an increase will involve a flood of Japanese money moving into the major world capital markets.[9]

---

[9]Part of this investment results from current Japanese accounting rules that prohibit insurance companies from using capital gains to pay out dividends on the portfolios they manage. As a result,

(continued)

TABLE 5–7
From Little Buyer to Big Investor:
Japanese Net Purchases of Foreign Securities
(in $ millions)

Year	Bonds	Stocks
1980	$ 4,285	− $344
1981	5,808	240
1982	6,066	151
1983	12,507	658
1984	26,773	51
1985	53,517	995
1986	93,024	7,048
1987	72,890*	16,870*

*Nearest ten million.

Source: Ministry of Finance.

Because the trust banks and life insurance companies have had small foreign offices, their active trading in foreign securities has been modest. They have often treated their securities investments like their investments in real estate, which are held for decades. Many of the life insurance companies and trust banks are now expanding their overseas operations and giving their foreign offices greater autonomy in investment decisions. As a result, their trading activities have been growing. Consequently, these financial institutions are beginning to train a new generation of fund managers in the intricacies and subtleties of international securities markets.

In March 1987, Nippon Life paid $538 million for a 13 percent stake in Shearson Lehman Brothers (the third biggest Wall Street securities firm in terms of capital and subordinated debt). Three months later, 28 Nippon Life trainees boarded Japan Air Lines flights for New York. They were to study the securities business at Shearson Lehman for a period of one to two years. Some of these trainees will eventually

---

the insurers have a strong motive for exposing some of their assets to the higher returns available in overseas markets. The Ministry of Finance is expected to change accounting regulations in 1988, permitting total return on assets (yield plus capital gains) to be used in paying dividends. Although this modification of accounting practice could reduce the need to seek higher returns abroad, the overall effect is not likely to be significant.

become fund managers in Tokyo, where they will use their knowledge of the American securities industry to manage portfolios that will include foreign, primarily U.S., issues.

Following the example of Nippon Life, Yasuda Mutual Life Insurance Company (Japan's fifth largest insurer) paid $300 million for an 18 percent voting share of the PaineWebber Group Inc. One component of the agreement reached between the two companies allows Yasuda to send up to 150 trainees to PaineWebber.

* * *

For the remainder of this century, Japanese financial institutions will continue to invest heavily in the United States because it represents an oasis where Japanese funds can flourish. The U.S. bond and stock markets are deep wells that can absorb huge capital infusions from Tokyo with little more than a ripple. They also provide a safe haven for Japan's enormous dollar earnings from trade, and they yield some of the best long-term returns in the world. Furthermore, because of its "quality, liquidity, and marketability," the dollar itself is seen as an indispensable receptacle for Japanese assets.

The life insurance companies and trust banks, which hold a vast segment of Japan's liquidity, will become ever more influential participants in the U.S. and other major capital markets. However, the Japanese securities companies are far better positioned than any other type of Japanese financial institution to direct the flow of Japan's domestic savings to international investments.

THE BIG FOUR SECURITIES COMPANIES

Sushi and Spumante

In terms of capitalization, the Italian stock market is less than 3 percent the size of the Tokyo or New York stock market. Its trading volume is minuscule by American or Japanese standards, and it has been of negligible interest to international investors. Most foreign securities firms have curtailed operations in Milan because of disappointing brokerage business. Nonetheless, in the fall of 1986, Daiwa and Nomura, the two biggest securities companies in the world, set up representative offices in Milan. Eight months later, Nikko and Yamaichi followed suit.

At one level, the Big Four are attempting to get closer to the Italian government bond market, where a massive public debt has resulted in high yields. In addition, they hope that representative offices in Italy will improve their chances of securing underwriting opportunities with Italian companies.

Meanwhile, in a private competition, each of the Big Four was striving to be the first securities company to arrange the listing of an Italian firm on the Tokyo Stock Exchange. Although little profit accrues to such participation, they believe that domestic prestige and the promise of future underwriting justify their efforts. However, all of these considerations only marginally justify the cost of setting up representative offices.

At a deeper level, the Japanese securities firms are seeking to establish a blanket presence in every major financial market. From this perspective, Milan is just one instance of a general expansion into all global securities markets. Short-term benefits are of little concern, and the representative offices are expected to lose money for many years. Eventually, Milan will be one unit in the multinational networks that each of the Big Four is now constructing at great expense and with high hopes.

Small Local Purveyors Become Giant International Agents

Japanese securities firms were born in the early 20th century and originally dealt largely in bonds. When Japan's stock exchanges reopened in 1949, these firms were a minor component of Japan's financial sector.

Under the protection of Article 65, the Big Four securities companies (Nomura, Daiwa, Nikko, and Yamaichi) grew rapidly and hundreds of smaller, second- and third-tier securities firms also thrived. The growth of the Japanese stock market, which paralleled Japan's economic expansion, led to big revenues for the securities industry.

The first foreign office of a Japanese securities firm appeared in New York in 1953, one year after the end of the Occupation. However, prior to the enactment of the new foreign exchange law in 1980, the securities companies were almost exclusively domestic affairs.

By 1987, the Big Four together maintained more than 40 wholly owned overseas units (representative offices or foreign subsidiaries) located in 11 countries. Nomura and Daiwa opened new banking units in London in late 1986, and Nikko and Yamaichi followed a year later.

Each of these firms had plans to expand its international business. The funds to do so were readily available.

The bull stock market of 1985–87 gave the Big Four record profits and astounding stock market capitalization. In 1986, for example, their aggregate net income was 2.5 times that of the four biggest firms on Wall Street.

By 1987, Nomura, the biggest securities firm in Japan, had grown to vast proportions. Its 155 offices serviced roughly 4 million clients who gave it customer assets of $237 billion—more than the assets of any commercial bank in the world. At the end of September 1987, Nomura's stock market capitalization was roughly $58 billion, more than triple the *combined* value of Salomon, Merrill Lynch, Shearson Lehman, and Goldman Sachs.

Initially, the Big Four's foreign operations specialized in the sale of Japanese equity to foreign investors and of foreign equity to Japanese investors, and for years most of these operations lost money. Nonetheless, each of the Big Four was determined to establish itself in leading American, European, and Asian financial centers in order to carve out and protect a long-term share of Japanese overseas securities business.

Competition for market share assured that as Daiwa and Nomura began to swiftly expand their London and New York operations in 1985, Nikko and Yamaichi would scramble to compete. Between 1985 and 1987, Nomura increased the staff of its U.S. subsidiary from 180 to 700; Daiwa, from 150 to 400; Nikko, from 70 to 260; and Yamaichi, from 45 to 275.

In fiscal 1986, each of the Big Four claimed to have derived about 10 percent of its pretax profits from overseas operations. Nomura has announced that it expects 50 percent of its profits to come from foreign markets by the turn of the century. Indeed, like a barbershop quartet, the Big Four harmoniously sing with optimism about their swiftly expanding international business.

Getting Settled in London

In October 1986, London's "Big Bang" marked the abandonment of fixed commission rates on bonds and equity transactions. The traditional distinction between jobbers (who execute trades) and brokers (intermediaries between the public and the jobbers) was terminated, and outside institutions were allowed to buy members of the London stock exchange.

In anticipation of a new and vital financial environment in London, brokers and jobbers merged or were acquired by foreign and domestic interests. More than 50 mergers and acquisitions of this type occurred in London during the period 1984–86. Leading banks from the United States, Canada, Switzerland, Belgium, France, and Hong Kong acquired London brokers or jobbers.

Japanese financial institutions were notably absent from the orgy of buying. Instead, Japanese securities companies and commercial banks substantially expanded their London subsidiaries, watched as events unfolded, and waited to see the outcome. They had little choice. The Ministry of Finance unofficially advised Japan's financial institutions to refrain from investing in the British financial services sector lest such investments exacerbate trade friction between Japan and the United Kingdom.

When the Big Bang began, 27 firms became market makers in gilt-edged securities. Competition within this market (about 20 percent the size of the U.S. Treasury market) and the London stock market was intense. Many of the newcomers found that they had overestimated the market share that they could procure and hold.

In March 1987, Greenwell Montagu Securities, the stockbroking arm of Midland Bank, decided to abandon equity market making. Two months later Lloyds Bank gave up trading gilts, and not long afterward Morgan Grenfell reduced its gilts staff by 50 percent. Other market makers in the gilts market followed Morgan Grenfell and reduced their trading staffs. In September 1987, the London branch of Shearson Lehman Brothers (the third largest investment bank in the United States) fired 150 employees and reduced the number of stocks in which it made markets from 400 to 200.

These cutbacks by major players were the result of excessive competition within the severely constrained British financial markets. Based in an economy about one seventh the size of the U.S. economy and about one third the size of the Japanese economy, Britain's indigenous financial markets cannot offer the depth of opportunity available in New York and Tokyo. Within this environment, British financial institutions (including those acquired by foreign firms prior to Big Bang) have insufficient capital to easily compete with better-capitalized foreign financial institutions.

It was within this environment that the Big Four decided to become market makers in British equities and eventually primary dealers in gilt-edged securities. Nomura, usually the leader of the Big Four, began making markets in shares in September 1987. At that time, it had expanded its London staff to more than 800, compared to 400 in 1986 and only 2 in 1964. It announced plans to increase its staff by an additional 75 percent by mid-1988.

Soon, the Big Four will be able to serve their domestic customers as market makers in British equities and as primary dealers in London. Of course, it will be quite some time before Japanese brokers are selected by significant numbers of British investors in preference to local firms. However, with overseas securities investments growing, Japanese clients will provide the Big Four with a respectable volume of brokering business. The short-term goals of these securities companies demand no more.

After less than one year as primary dealers in New York, Nomura and Daiwa developed close relationships with a number of state pension funds (which deal only with primary dealers). Eventually, the Big Four will establish similar relationships with British and other European clients.

The London subsidiaries of the Big Four were expected to employ several thousand British citizens by the end of 1987 and to be engaged in local brokering, banking, and underwriting. These activities are important as components of the total set of products, services, and capabilities that will serve to define the Big Four's market scope in the 21st century.

In the Euromarkets: Leaders of the League

Because of superior rates and easier issuing requirements, Japanese corporations have increasingly preferred to borrow in the Euromarkets rather than at home. Japan's Big Four securities companies and two long-term credit banks have become the lead underwriters for the plethora of Japanese issues floated in Europe.

Among Japan's financial institutions, in 1985 only Nomura ranked among the top 10 bookrunners in the prestigious Eurobond underwriting league tables. In 1986, three of the Big Four were there. One year later, 4 of the top 6 positions were filled by the Big Four, with three Japanese banks placed among the top 20. Thus, Japanese institutions accounted for roughly 25 percent of all Eurobond underwriting. By comparison, Merrill Lynch fell from 9th place in 1986 to 26th place in 1987.

The sudden ascendancy of Japanese institutions in the Euromarkets (displacing such entrenched firms as Goldman Sachs and Morgan Stanley) bore a striking resemblance to the powerful growth of the Japanese semiconductor industry in the 1980s. Domestic profits were used to cut margins to the bone, while predatory overseas pricing was common. Meanwhile, established domestic relationships assured a minimum market.

Concurrently, hundreds of Japanese corporations, flush with cash, turned to their familiar brokers to arrange Euroyen offerings. The money borrowed in this way was used for zaitek.

After securing impressive beachheads in the Eurobond market, Japan's Big Four set their sights on United Kingdom equities, big-block stock trading in New York, venture capital, leveraged buyouts, M&A, and (last but not least) the U.S. Treasuries market.

On Wall Street: Primary Dealers and Big Brokers

In 1985, Nomura and Daiwa decided to expand the government bond trading departments of their New York subsidiaries and to apply to the Federal Reserve Bank of New York for primary dealer status. Nikko and Yamaichi hastily followed suit. Each of the Big Four invested tens of millions of dollars to rent space, create trading rooms, and hire expensive local talent. Nikko, for example, hired the top-ranking staff official of the Federal Reserve System (the Fed) in 1986 and a vice president of the Federal Reserve Bank of New York a year later.

Virtually overnight, the Big Four became market movers in the U.S. government bond market, where at the end of 1987 they accounted for roughly 18–20 percent of long-term trading in U.S. Treasuries. Thus, on the one hand these securities firms have come to function as conduits, channeling Japan's domestic liquidity into the hungry maw of the U.S. government, while on the other hand they have grown to be leading traders of American debt.

Despite objections in Washington, in late 1986 the U.S. subsidiaries of the two biggest Japanese securities firms, Nomura and Daiwa, became primary dealers at the Fed. Primary dealer status involves special advantages and privileges in the $100 billion per day U.S. government securities market.

Although bidding at U.S. Treasury auctions for new issues is unrestricted, the Federal Reserve Bank of New York deals only with primary dealers when it trades government securities in the secondary market to implement monetary policy. While there are currently just 40 primary dealers, the secondary dealers number more than 400. Primary dealer status involves great prestige, and many companies will do business only with a primary dealer.

Eventually, Nikko and Yamaichi will also become primary dealers and a growing proportion of the Big Four's U.S. Treasury bond transactions will be with U.S. rather than Japanese customers. Meanwhile, during a period of just a few years the Big Four, which began as insignificant traders representing Japanese clientele, have become powerful forces in the Treasury market serving U.S. customers.

As with Treasuries, so with stocks. Although Japanese investors have been net buyers of foreign equities for many years, their total trading in such equities was never great and their annual net purchases of these equities always fell below $1 billion. In 1986, however, all of this began to change and Japanese institutional (and individual) investors began transacting a substantial number of small-lot and large-block trades in New York. By 1987, the Big Four accounted for an estimated 8 percent of all trading on the New York Stock Exchange (the bulk of it for Japanese customers) and had set their sights on making markets in United Kingdom equities.

Global Reach

The Big Four have been the traditional underwriters for Japan's biggest corporations, and they now control about 80 percent of Japan's underwriting business. Together, they account for roughly 40 percent of all bond trading in Japan and for nearly half of all equity trading. As a result, they have ridden on the shoulders of Japan's industrial success and its recent stock market boom. With pretax profits of $3.5 billion (¥450 billion) for the fiscal year ending September 1987, Nomura, for example, was the most profitable corporation in Japan.

The Big Four's burgeoning importance in international finance is not due to net income alone. Together, these firms have become the primary agent for the recycling of Japan's vast wealth. As a result, the Big Four (and the leading Japanese banks and insurance companies) have become instrumental in directing the deployment of Japan's overseas assets.

Overseas subsidiaries of the Big Four in leading world financial centers are growing like amoebas and are becoming an organic part of the national financial systems in which they participate. In some quarterly auctions of U.S. Treasury bonds, for example, Nomura alone has purchased more than 10 percent of the entire issue and the Big Four together have purchased one third of the total. As with the Japanese insurance companies, Big Four participation in Treasury auctions can move the market.

From Beijing to Bahrain, from Seoul to Singapore, from London to Luxembourg, the Big Four are extending their influence. Their vast equity capital, rich and loyal client base, and long-term strategy for international expansion enable them to disregard short-term return on investment and focus instead on market share. These companies know—from the example of Japan's manufacturing sector and from their own experience in Japan's financial markets—that securing a share of a market eventually yields stable profits. On the other hand, profits from a short-term situation are as evanescent as cherry blossoms.

THE CITY BANKS

Japan's biggest national banks are termed city banks. The strong yen has made these banks—13 in number—enormous in terms of assets, capital, and stock market capitalization. Despite a declining demand for loans, the elimination of interest rate ceilings on large deposits, and the strongest domestic banking competition of the postwar period, the city banks have been recording unprecedented profits (though their revenues have been flat). For the year ending March 31, 1987, their pretax profits increased an average of 40 percent (to ¥1.6 billion).

Beginning in 1985, U.S. and U.K. banks began to fall rapidly behind the top Japanese banks in their capacity to compete in international financial markets. While U.S. and U.K. banks have been progressively weakened by their insufficient reserves against loan losses to problem credits in the Third World, Japanese banks have grown stronger.

The bull stock market in Japan has caused the city banks' enormous holdings of stock to more than triple in value in dollar terms. Although traditionally concerned primarily with domestic business, during the 1980s the city banks began expanding their international activities.

Moving to the International Arena

As early as the 1960s, Japan's city banks purchased shares in international investment banks.[10] During the 1970s, the city banks set up joint venture financial subsidiaries throughout Europe and during the 1980s bought out their partners. Japan's global banking presence expanded steadily during the 1980s.

By 1986, the 13 city banks exceeded U.S. and U.K. banking institutions in volume of international lending. As the result of the sharp appreciation of the yen (which occurred during the period 1985–87), their reserves for overseas loan losses were drawn. At the same time, they seized a major portion of the burgeoning domestic credit flows being intermediated in the international financial markets. By fiscal 1987, an estimated 50 percent of the city banks' profits were derived from international business.

In 1985, Japanese banks marginally surpassed U.S. banks to become the world's leading international bankers. In 1986, Japan's city banks established a clear lead. According to the Bank for International Settlements, foreign lending by Japanese banks reached $1.1 trillion at the end of 1986, representing one third of all international loans extended by banks in the major industrial countries (the comparable figures for U.S. banks were $601 million and 18.6 percent, respectively). By 1987, Japan's banks provided most of the new international lending to the world's nonbanks and about 75 percent of the new loans to banks.

There are a number of reasons for Japan's emerging strength in international banking:

1. *High levels of liquidity*, resulting from Japan's high savings rate and large surpluses (for trade and the current account), have helped the city banks to aggressively increase their international lending activities.
2. Japanese banks have a *far lower overhead* than their U.S. or European counterparts. A major cause of their low overhead is that only a small portion of total bank lending is to individuals.

---

[10]F. N. Burton and F. H. Saelens, "The European Investments of Japanese Financial Institutions," *Columbia Journal of World Business*, Winter 1986, p. 29.

(Corporate lending requires far fewer employees than individual lending.) As a result, the top city banks, for instance, employ 60–80 percent fewer employees than the leading U.S. commercial banks.

3. *Low capital adequacy requirements* (discussed below) have helped Japan's banks provide cheap loans in the global markets. In this way, Japanese banks have been able to undercut the banks of other money centers. The average ratio of equity to assets for the city banks was 3.14 percent at the end of March 1987 (this compares with ratios of 5–6 percent for many U.S. and U.K. banks).

Japanese banks are swiftly becoming the largest foreign presence in every major financial center in the world. Since 1985, Japan's regional and specialized banks, determined to join the city banks and the long-term banks, have been busy opening overseas branches and representative offices in New York and London. As a result, there were 36 Japanese banks in New York and 40 in London at the end of 1986.

During the 1980s, Japanese banks became increasingly aggressive participants in the American and British banking sectors. By underpricing local banks, they swiftly acquired substantial market share.

Indeed, Japanese banks have replaced the banks of the United Kingdom as the biggest foreign banking presence in the United States, with roughly 8 percent of total banking assets, which represents more than half of the foreign sector's share. At the end of 1986, Japanese banks provided 9 percent of all U.S. business loans and controlled half of the U.S. market for municipal letters of credit.

Similarly, Japanese banks are the biggest foreign presence in the United Kingdom, accounting for 23 percent of the total assets held by banks, for 40 percent of foreign currency lending in London, and for about 5 percent of London sterling lending.[11] (By contrast, the total foreign banking presence in Japan—79 foreign banks—accounts for an aggregate share of just 3 percent of total yen lending, for a negligible portion of foreign currency loans, and for a less than 2 percent share of total deposits.) Leading Japanese banks have also been expanding their overseas branch networks to include Atlanta, Chicago, Dallas, and medium-sized European cities.

---

[11]These banking statistics are from *The Economist*, April 4, 1987, p. 72.

Japanese banks have been expanding their operations not only in the United States and Europe but also throughout the Pacific Basin. With 24 full banks and 28 registered deposit-taking companies, Japanese banks are now the largest foreign presence in Hong Kong's banking sector. In 1986, Dai-Ichi Kangyo bought a controlling interest in Hong Kong–based Chekiang First Bank.

In Australia, following the deregulation of the financial system in early 1985, the Bank of Tokyo, Mitsubishi Bank, and the Industrial Bank of Japan were among 15 foreign banks granted licenses. Despite terrible profit margins, these three Japanese banks will remain in Australia in anticipation of long-term growth.

The Achilles' Heel

Japan's major corporations, once vital customers of the city banks and long-term banks, now seek funds directly in the capital markets. Moreover, Japan's cash-rich manufacturing corporations have little need to borrow funds and most Japanese industries have vastly reduced their investments in plant and equipment.

As a direct consequence of these structural changes, the leading Japanese banks now hold a disproportionate share of "problem" credits in sunset industries. This, combined with troubled loans to the Third World (discussed below), has suggested to some observers that these banks have potential weaknesses that could undermine their powerful global stature.

Thus, the quality of the assets held by Japan's major banks has been declining as these banks have moved aggressively into international markets. Bank profitability (the return on assets), which has always been low for Japanese banks, has become lower. In addition, increased participation in the foreign exchange markets and the world's financial markets has increased the vulnerability of Japanese banks to interest rate instability and global financial market volatility.

Deregulation in Japan and throughout the world is enabling borrowers to bypass the banking system in their efforts to raise funds. This means that Japan's banks will be obliged to compete successfully with investment banks, which have far more experience in the securities industry. Thus, Japanese banks have been placing increasing emphasis on non-asset-related sectors—particularly bond and foreign exchange dealings and the promising mergers and acquisitions business (discussed above). The future strength of Japan's biggest banks will be determined by the extent to which they adjust to a changed world in which the lion's share of their profits is derived from new business areas in overseas capital markets.

Loans to the Third World

With international business accounting for more than a third of their operating profits, the city banks will vigorously oppose any decision that could impair their foreign lending opportunities. Meanwhile, these banks have been obliged to consider the inevitable need to make provisions for a portion of their nonperforming loans to the Third World. Japanese banks hold an estimated $35 billion of loans to 15 major Third World debtors, giving Japan the world's second largest Third World debt exposure after the $90 billion of the United States.

To offset the risk of default, West German banks have set aside funds to cover 60–70 percent of their Third World debt exposure. West German tax laws permit the banks to offset these funds against tax. U.S. and U.K. banks have set aside 25–30 percent of their outstanding loans to problem Third World debtors. By contrast, Japanese banks have established reserves for only a minuscule portion of their loans to high-risk countries. Japan's tax laws allow little opportunity to offset loan loss provisions against tax.

For many years, the International Finance Bureau of the Ministry of Finance has been at loggerheads with the ministry's Tax Bureau. The conservative Tax Bureau, which has sole authority to revise tax laws, has firmly opposed any change that would reduce tax revenues. A compromise solution was reached in 1987. Just before the end of the fiscal year, the city banks (along with 15 other major Japanese banks) set up IBA Investment.

Incorporated in the Cayman Islands, IBA is a shell company designed to take over some of the Japanese banks' loans to the less developed nations. The banks sold roughly $6 billion of Mexican loans to IBA at deep discounts and subsequently took tax deductions for the resulting losses.

In addition, the Ministry of Finance announced plans to increase the ceiling on the taxable loan loss reserves for financial institutions from 5 percent to 10–20 percent. It also indicated plans to increase the minimum volume of taxable loan loss reserves from 1 percent to 5 percent.

TABLE 5–8
Loans to the Third World by the Leading
City Banks*

Bank	Amount (¥ billions)
Bank of Tokyo	638
Sumitomo Bank	410
Dai-Ichi Kangyo Bank	406
Mitsubishi Bank	346
Sanwa Bank	330
Fuji Bank	326

*At March 31, 1987.

Source: Ministry of Finance.

Meanwhile, Japan's banks have placed most of the debt of Peru, Ecuador, and Costa Rica (all hopelessly impoverished small borrowers) on a nonaccrual basis. The February 1987 announcement by the Brazilian government that it would suspend interest payments on $67 billion of foreign bank debt will eventually force Japanese banks (which have loaned Brazil an estimated $9 billion) to place Brazilian debt in the same category as loans to the shattered economy of Ecuador. If the resulting losses are not counterbalanced by new earnings, the leading Japanese banks will suffer some decline in profitability at the end of March 1988.

Despite their considerable exposure to risky loans and their paltry reserves, Japanese banks are not worried, though they pretend to be. Each bank could sell a portion of its securities holdings, converting hidden assets to realized gains, and offset the losses. Thus, while Third World debt has been a specter haunting American banks (which have 40 percent more exposure than the Japanese banks), it is a minor headache for Japan's banks.

International Capital Convergence

As the world's financial markets become increasingly integrated, the need for uniformity grows proportionally. Like futures contracts, which must be identical in order to be traded, banking regulations among the major nations will inevitably be forced from their current national diversity into the straitjacket of homogeneity.

This is but one instance of a global trend that has characterized the "age of information." Sociocultural features that have developed over decades and centuries are instantly cast away in favor of a narrow, predominantly Western, tradition that is loosely shared by all of the free world's nations. This new standardization, which will be a central feature of 21st century international finance, could increase global harmony, but it could also lead to the dull, gray tyranny of a handful of giant financial conglomerates.

In 1986 and early 1987, considerable U.S. and European pressure on the Ministry of Finance to increase the capital adequacy ratios (the level of shareholders' equity and reserves) of Japan's banks led to intense discussions. Ministry of Finance officials met frequently with representatives of the city banks to debate the necessity for raising the ratio of capital to assets.

A bank's capital is a significant expense and a crucial reserve against bad debts. Because Japan's banks maintain lower capital adequacy ratios than their leading global competitors, they have the advantage of a very cheap cost of funds. American and British banks have complained bitterly about their Japanese rivals' low capital, and international banking authorities have expressed concern that in the event of a crisis the global banking system could be undermined by the insufficient capital of Japanese banks.

In February 1987, in a lengthy joint proposal, the U.S. Federal Reserve System and the Bank of England urged commercial banks throughout the world to raise their minimum capital adequacy ratios. This proposal was the product of the sober recognition that loans to the Third World had lost a substantial proportion of their value. Meanwhile, many American and European banks insisted that the 4 percent capital to assets ratio approved by the Ministry of Finance in May 1986 was not high enough.

Japan's banks balked at the suggestion of higher ratios. Banking losses in Japan are covered by the liquidation of equities rather than by reductions in capital (the differences between the market value and the book value of portfolio holdings are applied to cover losses). Therefore, the banks argued, if 70 percent of their hidden reserves were taken into account, then the average ratio for the city banks would more than triple, to 9–11 percent. Indeed, if 70 percent of the hidden assets of the trust banks were taken into account, *their* capital ratios would more than quadruple.

Furthermore, Japanese bankers pointed out, many U.S. banks, for example some of New York's money-centered banks, had suffered severe declines in their capital ratios as a result of their big reserves against loans to Latin America. Manufacturers Hanover, Citicorp, and Chase Manhattan (three of America's biggest money-centered banks) all had equity to assets ratios of less than 3 percent at the end of August 1987 (prior to their new stock issues).

American and European bankers, participating in the Cooke Committee of bank supervisors meeting in Basel (where the Bank for International Settlements is located), responded to these claims by arguing that the valuation of hidden assets at 70 percent of their market value was unreasonably high in light of market volatility. In 1986, Japan's stock and real estate markets had reached exceptionally high levels. For example, spurred by excess liquidity and speculation, land prices in Tokyo during the 12 months ending June 30, 1987, rose by an average of 85.7 percent, with residential land prices soaring by 93 percent.[12]

The Ministry of Finance countered that the figure of 70 percent took into account *all* likely fluctuations in the market values of real estate or securities. At the end of March 1987, for example, the four biggest city banks held invisible assets of roughly ¥14 trillion (about $10 billion). These hidden assets would cushion loan losses even if the stock and real estate markets lost 70 percent of their current market values.

Moody's Investors Service, a leading U.S. credit rating agency, did not agree with the Ministry of Finance's optimistic assessment. In June 1987, Moody's placed the Bank of Tokyo, the Long-Term Credit Bank of Japan, Mitsubishi Trust and Banking, and Sanwa Bank under review for possible downgrading. It indicated that these institutions suffered from weaknesses and might not be able to deal successfully with a drastic downswing in domestic or international markets.

Nonetheless, in late 1987, under administrative guidance from the Ministry of Finance, Japan's leading banks began reviewing their total assets in the expectation that 40–50 percent of their hidden assets would

---

[12]According to National Land Agency statistics. Land in the Ginza, the most expensive area, was valued at ¥32 million (about $220,000) per square meter.

be approved by the Cooke Committee as applicable toward total banking capital. Through such asset reviews, the banks intended to cut their assets and raise their capital to assets ratios to the international standards determined by the banking regulators of the 17 industrial nations.

As a result, the city banks will be obliged to sharply curtail their practice of taking short-term deposits in the Euromarket (far in excess of necessary funds for loans) and managing the funds in the domestic short-term markets. More importantly, they will be forced to restrain the practice of extending loans at thin profit margins. Instead, the city banks will be driven to pursue high returns from high return businesses. Consequently, potentially profitable overseas companies (such as the Walter E. Heller subsidiaries mentioned above) will be purchased and exploited.

In addition, many leading banks issued new shares or convertible bonds to strengthen their capital ratios. In 1987, Dai-Ichi Kangyo, Sanwa, Sumitomo, Mitsubishi, and three long-term banks issued new securities. The biggest new stock issue, floated by the Industrial Bank of Japan, was worth roughly $1.5 billion (¥218 billion). Such issues will raise the banks' capital adequacy ratios by at least 0.5 percent.

Furthermore, the Ministry of Finance, in an effort to tighten curbs on overseas loans and other foreign assets, reduced the maximum ratio of foreign assets to foreign net worth from 3.5 times to 2.5 times. This decision will temporarily impede the city banks' efforts to increase overseas market share.

In the course of improving their capital adequacy ratios, however, the banks will be forced to reduce the growth of low-quality assets. While this may impede short-term growth, over the long-term it will result in greater rationalization of banking operations. Indeed, if Japan's banks raise the levels of their capital adequacy to international standards with only modest recourse to hidden assets, they will emerge as the most creditworthy banks in the world. By becoming more efficient, Japan's banks will ultimately become stronger global competitors.

ALL ABOARD!

Japan's general trading companies (sogo shosha) were one of the pillars supporting the prewar zaibatsu. During the postwar period, they functioned as vital intermediaries, trading commodities and capital

TABLE 5–9
Equity to Assets Ratios of the 13 City Banks, though Low,
Will Improve Steadily

	Equity to Assets Ratio	
Institution	31 March 1986	31 March 1987
Dai-Ichi Kangyo Bank	2.04	2.87
Fuji Bank	2.56	3.31
Sumitomo Bank	2.62	3.11
Mitsubishi Bank	2.43	3.22
Sanwa Bank	2.26	3.02
Tokai Bank	2.09	2.92
Mitsui Bank	2.07	2.97
Taiyo Kobe Bank	2.02	2.77
Bank of Tokyo	2.57	3.53
Daiwa Bank	1.51	3.59
Kyowa Bank	2.02	3.81
Saitama Bank	2.31	3.09
Hokkaido Takushoku Bank	1.98	2.59
Average	2.19	3.14

Source: Ministry of Finance.

goods in large quantities with low margins. Involved in every area of production and sales, the sogo shosha grew to enormous proportions during the era of Japan's rapid economic growth. The biggest (Mitsui Fudosan, Mitsubishi Shoji, Marubeni, C. Itoh, Sumitomo, and Nissho Iwai) became some of the largest corporations in the world.

Today, the sogo shosha are in decline because of structural changes in the Japanese and world economies. Japan's demand for raw materials decreased as the service sector grew. Simultaneously, many Japanese manufacturers began bypassing their traditional sogo shosha linkages.

As a result of these changes, the trading companies have been forced to develop new business areas in order to survive. They have become international project managers, overseeing every aspect of major undertakings from the financing of plant and equipment to final sales. Recently, the trading companies have tried their hand at third country trade (trade excluding Japan), countertrade (barter), biotechnology, telecommunications, and *financial services*.

During 1984–86, the big sogo shosha set up finance subsidiaries in

New York, London, and a number of offshore banking centers. They hoped to use their expertise in risk management and their well-established global networks to trade financial services just as they had traditionally traded goods. In 1987, overseas sogo shosha financial subsidiaries offered a broad range of financial services that included leasing, export finance, project finance, and the handling of many financial instruments.

Although still at an early stage of development, these subsidiaries promise to transform the trading companies into financial service vendors. It is likely that by the turn of the century Japanese domestic regulations will no longer prevent the sogo shosha from functioning as domestic bankers and brokers. When that day arrives, the trading companies will be ready. Meanwhile, they are positioning themselves to compete with the overseas financing operations of the securities companies and the commercial banks.

Like the sogo shosha, a broad range of leading Japanese manufacturers have also recognized the advantages of diversification into financial services. Matsushita Electric Industrial Company created New York–based Panasonic Finance in 1985. Like hundreds of similar Japanese corporate subsidiaries in New York and London, Panasonic Finance sells its parent's commercial paper to foreign buyers.

Many of these financial subsidiaries participate in the securities markets to maximize the return of an assigned portion of the parent's cash assets. At the end of 1986, the Ministry of Finance counted 3,196 overseas financial subsidiaries belonging to Japanese financial institutions and corporations. During the next five years, these subsidiaries will grow and multiply.

JAPAN VERSUS WORLD FINANCE?

By 1986, Japan's six major city banks had achieved notoriety within the world's club of international bankers. If the 1988 Olympic Games offered a banking competition, Japan's Club of Six would have a collection of medals dangling from its collective neck:

- The biggest five in the world in terms of assets.
- The biggest six in the world in terms of equity capital
- The largest international lenders to final borrowers

- The biggest national group of international lenders.
- The largest foreign currency lenders from London.
- The biggest foreign banking presence in the United States and the United Kingdom.

Like all Japanese businesses, Japan's banks have focused their attention on the acquisition of market share at the expense of short-term profitability. Because of their size and their powerful collective presence in the world's leading international banking centers, some financial commentators have expressed anxiety (occasionally panic) that Japanese banks will soon establish dominance of world banking, matching the startling success of Japan's auto and semiconductor industries.

Japan's big banks, particularly Sumitomo and the Industrial Bank of Japan, have looked to Citibank as the international grand master of banking strategy. Citibank has shown the world how daring innovation and aggressive retailing can conquer world markets. Japan's big banks are determined to do the same. *Will they?*

Some Western financial specialists point out that while these banks have the biggest assets and capitalizations in the world, scarcely any of their employees are the proud owners of undergraduate degrees from Oxford University or parchment from the Harvard Business School. In the world of international finance, flawless English and Western marketing etiquette are *de rigueur*. Japanese businessmen have been notoriously weak at marketing their international financial services. How can they hope to compete over the long-term with the leading banks of America and Britain?

Until very recently, Japanese banking was a domestic and heavily protected business. Furthermore, Japan's banking leaders, and the army of deal makers and planners who carry their briefcases, began their careers as bank clerks. They rose through the ranks in a system that offered no battlefield promotions—a system that discouraged individuality and daring decisions. Do they have the imagination, the cunning, and the independent flexibility to excel in an ultracompetitive field with shrinking margins?

The same question could be posed about Japan's Big Four securities companies. Yes, they have money. Yes, they are determined. They have decided to move swiftly into the international sector, and like the city banks, they are planning to derive half of their total revenues from international operations well before the year 2000 But are money and determination enough to buy a durable share of the global financial services industry? Are Japanese bankers and brokers such brilliantly innovative financiers, such suave marketers, that they can permanently take significant portions of market share away from the Morgan Stanleys or the Citibanks or the S. G. Warburgs of this world?

* * *

Those who without hesitation answer these questions with a confident "Nay" should pause for a moment. Consider, for example, the rise of the Big Four securities firms to top places in the Eurobond underwriting league tables. Consider Nomura's and Daiwa's status as primary dealers in the U.S. Treasury market and their new banks in London. Consider Industrial Bank of Japan's purchase of Schroder Bank & Trust and its acquisition of Aubrey G. Lanston, Sumitomo's purchase of a Swiss bank (Banca del Gottardo) and its investment in Goldman Sachs, Nippon Life's share of Shearson Lehman, Yasuda Mutual Life's share of the PaineWebber Group, Fuji's ownership of the Heller subsidiaries, and Sanwa's leasing operations in Chicago and its likely purchase of a primary dealer in New York. Consider that 5 of the 11 biggest banks in California are Japanese and that in 1986 Japanese banks accounted for 16 percent of California's total banking assets.[13]

Japanese financial institutions are at the beginning of a decade-long process of slowly buying what they do not have—overseas business. Many of the ventures and acquisitions mentioned in the preceding paragraph are now low losing money or are only marginally profitable. The parent institutions are preparing to absorb losses for as long as necessary. They are hiring high-quality foreign executives and they are training (often in foreign institutions) a new generation of Japanese employees who will devote their lives to international business.

This new generation of Japanese inhabitants of the world of international finance will be as capable as their Western counterparts at contriving new products. The whiz kids of Nomura and other Japanese securities firms have already developed a few innovative instruments for the Euromarkets. In far less than a decade, they will master the finan-

---

[13]As this book goes to press, Standard Chartered PLC is planning to sell its California subsidiary, Los Angeles-based Union Bank. The winning bid for Union Bank, the fifth largest bank in California, is likely to fall in the range of 1.5–2 times shareholder's equity—in the neighborhood of $1 billion. I believe that there can be little doubt that a Japanese bank will submit the highest bid.

cial theory and market timing so vital to success in the new world of finance. It would be foolhardy to assume that because Japanese investment bankers and commercial bankers lack fashion today, they will not be inventing the fashion of tomorrow.

Of course, the international financial services industry is not comparable to the auto industry. It is not as inevitable as sunrise that the strategy of Japanese manufacturers can be applied to global banking, investment, and securities. However, there is little persuasive evidence that Japanese institutions will fail in their plan to become the world's leading provider of financial services.

It has been alleged that money cannot buy lasting love. It has, on occasion. It has been argued that money cannot buy a durable and substantial share of global financial services. It can and it will.

CHAPTER 6

"THE FUTURE BELONGS TO US"

The war fleet will still be in Japan but
we will have more cruisers and destroyers
abroad.[1]

Tsunehiko Ishizuka, managing director,
Sony Corporation (1986)

A VAGUE BUT MEANINGFUL RESEMBLANCE

Long ago, the observation that certain aspects of business resemble war
became trite. Although, of course, scrutiny of classic works of military
strategy may improve business acuity, in most countries the relationship
between business and war is metaphoric. Associating business strategy
with military strategy may help improve tactical thinking, but a direct
correlative relationship between the two does not exist.

In Japan, however, the parallels between military structure and
martial attitudes, on the one hand, and business corporations and business attitudes, on the other, are particularly pronounced. Japanese
corporations, perhaps more than the corporations of other nations,
resemble the military in a number of respects: recruitment (mentioned in
Chapter 3), strong hierarchical structure (individual status and behavior
are rigidly defined), stability (only mercenaries, who are social
deviants, move from army to army or from job to job), and impenetra-
bility (discussed below).

---

[1]Quoted in Kevin Rafferty, "Japanese Corporate Finance Goes Global," *Institutional Investor*,
November 1986, p. 293.

IMPERVIOUS

When a military force positions itself outside its national borders (as an occupier or a friendly ally), it does not hire local nationals as generals or colonels or even privates. Foreign embassies may hire local recruits, but not the army or navy. Nor does the military attempt to imitate local customs. Learning a foreign language is always useful, and speaking the language of an occupied country is vital to maintaining security. Soldiers, however, are discouraged from adopting native garb, native cuisine, and native spouses. The military protects its interests, and if those interests cease to exist in a location, the military goes away. It goes to wherever its interests can be served best.

Like the military, the Japanese corporation that sets up units in overseas markets remains impervious to the environment. Unlike Western corporations, which view themselves as immigrants in new markets, Japanese companies do not "go native." The managers sent by the parent company, like officers sent overseas, give key commands and report to headquarters.

The citizens of a democracy own the military, but they have remarkably little authority over it. In much the same way, the shareholders own a public Japanese company but have virtually no de facto control of management.

Although a special arm of the military can be discontinued, reduced in size, or merged with other units, it cannot go bankrupt. Similarly, large Japanese corporations have been heavily protected by MITI from the oblivion of insolvency.

MANAGERS AND GHOSTS

Like the army, Japanese corporations have not traditionally established local subsidiaries with high-ranking foreign staff. Japanese management is exported by the parent company to the overseas units, as a matter of course. Just as the career soldier is routinely moved from post to post, limiting the duration of his exposure to a particular foreign country, the Japanese businessman's average foreign tour of duty is also limited.

To maintain maximum control of the foreign workers who must be hired, every effort is made to avoid establishing factories in areas where labor unions are strong. Whenever possible, young nonunion employees are hired.

Increasingly, Japanese subsidiaries in the United States and the European Community have created high-ranking positions for "local hires." Foreign senior executives close to retirement are often hired as "senior executive vice presidents" and "vice chairmen." A small number of Japanese manufacturing firms have instated Americans and Britons as chief executive officers of a local subsidiary. These individuals create the appearance of foreign management within the Japanese overseas unit. Needless to say, none of these "top executives" has risen through the ranks.

However (with one recent exception), these "foreigners" do not have executive positions with the parent corporation. In nearly all instances, the parent corporation regards "local hires" as a component of a subsidiary's operating expense rather than as a part of the corporation.

The authority of the foreign employee extends only to the foreign aspects of the overseas unit. Japanese citizens who are recruited locally also fall into the "foreign" category (they are not part of the parent organization).

Take for example, a 57-year-old American senior executive vice president at the overseas subsidiary of a Japanese company. Dissatisfied as he may be with a 27-year-old Japanese assistant vice president under his jurisdiction, under no circumstances will he have the authority to fire or even reprimand the assistant vice president. The Japanese employee, though officially employed by the subsidiary corporation, is actually seconded by the parent company to the subsidiary. Of course, every effort is made to avoid giving foreign employees authority over Japanese (parent company) staff.

From the perspective of the parent corporation in Japan, foreign executives have form without content. They are ghosts. They are employed to act as an interface between the foreignness of the overseas market and the Japanese management of the subsidiary.

In Japanese folklore, ghosts have no feet. This missing attribute is significant. These unwholesome and disturbing apparitions do not walk on the land of Japan and thus are not connected to it. Ghosts, like foreigners, are not Japanese people, and they acquire much of their repugnance from that irreversible fact.

Similarly, the Japanese overseas subsidiary is itself a ghost. It appears at first glance to be an accurate replica of other multinational

TABLE 6–1
The Foreign Employees of Some Major Japanese Corporations*

Corporation	Number of Foreigners	Total Number of Employees
Sony	30	15,000
NEC	30	38,364
Kobe Steel	30	26,151
Marubeni	29	7,678
Nikko Securities	25	8,637
Dentsu	19	5,760
Toyota Motor	18	62,530
Nippon Kokan	17	31,660
Ricoh	15	11,358
Fuji Bank	14	15,000
Mitsubishi Corporation	13	8,820

*These data refer to the Japan-based parent corporation *only.*

Source: "Special Survey, Japanese Management," *Japan Economic Journal*, September 5, 1987, p. 5.

companies, just as a ghost appears to be a living person. However, its management (consisting of expatriated Japanese and foreigners) is not grounded abroad. Its feet are in the parent company; the subsidiary has no feet.

FOREIGN SUBSIDIARIES (WHERE ARE THE FEET?)

The majority of the West's multinational corporations have established overseas subsidiaries in dozens of nations. Generally, however, each of these subsidiaries is based on a local management structure that transforms it (in essence if not in fact) into a national company.

These "overseas nationals" must contend with the union demands of their workers and the exigencies of the local markets that they serve. The greater the subsidiary's obligations to local employees, local conditions, and local markets, the less free the subsidiary is to pursue the international strategy of the parent organization.

As a result, the overseas operations of multinational corporations usually compromise their greatest asset: the potential to *freely* allocate the corporation's total resources. In this way, the overseas units of multinationals become embedded in local markets. Instead of rising above a particular domestic market, the overseas subsidiary becomes a provincial unit. It is as though Marco Polo had journeyed to Cathay only to settle there permanently and set up shop. Instead of being a component of an international marketing structure, the overseas subsidiary is a foreign business. Instead of becoming a galaxy in a universe, each overseas subsidiary becomes a lone star.

By contrast, for Japanese corporations the overseas subsidiary never ceases to be a local production unit fully integrated into the parent organization. Top (and sometimes middle) management is predominantly Japanese and the total activities of the subsidiary serve to fulfill the international goals of the parent. This means that the product being produced or marketed takes precedence over the subsidiary. This distinction between Japanese and Western overseas subsidiaries may appear to be vague and inconsequential, but it is not.

Although Japanese corporations sometimes claim that their overseas subsidiaries are separate profit centers, such a view is equivocal. Employees of Japanese companies, including the overseas subsidiaries, do not traditionally receive bonus payments based on their performance, and a subsidiary is not awarded new equipment on the basis of its profitability. The total pretax profits of the overseas subsidiary belong to the parent company and can be directed by the home office to other overseas units or to domestic operations. Therefore, unprofitable subsidiaries can float indefinitely on the profits of the parent corporation or its other subsidiaries.

Some of the most successful foreign corporations bear close resemblances to their Japanese counterparts in many respects. International Business Machines Corporation (IBM), for instance, has been identified as one example of Japanese organizational structure in a non-Japanese company.[2] However, IBM Japan is a Japanese corporation with a Japanese president, Japanese management, and Japanese staff.

When, in 1987, the U.S. Defense Department vetoed the sale of an IBM computer by IBM Germany to Transnautic, a Soviet-owned West German corporation, West German diplomats in Washington objected that the Pentagon exceeded its authority by prohibiting a transaction between two *German* entities. The fact that West German represen-

---

[2]See, for example, William G. Ouchi, *Theory Z: How American Business Can Meet the Japanese Challenge* (New York: Avon Books, 1982), p. 58.

tatives could make such a claim is indicative of the extent to which the subsidiaries of multinational corporations have become national companies.

By contrast, the Japanese overseas subsidiary is *subsidiary* in the literal sense—its essential purpose is to *support* the parent company. Thus, it serves to assist or supplement the creation and distribution of products. It is *always* subordinate or secondary to the product and to the parent company. Unlike Western multinational corporations or British social anthropologists, Japanese companies do not go native when they go abroad. Their feet as well as their heartbeats remain in Japan.

PRODUCTS WITHOUT COUNTRIES

Western firms, like dairy farmers, give priority to the cow—its health, its feed, its barn. They assume that if the cow is given the best possible conditions its milk production will be outstanding. Conversely, Japanese corporations give primary attention to the milk (the product) and only secondary attention to the cow (the local production unit). If the cow does poorly, others can be purchased in the same country or in another country.

Although Japanese corporations scour the world for the best and most economical equipment, raw materials, and unskilled labor, management remains a domestic component of production. Even if the overseas subsidiary is operated on a day-to-day basis by a local (foreign) president and managing director, the native management remains a puppet. The strings are controlled by puppet masters at the parent company in Japan.

Just as troops can be pulled out of a foreign city, Japanese management can be pulled out of a troubled overseas subsidiary. The product can then be produced by the means and in the place offering maximum efficiency. In this way, it is the product, *not the producer*, that is truly international.

Thus, while Western corporations invest heavily in the creation of global networks, Japanese corporations focus on the creation of global products. The product takes precedence over the foreign unit.

Of course, a general product line may be adjusted to a particular local market. For example, Sony Corporation produces different *models* of its Walkman for markets in Japan, the United States, West Germany, and France. However, the creation of these country-specific models does not *necessarily* involve local-level manufacture. Much the same can be said about other Japanese products.

Japanese manufacturers devote their research and development to the creation of products that are tailored to the needs, expectations, and tastes of foreign markets.[3] Just as soldiers are equipped in accordance with the terrain and climate where they will be deployed, the global product is directed and finely tuned to the characteristics of each marketplace. The child of the parent corporation is *not* the subsidiary company; it is the product.

Given the preeminence of the product over all other factors in the Japanese corporate world view, it becomes easily understandable why in Japanese corporate culture long-term strategic goals *always* override short- and medium-term costs and obstacles. The month-to-month and year-to-year losses of a particular subsidiary are viewed within the total context of the creation and marketing of particular products.

THE FUTURE BECKONS

Gradually, the world's markets for manufactured goods will come to resemble the global financial markets. Just as a Japanese bond futures contract can be purchased on the Tokyo Stock Exchange in the morning and sold on the London International Financial Futures Exchange the following night (afternoon in London), goods will increasingly become as interchangeable as raw commodities and will transcend national borders. Hence, Kenichi Ohmae's observation that "today, new products circle the globe with the speed of a satellite. It no longer holds that innovations trickle down like a cascade or waterfall from the most to the least technologically advanced countries."[4]

What will distinguish the future from the past, however, is not so much the development of "companies without countries" as the evolution of *products without countries*. Like today's incipient 24-hour finan-

---

[3]Many Japanese corporations, far more than the corporations of other nations, are able to flexibly mobilize their total resources in order to efficiently maximize the effectiveness of their production and marketing functions. As a result, certain corporate sectors (such as research and development) are more centrally integrated into corporate structure than other sectors (such as overseas marketing).

[4]Kenichi Ohmae, *Beyond National Borders* (Homewood, Ill.: Dow Jones-Irwin, 1987), p. 84

cial markets, where uniform products are bought and sold independently of geography and politics, tomorrow's electronics or auto markets will not be based on location.

The supreme measure of the manufacturing industries of tomorrow will be product quality and universality. The arrangement or placing of the source of production will become irrelevant to the global manufacturing market of the future, in which success will hinge upon product selection, design, price, and financing.

Recall from the previous chapter that Honda Motors intends to export 70,000 automobiles per year from the United States by 1989. Aiwa Corporation now produces 50 percent of its total output in Singapore and exports more than half of its Singapore production to Japan. The Toshiba Corporation imports into Japan microwave ovens and color televisions manufactured by its United States' unit, Toshiba America.

Soon, the proliferating overseas units of Japanese corporations will be routinely exporting a significant portion of their production. Before long, Japanese cars made in Tennessee or Wales, for example, will be more threatening to European manufacturers than was General Motors in its heyday.

Japan's third country ("triangular") trade will become ever more predominant and will serve to deflect protectionist outcries. Gradually, Japan will become a major importer of its own foreign-produced goods. This, in turn, will stabilize its growing current account surpluses. The potential destabilizing force behind the excessive accumulation of money will be ameliorated. The hurricane, traveling from ocean to land, spends its force and becomes a gale wind.

As a direct result of overseas production, pressure on the yen (which will drive it higher during the next several years) will relax. The yen, following Japan's surpluses, will rise to a plateau in a range that Japanese manufacturers now equate with death: 100–110 yen to the dollar. In this new world, which resolutely approaches, Japan's manufacturers will reside abroad—but few indeed will become expatriates.

THE YEN AS A WORLD CURRENCY

Gaining Strength

Although foreign exchange traders and central banks are loath to admit it, exchange rates are impossible to forecast. For example, in early 1985, when the dollar traded at $1.03 to the pound sterling, many experts predicted that the dollar and pound would soon attain parity. They were wrong, of course, and the dollar stabilized in the range of $1.60–1.75 to the pound. No forecasters predicted in early 1985 that within two years, in terms of purchasing power parity, the overvalued dollar and the undervalued yen would become an undervalued dollar and an overvalued yen.

Traditionally, central banks (which hold the banking reserves of nations) have been responsible for intervening in foreign exchange markets in order to stabilize the foreign exchange value of their national currency. The internationalization of world markets has caused an inevitable reduction in the power of the individual central banks. Partially as a result, during the past several years the world's major central banks (the Federal Reserve System, the Bundesbank, and the Bank of Japan) have usually intervened significantly only when forced to do so by the threat of severe imbalances.

The agreement reached at the Plaza Hotel (in September 1985) and the later Louvre agreement (reached in February 1987) have become landmark examples of today's central bank approach to intervention. These agreements, reached by the major industrial nations, resulted in coordinated intervention designed to force the dollar down from its overvalued level and subsequently to maintain it within an undisclosed range of stability.[5] Measured against many major currencies, the dollar fell 40 to 50 percent during the period between the Plaza Hotel and Louvre accords.

The swift decline of the dollar in 1985–87 was more than Japan bargained for. From its trough of ¥263 to the dollar in February 1985, the yen appreciated to a postwar high of ¥129 per dollar in November 1987.[6] Subsequently, Japanese industry revealed (to the chagrin of overseas competitors) that not only was adjustment to a strong yen possible but that it could be achieved quickly. Can the yen strengthen further during the next five years? Will Japanese companies adjust (rationalize) successfully to an even stronger yen?

---

[5]Thus, for example, during the first three quarters of 1987, the dollar was prevented from tumbling by the weight of $90 billion of central bank interventions.

[6]In April 1949, the official Japanese exchange rate was set at ¥360 to the U.S. dollar. (On December 20, 1971 the yen was revalued to ¥308 to the dollar.) In late 1987, this was the highest level reached by the yen since April 1949.

Still a Provincial Currency

Japan has been reluctant to adopt a significant role in financing world economic growth. Domestic demand for manufactured goods has been modest and aid to the Third World unimpressive (recall the discussion of aid in Chapter 1). Within this context, the yen has been a provincial currency. In fiscal year 1986, only 35.5 percent of Japan's exports and 9.7 percent of its imports were denominated in yen.

Foreign holdings of yen have been primarily confined to the Eurobond market and the Japanese stock market. Yet, the Euroyen bond market is *functionally* a segment of Japan's domestic capital markets.[7] (Nonetheless, the supranational World Bank, a leader in yen financing, now raises 20 percent of its funding requirements in yen.) Meanwhile, although foreign investors have been drawn to Japan's stock market, since 1983 they have been net sellers of Japanese equities and incremental increases in their holdings have been due to share price appreciation.

As a result, the world's central banks used the yen only marginally as a reserve currency. The member countries of the International Monetary Fund hold 70 percent of their foreign exchange reserves in dollars, 13 percent in deutsche marks, and only 7.6 percent in yen. Given Japan's role in the global economy (in which it is the biggest creditor nation and represents about 15 percent[8] of the free world's gross national product and about 9.5 percent of *all* world trade), the yen should constitute at least 25–30 percent of currency reserves, while the overrepresented and now weak dollar should decline to about 40–50 percent. As a result, an imbalance has arisen between the role of the dollar in the global monetary system and the U.S. role in the world economy.

Japan and West Germany cannot permit such an imbalance to continue for long. Therefore, it is likely that a multicurrency system, which has already been proposed by central bankers, will be established. In such a system, the U.S. dollar would cease to function as the primary unit of value in international trade and would be replaced by a systemic arrangement of the dollar, the yen, and the deutsche mark.

---

[7]However, because yen raised in the Euroyen bond market are usually swapped into floating rate dollar securities, the Euroyen market is a technical extension of the dollar based international capital markets.

[8]By contrast, in 1984 the United States and Germany accounted for 34 percent and 6 percent respectively of the free world's GNP.

As mentioned above, the yen will remain strong and will gradually achieve stability. A strong and stable yen will pressure Japan to internationalize its currency. The steady opening of Japan's financial markets will contribute to an increased use of the yen as a reserve currency.

Suppliers of vital commodities (such as oil) will someday demand that Japan pay them in yen. Expectations that the yen will appreciate against the dollar over the long term should further encourage producers to seek payment in a currency that may gain in value. This, in turn, would lead to an accumulation of yen assets abroad (and yen liabilities in Japan). Under such circumstances, the yen will remain strong indefinitely.

The stronger the yen, the greater is the pressure on Japanese industry to produce abroad. Thus, the inevitable trend of the strengthening yen will involve a steady emigration of Japanese production facilities and marketing organizations from Japan to all of the world's major markets.

THE EMERGING POWER OF JAPANESE MONEY

Strengthening Hand

Thousands of tributaries of dollars, deutsche marks, and other currencies now flow from Western nations to Japan. These streams and rivers of money pour into corporate treasuries. The corporate treasuries direct a large portion of the flow of funds to Japan's commercial banks. Japan's individual savers do the same thing.

About half of Japan's surplus stays at home, contributing to the world's greatest reservoir of liquidity. The other half is "recycled." Japan's recycled funds form distributaries that flow out to the United States, Europe, and Hong Kong. A tiny brook even meanders its way to the governments of the Third World in the form of development assistance.

During the next decade, the distributaries will grow deeper as Japan's surpluses increase and domestic funds seek higher returns (and diversity) abroad. Japan's financial industry will be the corps of engineers that decides how these brooks, streams, and rivers will flow— fast or slow, deep or shallow, East or West. The decisions, of course, will be largely determined by overseas interest rates, foreign exchange markets, and, perhaps, protectionist legislation.

"Money Is Power"

The hackneyed expression "Money is power" may be as old as Croesus. While money can be used to promote ascendancy, authority, or influence, it does not in and of itself embody power. Money, like the financial services that help deploy it, is only a means to an end. A medium of exchange, a unit of account, or a store of value will facilitate the production of real goods and services, but it will not create them.

Today, money is flowing among financial institutions and across national borders at an increasing velocity that promises only to accelerate further. Throughout the free world, interest rates, securities prices, and asset valuation are becoming ever more volatile. Foreign exchange rates—if the trading activities of Japan's life insurance companies are any indication—have become susceptible to the trading practices of private companies as well as central and commercial banks.

Japan's accumulation of domestic liquidity, the strength of the yen, and the consequent growth of overseas assets do not necessarily imply a parallel increase in Japanese power. It is inevitable, however, that the ascendancy, authority, and influence of Japanese investors will increase as the actions of these investors increasingly affect overseas markets and the pattern of the flow of funds. Toshiba Corporation's likely deflection of some sanctions under the Omnibus Trade Bill is a demonstration of how *foreign market penetration carries with it the distinctive power to influence events abroad*. Therein lies evidence of the truth embedded in the old cliché.

Japan Joins the Financial World, and the Financial World Joins Japan

Ongoing developments in the world's financial markets are gradually encompassing Japan. Regulations inhibiting the development of domestic futures and options are being revised, while simultaneously restrictions excluding Japanese participation in the derivative securities of overseas markets are being demolished.

Meanwhile, as new financial instruments are proliferating throughout the world, some are percolating into Japan's tightly regulated markets. Global futures and options markets have caused a shotgun marriage to take place between the financial and commodity markets. In Japan, commodities trading (traditionally the country's sleaziest market sector) will grow in importance. The global trend favoring automation will encourage Japanese investors to participate ever more in new markets and the trading of new vehicles.

Global financial competition will increase in intensity as the integration of financial markets and financial systems becomes more complete. The ongoing process of the globalization or standardization of finance is the product of financial deregulation in each nation. As legal and regulatory barriers fall in one country, the likelihood of parallel changes in other nations increases.[9] Japan's Ministry of Finance, the most powerful arm of the Japanese government, has traditionally opposed financial innovation. Now, however, under the pressure of precedents set elsewhere, the ministry (with Japan at its heels) is changing.

Two powerful cultural forces within Japan have begun to merge. On the one hand, a centrifugal force that with xenophobic zeal excluded foreign incursions has been forced to compromise, while, on the other hand, a centripetal force that stressed internal conformity has reached outward. In a process that began with the Meiji Restoration, pressures inside and outside Japan have precipitated a drive to conform to foreign financial market patterns and practices.

Thus, global financial deregulation will lead Japanese institutions to move directly and swiftly into the future. They will become increasingly proficient in their overseas participation in securities trading, mergers and acquisitions, joint venture investments, real estate investments, and project finance.

While these changes occur, structural transformation in the U.S. financial system—which is resulting in dramatic modification of the Glass-Steagall Act and other restrictive legislation—will be mimed or anticipated by Japan's Ministry of Finance. Already, American banks have been authorized by the ministry to set up securities subsidiaries in Tokyo and Japanese banks have been actively engaged in investment banking in foreign markets.

In the near future, banks and securities companies will be permitted by the Ministry of Finance to encroach on each other's domestic territories through subsidiaries. Key distinctions between long-term credit

---

[9]Thus, for instance, the impending "*Petit* Bang" in Paris (scheduled for 1992) is a direct result of London's "Big Bang" of 1986. Faced with the deregulation of markets in New York, London, Tokyo, and Toronto, Paris was *forced* to deregulate in order to become competitive. As in London, France's financial markets will be significantly opened, enabling foreign and domestic banks, insurers, and other companies to buy into French brokerage firms beginning in 1988.

banks, trust banks, and commercial banks will disappear. During the next several years, financial reforms will transform Japan's highly segmented and rigid financial world into a new fluid system. The Chinese walls will crumble and foreign barbarians will travel freely across Japan's financial borders.

The realignment of the world's currencies, which has resulted in a sharp appreciation of the yen against the dollar and other major currencies, enhances the current ability and motivation of Japanese investors to engage in foreign investments. Simultaneously, official ceilings inhibiting overseas investments are being raised.

Today, Japanese investors are scrutinizing the investment universe with single-minded absorption. As Japan's portfolio managers master new investment techniques, they will become like astronomers with ever more powerful telescopes. Japanese knowledge and understanding of overseas markets will become increasingly sophisticated. Thus, by being obliged to internationalize (changing in step with global financial markets), Japan will benefit immeasurably from the transformation that has been occurring in the world of finance. As a direct result, the incipient power of Japanese money will grow and amplify.

Within this environment, the institutions that control Japanese money have acquired considerable power. Were Japan's leading investors to simultaneously sell most of their U.S. securities holdings, for example, U.S. interest rates would rise like a hot-air balloon while the black curtain of recession would fall on America's financial stage.

Of course, the consequences of a U.S. recession and spiraling dollar inflation would damage Japan's economy too. Nonetheless, the fact that a handful of Japanese institutions has the power to ravage the American economy is awesome. It means that the motivations of Japanese investors have become a key factor in global economic and political stability. The complex psychology and opportunistic philosophy that inspire these motivations cannot be ignored.

The Emerging Power of Japanese Fund Managers

There are few current indications that the U.S. current account deficit (which measures the deficit in trade in goods and services) will decline significantly during the next five years from its level of about $150 billion (or three percent of GNP) in 1987. Meanwhile, the proportion of American debt owned by foreign interests is likely to soar steadily and will exceed 20 percent of GNP (gross national product) by the early 1990s, up from less than 10 percent in 1986. Japanese institutions will control the lion's share of this foreign-owned American debt.

Concurrently, the magnitude of Japanese overseas investments will parallel Japan's growing surplus. Japan was a net creditor of nearly $100 billion in 1986, and its surplus is likely to at least triple by the early 1990s. Japan's overseas investments will similarly climb steadily and will certainly double before the end of 1990.

Japan's towering surplus is being created primarily by the private sector, and it will be managed by financial institutions within the private sector. Because big institutional investors in Japan tend to reason along similar lines (and thus to act in concert without collusion), a decision to shift a portion of foreign investments from one country to another often involves the vast holdings of many big institutions. Thus, the inclinations of a small number of Tokyo- and Osaka-based fund managers can already have an instantaneous impact not only on specific markets but on national economies. During the next five years, the magnitude of that potential impact will expand in breadth and severity.

The strong Japanese penchant for bond investments in preference to the stock or money markets has caused a large proportion of Japanese overseas investments to be positioned in fixed income assets, particularly government issues. It is precisely these issues that help determine the entire spectrum of interest rates—from mortgages to consumer credit. Thus, as Japan's increasingly sophisticated portfolio managers begin to maneuver their holdings, shifting funds from nation to nation according to global trends, domestic pressures, and inflationary concerns, economic growth in particular countries will be promoted or inhibited by Japanese decisions.

At the same time, Japan's trust banks, life insurance companies, and other asset managers have initiated new policies intended to improve overall portfolio performance. A traditional focus on yield has been shifting to a concern with total return.[10] This shift has been prompted by complaints about poor performance by the clients of the managing institutions. It has also been stimulated by a recent change in regulations that permits trust banks to trade for their own accounts. In

---

[10]See Chapter 5. See also Aron Viner, *Inside Japanese Financial Markets* (Homewood, Ill.: Dow Jones-Irwin, 1987), pp. 284, 290–92.

1986, bond dealing became a meaningful contributor to the pretax profits of the trust banks.

As a direct result of the shift from yield to total return, Japanese institutional fund managers have been steadily increasing the turnover of their bond portfolios. This has triggered a significant growth in bond trading volume in Tokyo, New York, and London. The volume of the Tokyo dollar bond market, where U.S. Treasury issues are traded while New York sleeps, has grown enormously and will continue to increase. And, of course, the greater the overall Japanese trading volume, the more volatility there is in the world's major bond markets and the greater is the influence of Japanese traders.

Finally, Japan's burgeoning investments in the U.S. stock market and the U.S. commercial real estate market will result in increased Japanese influence on those markets. Prices at the high end of the commercial real estate market in New York and Los Angeles are believed to have risen 8–15 percent because of aggressive Japanese buying.

Although they are far smaller than the U.S. markets, the stock and bond markets of the United Kingdom, West Germany, and Australia will also be the objects of increased Japanese buying and thus increased Japanese influence. The Big Four securities companies have branches near all of the world's leading stock markets. Their role as brokers and investors can only grow.

THE CONSOLIDATION OF FINANCIAL POWER

The government and the major financial institutions of Japan have a powerful and durable commitment to global economic stability. From their perspective, Japan is a nation with few natural resources and no natural allies. Japan's dependence on exports of its goods and its equal and parallel dependence on imports of its food, render the nation perpetually vulnerable to trade sanctions. Furthermore, the recent growth of Japan's investments in overseas assets has heightened its concerns regarding foreign exchange and interest rate stability (as well as protectionist legislation).

During the next five years, Japan will consolidate its position as the world's greatest capital exporter. Unlike the surplus of OPEC (Organization of Petroleum Exporting Countries), Japan's surplus is controlled by Japanese institutions. Thus, while capital surpluses strengthened OPEC governments during the 1970s, Japan's surplus is serving to strengthen Japanese financial institutions and to extend *their* power. Japan's multitude of private financial firms have far more flexibility and far greater skill at handling money than do the handful of OPEC governments, which in the 1970s had barely entered the 20th century.

The deregulation of Japan's domestic banking and securities sectors will result in insolvencies (or mergers to avert them) and acquisitions that will increase the size of the major banks and securities firms. Sumitomo Bank's decision to merge with Heiwa Sogo (a beleaguered mutual savings bank) in 1986 foreshadowed this trend.

As a result, Japan's banks and securities companies will be in a position of outstanding strength in the 21st century. At that time, there are likely to be no more than three or four dozen fully international "banks" in the global arena. It is probable that within 12 years Japanese and American financial institutions will have been permitted to evolve into financial department stores. Thus, by the end of the 1990s a small number of Japanese and American universal financial institutions will compete among themselves and with the Big Three German banks, the Big Three Swiss banks, and a few London-, Paris-, and Hong Kong–based establishments.

Concurrently with the concentration and liberalization of Japan's financial sector, diversification into foreign markets (through both acquisition and the creation of new businesses) will continue unabated. A relaxation of Japan-U.S. and Japan-U.K. trade tensions will enable the Ministry of Finance to approve further acquisitions of American financial firms and their more vulnerable British counterparts.

TO THE VICTOR BELONG THE SPOILS

In less than a decade, Japan's share of world trade will surpass that of the United States. Within Japan, pressures to improve infrastructure will inexorably lead to improvements in the standard of living. Not only will Japan boast the world's highest per capita income, but it will eventually provide its citizens with a "quality of life" comparable to the best of Western Europe. Holding more foreign assets than any nation in the world, Japan will become a 21st-century version of 20th-century American affluence

Japan's sudden global financial ascendancy during the late 1980s took it by surprise. Despite Japan's importance within the world economy, its bureaucratic, industrial, and financial leaders were unprepared and unwilling to assume international leadership roles.

Japan has long provided modest contributions to the major supranational organizations. However, with the sole exception of the Manila-based Asian Development Bank (which Japan has been seeking to dominate), no Japanese representative has publicly expressed a willingness to accept a major role in the governance of a multilateral institution such as the World Bank.

Although Japan is the largest supporter of the World Bank after the United States, in 1986 there were 18 Americans for every Japanese on its professional staff. The limited Japanese participation in international organizations has long been regarded as an indication of Japan's reluctance to assume a leading role in global finance.

Unable to choose its own direction and not fully in control of the developments that have drawn it into international financial markets, Japan has failed to apply its skills at long-term planning to its political and economic destiny. With the future in the palm of its hand and "internationalization" a buzzword for all imported ideas (and people), Japan remains wrapped in the cloak of Tokugawa-era provincialism.

A massive wave of modernization that began in 1868 had raised Japan from feudal economy and technology to the highest levels of technological development 70 years later. The wave spent itself on war. Beginning in the 1950s, another wave raised Japan to economic and financial power unprecedented in modern Asia. The Japanese themselves will decide how much higher the ascent will be and how long it will last.

THE POWER OF MONEY IN THE 21ST CENTURY

Weapons are at a standoff. In the 19th and early 20th centuries, concentrations of arms served to assure power. The most heavily armed nation was the mightiest. Paradoxically, perhaps, nuclear weapons have altered the sheer power of accumulation. The superpowers cannot gain supremacy through military means without mutual destruction.

Manufacturing has ceased to stoke the fires of the developed nations' economic growth. The postindustrial era is now at midday. The free world's industrial leaders represent economies that derive the largest portion of GNP from the services sector. Within this area, financial services are growing.

The industrial revolution once enabled Great Britain to rule the waves. During the 21st century, new leaders with a new basis of power will call the shots. Money will replace weapons as a vital means of wielding influence, *making capital a crucial strategic asset*. The nation with a surplus of money will use that money to accomplish political and military aspirations by supplying funds and influencing the integrated world economy.

Although glib and perfunctory, this quick appraisal is not devoid of immediacy. Recent economic reforms initiated by Deng Xaoping and Mikhail Gorbachev are expressions of a vital realization: In the 21st century, international power will be the *direct* outcome of economic strength, which in turn will rest upon the prosaic capitalist activities of universal banking. Within this new environment, Japanese financial influence will hold the world in a tight embrace.

BIBLIOGRAPHY

Abegglen, James C., et al. *U.S.-Japan Economic Relations*. Berkeley: University of California Institute of East Asian Studies, 1980.

Abegglen, James C., and George Stalk, Jr. *Kaisha: The Japanese Corporation*. New York: Basic Books, 1985.

Adams, T. F. M., and Iwao Hoshii. *A Financial History of the New Japan*. Tokyo: Kodansha, 1972.

Allen, G. C. *A Short Economic History of Modern Japan*. 4th ed. New York: St. Martin's Press, 1981.

Azumi, K. *Higher Education and Business Recruitment in Japan*. New York: Columbia University Press, 1969.

Ballon, Robert J., ed.. *The Japanese Employee*. Tokyo: Sophia University Press, 1969.

Ballon, Robert J., and Eugene H. Lee, eds. *Foreign Investment and Japan*. Tokyo: Sophia University Press, 1972.

Befu, Harumi. *Japan: An Anthropological Introduction*. San Francisco: Chandler, 1971.

Behrman, J. N. *Some Patterns in the Rise of the Multinational Enterprise*. Chapel Hill: University of North Carolina Press, 1969.

Bellah, Robert N. *Tokugawa Religion: The Values of Pre-Industrial Japan*. Boston: Beacon Press, 1970.

Benjamin, Roger, and Kan Ori. *Tradition and Change in Postindustrial Japan: The Roles of the Political Parties*. New York: Praeger Publishers, 1981.

Bergsten, C. Fred, and William R. Cline. *The United States-Japan Economic Problem*. Washington, D.C.: Institute for International Economics, 1985.

Bisson, T. A. *Zaibatsu Dissolution in Japan*. Berkeley: University of California Press, 1954.

Burks, Ardath W. *Japan: A Postindustrial Power*. 2nd ed. Boulder, Colo.: Westview Press, 1984.

Castle, Emery N., and Kenzo Hemmi, eds. *United States-Japanese Agriculture Trade Relations*. Baltimore: Johns Hopkins University Press, 1982.

Caves, Richard E., and Uekusa, Masu. *Industrial Organization in Japan.* Washington, D.C.: Brookings Institution, 1976.

Christopher, Robert C. *The Japanese Mind: The Goliath Explained.* New York: Simon & Schuster, 1983.

Clark, Rodney. *The Japanese Company.* New Haven: Yale University Press, 1979.

Cole, R. E. *Work, Mobility, and Participation: A Comparative Study of American and Japanese Industry.* Berkeley: University of California Press, 1979.

Crocker, Olga L; Syril Charney; and Johnny Sik Leung Chiu. *Quality Circles, and How We Can Make It Work for Us.* New York: Methuen, 1984.

De Vos, George. *Socialization for Achievement: Essays on the Cultural Psychology of the Japanese.* Berkeley: University of California Press, 1973.

Dore, Ronald. *Aspects of Social Change in Modern Japan.* Princeton, N.J.: Princeton University Press, 1971.

————. *British Factory—Japanese Factory: The Origins of National Diversity in Industrial Relations.* Berkeley: University of California Press, 1973.

Goldsmith, Raymond W. *The Financial Development of Japan, 1868–1977.* New Haven: Yale University Press, 1983.

Hadley, Eleanor M. *Antitrust in Japan.* Princeton, N.J.: Princeton University Press, 1970.

Hanabusa, Masamichi. *Trade Problems between Japan and Western Europe.* Farnsborough, England: Saxon House, 1979.

Hasegawa, Nyozekan. *The Japanese Character: A Cultural Profile.* Trans. John Bester. Tokyo: Kodansha, 1966.

Havens, Thomas R. H. *Farm and Nation in Modern Japan.* Princeton, N.J.: Princeton University Press, 1974.

Hayashi, Shuji. *Culture and Management in Japan.* Tokyo: University of Tokyo Press, 1986.

Higashi, Chikara. *Japanese Trade Policy Formulation.* New York: Praeger Publishers, 1983.

Hirschmeier, J., and T. Yui. *The Development of Japanese Business.* 2nd ed. London: Allen & Unwin, 1981.

Ho, Alfred K. *Japan's Trade Liberalization in the 1960s.* New York: International Arts and Sciences Press, 1973.

Hollerman, Leon. *Japan's Dependency on the World Economy: The Approach toward Economic Liberalization.* Princeton, N.J.: Princeton University Press, 1967.

Hori, Ichior. *Folk Religion in Japan: Continuity and Change.* Ed. Joseph M. Kitagawa and Alan L. Miller. Chicago: University of Chicago Press, 1968.

Hyoe, Murakami, and Johannes Hirschmeier, eds. *Politics and Economics in Contemporary Japan.* Tokyo: Kodansha, 1983.

Japanese Ministry of Finance and the United States Department of the Treasury

Working Group on Yen/Dollar Exchange Rate Issues. *Report by the Working Group on Yen/Dollar Exchange Rate, Financial, and Capital Market Issues to Japanese Minister of Finance Noboru Takeshita [and] U.S. Secretary of the Treasury Donald T. Regan*. Tokyo, May 1984.

Japan External Trade Organization (JETRO) Staff, ed. *White Paper on International Trade: Japan*. Tokyo, 1981.

Johnson, Chalmers. *MITI and the Japanese Miracle: The Growth of Industrial Policy, 1925–1975*. Stanford, Calif.: Stanford University Press, 1982.

Kahn, Herman. *The Emerging Japanese Superstate*. Harmondsworth, England: Penguin Books, 1973.

Kahn, Herman, and Thomas Pepper. *The Japanese Challenge*. Harmondsworth, England: Penguin Books, 1973.

Kaplan, David E., and Alec Dubro. *Yakuza: The Explosive Account of Japan's Criminal Underworld*. Reading, Mass.: Addison-Wesley Publishing, 1986.

Kaplan, Eugene J. *Japan: The Government-Business Relationship*. Washington, D.C.: U.S. Department of Commerce, 1972.

Lincoln, Edward J. *Japan's Industrial Policies*. Washington, D.C.: Japan Economic Institute of America, 1984.

Lockwood, William W. *The Economic Development of Japan*. Princeton, N.J.: Princeton University Press, 1954.

McCraw, Thomas K., ed. *America versus Japan*. Boston: Harvard Business School Press, 1986.

Magaziner, Ira C., and Thomas M. Hout. *Japanese Industrial Policy*. Berkeley: University of California Institute of International Studies, 1981.

Marsh, R. M., and H. Mannari. *Modernization and the Japanese Factory*. Princeton: N.J.: Princeton University Press, 1976.

Marshall, Byron K. *Capitalism and Nationalism in Prewar Japan: The Ideology of the Business Elite, 1868–1941*. Stanford, Calif.: Stanford University Press, 1967.

Mayer, Fanny Hagin, trans. and ed. *The Yamagita Kunio Guide to the Japanese Folk Tale*. Bloomington: Indiana University Press, 1986.

Morishima, Michio. *Why Has Japan 'Succeeded'?: Western Technology and the Japanese Ethos*. Cambridge: Cambridge University Press, 1982.

Nakamura, James I. *Agricultural Production and the Economic Development of Japan, 1873–1922*. Princeton, N.J.: Princeton University Press, 1966.

Nakane, Chie. *Human Relations in Japan*. Tokyo: Ministry of Foreign Affairs, 1972.

———. *Japanese Society*. Berkeley: University of California Press, 1972.

Nakane, Fukio, trans. and ed. *Japanese Laws Relating to Banks*. Tokyo: Eibun-Horei-Sha, 1977.

Nishikawa, S., ed. *The Labor Market in Japan*. Tokyo: University of Tokyo Press, 1980.

Nitobe, Inazo. *Bushido: The Soul of Japan*. Rutland, Vt.: Tuttle, 1969.

Norman, E. H. *Origins of the Modern Japanese State: Selected Writings.* Ed. John W. Dower. New York: Random House, 1975.

Okimoto, Daniel I.; Takuo Sugano; and Franklin B. Weinstein, eds. *Competitive Edge: The Semiconductor Industry in the U.S. and Japan.* Stanford, Calif.: Stanford University Press, 1984.

Ouchi, William G. *Theory Z: How American Business Can Meet the Japanese Challenge.* Reading, Mass.: Addison-Wesley Publishing, 1981.

————. *The M-Form Society.* Reading, Mass.: Addison-Wesley Publishing, 1984.

Ozawa, T. *Multinationalism, Japanese Style: The Political Economy or Outward Dependency.* Princeton, N.J.: Princeton University Press, 1979.

Pascale, R. T. "Zen and the Art of Management." *Harvard Business Review*, March–April 1978.

Pascale, Richard Tanner, and Anthony G. Athos. *The Art of Japanese Management.* New York: Simon & Schuster, 1981.

Passin, Herbert, ed. *The United States and Japan.* 2nd ed. Washington, D.C.: Columbia Books, 1975.

Patrick, Hugh. *Japanese Industrialization and Its Social Consequences.* New York: Columbia University Press, 1976.

Patrick, Hugh, and Henry Rosovsky, eds. *Asia's New Giant: How the Japanese Economy Works.* Washington, D.C.: Brookings Institution, 1976.

Patrick, Hugh, and Ryuichiro Tachi, eds. *Japan and the United States Today: Exchange Rates, Macroeconomic Policies, and Financial Market Innovations.* New York: Center on Japanese Economy and Business, Columbia University, 1986.

Perrin, Noel. *Giving Up the Gun: Japan's Reversion to the Sword, 1543–1879.* Boulder, Colo.: Shambhala, 1979.

Petri, Peter A. *Modeling Japanese-American Trade: A Study of Asymmetric Interdependence.* Cambridge, Mass.: Harvard University Press, 1984.

Reischauer, Edwin O. *The Japanese.* Cambridge, Mass.: Harvard University Press, 1977.

Roberts, John G. *Mitsui: Three Centuries of Japanese Business.* New York: John Weatherhill, 1973.

Rohlen, T. P. "Spiritual Training in a Japanese Bank." *American Anthropologist* 75 (1973).

————. *For Harmony and Strength.* Berkeley: University of California Press, 1974.

Sansom, G. B. *The Western World and Japan.* New York: Alfred A. Knopf, 1950.

Sasaki, N. *Management and Industrial Structure in Japan.* Oxford: Pergamon, 1981.

Schonberger, Richard J. *Japanese Manufacturing Techniques: Nine Hidden Lessons in Simplicity.* New York: Free Press, 1982.

Shirai, Taishiro, ed. *Contemporary Industrial Relations in Japan*. Madison: University of Wisconsin Press, 1983.

Smith, Thomas C. *The Agrarian Origins of Modern Japan*. Stanford, Calif.: Stanford University Press, 1959.

Sperelakis, N. "Electrical Properties of Embryonic Heart Cells." In *Electrical Phenomena in the Heart*. ed. W. C. DeMello. New York: Academic Press, 1972.

Spindler, J. Andrew. *The Politics of International Credit, Private Finance, and Foreign Policy in Germany and Japan*. Washington, D.C.: Brookings Institution, 1984.

Stone, P. B. *Japan Surges Ahead: The Story of an Economic Miracle*. New York: Praeger Publishers, 1969.

Tatsuno, Sheridan. *The Technopolis Strategy: Japan, High Technology, and the Control of the 21st Century*. Englewood Cliffs, N.J.: Prentice-Hall, 1986.

Tokyo Metropolitan Government, ed. *Financial History of Tokyo: A Century of Growth amid Change*. Tokyo: Tokyo Metropolitan Government, 1972.

Toyo Keizai Shinposha (Oriental Economist). *Japan Company Handbook*. Tokyo, annual.

Trevor, Malcolm. *Japan's Reluctant Multinationals: Japanese Management at Home and Abroad*. New York: St. Martin's Press, 1983.

Tsunetomo, Yamamoto. *Hagakure*. Trans. William Scott Wilson. Tokyo: Kodansha, 1979.

Vernon, R. *Storm over the Multinationals: The Real Issues*. Cambridge, Mass.: Harvard University Press, 1977.

Viner, Aron. *Inside Japanese Financial Markets*. Homewood, Ill.: Dow Jones-Irwin, 1987.

Vogel, Ezra, ed. *Modern Japanese Organizations and Decision Making*. Berkeley: University of California Press, 1975.

————. *Japan as Number One*. Cambridge, Mass.: Harvard University Press, 1979.

————. *Comeback: Building the Resurgence of American Business*. New York: Simon & Schuster, 1985.

Wildes, Harry Emerson. *Typhoon in Tokyo: The Occupation and Its Aftermath*. New York: Macmillan, 1954.

Yoshino, M. Y. *Japan's Managerial System: Tradition and Innovation*. Cambridge, Mass.: MIT Press, 1971.

————. *Japan's Multinational Enterprises*. Cambridge, Mass.: MIT Press, 1976.

Yoshino, M. Y., and Thomas B. Lifson. *The Invisible Link: Japan's Sogo Shosha and the Organization of Trade*. Cambridge, Mass.: MIT Press, 1986.

Young, Alexander K. *The Sogo Shosha: Japan's Multinational Trading Companies*. Boulder, Colo.: Westview Press, 1979.

GLOSSARY

Amakudari The term ("descent from heaven") refers to the acceptance of private sector positions by bureaucrats retiring from the ministries. Most companies providing the jobs have been regulated by the officials during their government service.

Article 65 (of the Securities and Exchange Act of 1948) Prohibits banks from participating in the domestic securities industry and bans securities companies from domestic banking activities. Banks are not permitted to own more than 5 percent of a Japanese securities company and they are banned from selling equity or underwriting primary securities issues in Japan. At the same time, securities companies are not allowed to take deposits or give loans in the home market.

Bank of Japan Japan's central bank. The sole issuer of currency and the lender of last resort; the bank determines and implements monetary policy and is the defender of the yen.

Big Four The four largest securities companies in Japan: Nomura, Daiwa, Nikko, and Yamaichi.

City bank A name for the 13 largest domestic commercial banks, so called because they are based in cities. The term includes the Bank of Tokyo which is also classified as a foreign exchange bank.

Daimyo Territorial lords in feudal and Tokugawa era Japan.

Endaka Literally, the "high yen." The term refers to the substantial appreciation of the yen against the dollar and other currencies, which occurred after the September 1985 meeting of the Group of Five at the Plaza Hotel in New York.

Euroyen Yen deposits and yen currency held outside Japan (currently equal to about 2.7 percent of international banking assets).

Euroyen bond The first Eurobond issue denominated in yen was not floated until 1977, more than a decade after the emergence of the Eurobond market. Domestic entities were probhited from issuing **Euroyen** instruments and inhibiting regulations were not significantly altered until December 1984.

Keidanren The Federation of Economic Organizations. Composed of more than 700 major domestic corporations as well as about 30 foreign firms, this is the leading representative organization of private sector Japanese industry. The organization's chairman has often been referred to as the "Prime Minister of Japanese Industry."

Keiretsu Groupings of companies. Some groupings were successors of the prewar **zaibatsu**, while others developed during the postwar period. Usually bank-centered and invariably using interlocked cross-shareholding, credit, management, and marketing to maintain and promote cohesion, the groups continue to exercise a decisive influence.

Meiji Restoration A period in Japanese history which began in January 1868, following the surrender of power by the Tokugawa shogunate directly to Emperor Meiji and indirectly to the imperial family. The period ended in 1912 with the death of Meiji and the beginning of the Taisho period. This "restoration" of imperial power lasted until 1945 when it was terminated by the Occupation.

Ronin **Samurai** (warriors) with no **daimyo** (lord) to serve.

Samurai Warrior retainers of the **daimyo**. (See Chapter 3, pp. 110–13.)

Tokugawa Era Period (1603–1868) during which Japan was ruled by a shogunal government. Each shogun was a leader of the Tokugawa family.

Zaibatsu Literally, "financial cliques." Pre-1945 conglomerates clustered around a central bank or a trading company or both. Mitsui and Sumitomo, the two largest *zaibatsu*, developed from merchant families who had risen to prominence during the Tokugawa period. Other major *zaibatsu* such as Mitsubishi, Yasuda, and Dai-Ichi, were created by entrepreneurs during the first 20 years of the Meiji Restoration. Dismantled but not destroyed by the Occupation.

Zaitek A slang neologism coined from part of *zaimu*, the Japanese word for finance, and part of the English word *technology*. A vague term referring to domestic and international financial arbitrage conducted by treasurers of Japanese corporations.

INDEX